Walt Whitman's
"Song of Myself"

Walt Whitman's "Song of Myself" (1855) has been enjoyed, debated, and imitated by readers, critics, and poets around the world since its publication. Many now argue that it is the most influential poem written by an American.

Functioning as both sourcebook and critical edition of Whitman's extraordinarily creative and controversial poem, this book offers:

- key passages from the 1855 edition, with full commentary, and the complete "final" 1881 edition of the poem
- extensive introductory comment on the contexts and many interpretations of the text, from publication to the present
- annotated extracts from key contextual documents, reviews, critical works, and the text itself
- cross-references between documents and sections of the guide, in order to suggest links between contexts and criticism
- suggestions for further reading.

Part of the *Routledge Guides to Literature* series, this volume is essential reading for all those beginning detailed study of "Song of Myself" and seeking a way through Whitman's text and the wealth of contextual and critical material that surrounds it.

Ezra Greenspan is Kahn Chair in the Humanities and Professor of English at Southern Methodist University in Dallas. He is the author and editor of several books on Walt Whitman.

Routledge Guides to Literature*

Editorial Advisory Board: Richard Bradford (University of Ulster at Coleraine), Jan Jedrzejewski (University of Ulster at Coleraine), Duncan Wu (St. Catherine's College, University of Oxford)

Routledge Guides to Literature offer clear introductions to the most widely studied authors and literary texts.

Each book engages with texts, contexts and criticism, highlighting the range of critical views and contextual factors that need to be taken into consideration in advanced studies of literary works. The series encourages informed but independent readings of texts by ranging as widely as possible across the contextual and critical issues relevant to the works examined and highlighting areas of debate as well as those of critical consensus. Alongside general guides to texts and authors, the series includes "sourcebooks", which allow access to reprinted contextual and critical materials as well as annotated extracts of primary text.

Available in this series:

* Some books in this series were originally published in the Routledge Literary Sourcebooks series, edited by Duncan Wu, or the Complete Critical Guide to English Literature series, edited by Richard Bradford and Jan Jedrzejewski.

Kate Chopin's The Awakening: A Sourcebook edited by Janet Beer and Elizabeth Nolan

D. H. Lawrence by Fiona Becket

The Poems of W. B. Yeats: A Sourcebook edited by Michael O'Neill

E. M. Forster's A Passage to India: A Sourcebook edited by Peter Childs

Samuel Beckett by David Pattie

Walt Whitman's
"Song of Myself"
A Sourcebook and Critical Edition

Edited by Ezra Greenspan

Routledge
Taylor & Francis Group

NEW YORK AND LONDON

First published 2005
by Routledge
711 Third Avenue, New York, NY 10017

Simultaneously published in the UK
by Routledge
2 Park Square, Milton Park, Abingdon, Oxfordshire, OX14 4RN

Routledge is an imprint of the Taylor & Francis Group, an informa business

Editorial material and selection © 2005 Ezra Greenspan

Typeset in Sabon and Gill Sans by RefineCatch Limited, Bungay, Suffolk

British Library Cataloguing in Publication Data
A catalogue record for this book is available from the British Library

Library of Congress Cataloging in Publication Data
Whitman, Walt, 1819–1892.
    Song of myself : a sourcebook and critical edition / edited by
Ezra Greenspan.
        p. cm. – (Routledge guides to literature)
    Includes bibliographical references and index.
    1. Whitman, Walt, 1819–1892. Song of myself.   I. Greenspan, Ezra.
II. Title.   III. Series.
    PS3222.S6 2004
    811'.3 – dc22   2004002709

ISBN 13: 978-0-415-27543-9 (hbk)
ISBN 13: 978-0-415-27544-6 (pbk)

Contents

Nineteenth-Century Responses and Criticism   **38**

Twentieth-Century Responses and Criticism   **74**

Figures

Annotation and Footnotes

Annotation is a key feature of this series. Both the original notes from reprinted texts and new annotations by the editor appear at the bottom of the relevant page. The reprinted notes are prefaced by the author's name in square brackets, e.g. [Robinson's note].

Acknowledgments

I owe thanks to Rare Book Librarian Patrick Scott, and the staff of Special Collections, Thomas Cooper Library, University of South Carolina, for their cooperation in making first editions of Whitman's work available to me and for permitting me to have photographs made from works in their collections. I also owe thanks to my research assistants, Jessica Wissel and Jamie Self, for their efficient help in finding materials and verifying textual accuracy. And thanks go, as always, to my constant companion, Riki.

The editor and publishers would like to thank the following for permission to reprint copyright material:

David Higham Associates for "I, Too" by Langston Hughes, from *The Collected Poems of Langston Hughes* in the UK and Commonwealth.

Department of Rare Books and Special Collections, Thomas Cooper Library at University of South Carolina for the frontispiece illustration from *Leaves of Grass*, 1855, the title page from *Leaves of Grass*, 1855, the frontispiece illustration from *Leaves of Grass*, 1860, the illustrations of Whitman from the 1889 pocket edition of *Leaves*, and the title page from the 1881–82 edition of *Leaves*.

Duke University Rare Book, Manuscript and Special Collections Library for permission to reproduce first page of text of "Song of Myself", Trent 1-J, No. 2, Trent Collection of Whitmaniana, Rare Book, Manuscript and Special Collections Library, Duke University.

Faber and Faber Ltd for Ezra Pound, "The Pact," from *Personae*, copyright © by Ezra Pound. Reprinted in the UK and Commonwealth by permission of Faber and Faber Ltd.

Harper Collins for the entire text of "A Supermarket in California" from *Collected Poems 1947–1980* by Allen Ginsberg, reprinted in the United States and Canada by permission of Harper Collins.

Harvard University Press for the excerpt from Lawrence W. Levine, *Highbrow/Lowbrow: The Emergence of Cultural Hierarchy in America*. Copyright © 1988 by the President and Fellows of Harvard College.

New Directions Publishing Corp. for Ezra Pound, "The Pact" from *Personae*, copyright © by Ezra Pound. Reprinted in North America by permission of New Directions Publishing Corp.

New-York Historical Society for the photograph of Hudson St., Nos. 2, 3 and 5, John Peake, Druggist, *c*. 1865.

Pollinger Ltd for D. H. Lawrence, "Whitman", in *Studies in Classic American Literature*, Thomas Seltzer, New York, 1923. Reprinted in the UK by permission of Pollinger Ltd.

Random House Inc. for "I, Too" by Langston Hughes, from *The Collected Poems of Langston Hughes* in North America.

University of California Press for Karen Sánchez-Eppler, *Touching Liberty: Abolition, Feminism, and the Politics of the Body*, 1993.

University of Iowa Press for Alicia Ostriker, "Loving Walt Whitman and the Problem of America," from Robert K. Martin, ed., *The Continuing Presence of Walt Whitman*, 1992.

University of Pennsylvania Press for Susan S. Williams, *Confounding Images: Photography and Portraiture in Antebellum American Fiction*. Copyright © 1997.

Viking Penguin for "Whitman," from *Studies in Classic American Literature* by D. H. Lawrence, copyright 1923 by Thomas Seltzer, Inc., renewed 1950 by Frieda Lawrence. Copyright © 1961 by The Estate of the Late Mrs. Frieda Lawrence. Reprinted in North America by permission of Viking Penguin, a division of Penguin Putnam Inc.

Every effort has been made to trace and contact copyright holders. The publishers would be pleased to hear from any copyright holders not acknowledged here so that this acknowledgments page may be amended at the earliest opportunity.

Introduction

"Song of Myself" is the most acclaimed and influential poem written by an American. As Walt Whitman (1819–92) has been called "America's ur-poet," one may call "Song of Myself" an American "ur-poem." It has been extensively discussed, studied, imitated, parodied, translated, and incorporated into other art forms for 150 years by writers, artists, composers, film makers, and general readers across national and linguistic boundaries.

Its author was, in 1855, as unlikely a candidate as Herman Melville or Emily Dickinson[1] for canonical authorship. When Ralph Waldo Emerson, arguably the most prestigious American writer of his time, received an unsolicited review copy of the 1855 *Leaves of Grass*, in which "Song of Myself" first appeared, he was so unsure about the identity of the author that he sent his letter of appreciation to the Manhattan office of the book's distributor (no commercial publisher would stake its budget or reputation on the self-published work). Emerson also expressed an opinion that has proven prophetic: "I greet you at the beginning of a great career, which yet must have had a long foreground somewhere for such a start" (the full text of his letter is printed in Interpretations, **pp. 38–39**).

The poet's start was inauspicious. Whitman left formal schooling in 1831 at age eleven, apprenticing for the next five years in Brooklyn printing shops, where, as he told his protégé Horace Traubel late in life, "you get your culture direct: not through borrowed sources – no, a century of college training could not confer such results on anyone."[2] After "graduating" to journeyman status in 1835, Whitman found printing work hard to come by in economically depressed Manhattan, abandoned hope of locating steady work, and moved aimlessly for half a dozen years through a series of mostly short-term teaching stints on Long Island before returning to the New York area in 1841. He found work initially in the press-room of a popular periodical, then the next year in the editor's office of a New York City daily newspaper, the first of a string of New York and Brooklyn dailies he edited over the course of the decade. In addition, he published his own convention-bound poems, one by one, in local newspapers and national

---

1   For information on figures mentioned in the Introduction, see the Directory of Contextual Figures, **pp. 30–33**.
2   Horace Traubel, *With Walt Whitman in Camden* (Philadelphia: University of Philadelphia Press, 1953), 4: 505–06.

magazines. His commitment to journalism waned, however, by the time he left the *Brooklyn Daily Eagle* in 1848 after a two-year stay, and his career compass once again wavered as he moved during the next half-dozen years through a series of short-term jobs in journalism and – a trade he learned from his father – housebuilding.

Whitman left a faint biographical trail during the years 1848–54, but we do know for sure that during this period he began a sweeping artistic transformation that culminated in 1855 in the publication of *Leaves of Grass*. When and by what process Whitman composed its innovative poems is not precisely known. What is known is that they grew out of a prolonged process of poetic experimentation, perhaps beginning in the late 1840s, probably continuing through the early 1850s, and definitely culminating in the year and a half before his volume's July 1855 publication. The clearest record of that experimentation appears in the home-made notebooks Whitman kept during this period, into which he jotted trial lines, stanzas, titles, lists of words and expressions, and ideas.[3] That period of experimentation transformed his earlier conventional verse into an innovative, emboldened free verse and himself concurrently from an unknown, occasional poet into a self-styled workingman, national poet – the self-proclaimed poet of the modern democratic experience. The visual proof was in the engraved illustration he used as the frontispiece to his first volume of poems, produced from a daguerreotype Whitman had posed for the previous summer and set opposite the title page, featuring a casually dressed and posed portrait of the new American poet (see Figure 2, **p. 16**). That illustration, in effect, took the place of the poet's name on the title page, but the corresponding, printed signature appeared in the volume's feature poem (untitled in 1855 but later called "Song of Myself") as "Walt" rather than "Walter" Whitman (l. 497).

By the time the twelve poems he intended for his volume were completed in spring 1855, Whitman was presumably casting about in Manhattan and possibly in Brooklyn for a publisher. Years of work as a printer and newspaper editor had given him an extensive – and in some cases, as with Harper and Brothers, a personal – knowledge of publishing houses on both sides of the East River. But whatever connections he attempted to make, even at a time of vigorous activity in the publishing sector locally and nationally, proved unavailing: no commercial publisher would risk its money or reputation on a volume of poems that looked likely to result in a commercially – and, perhaps, morally – suspect venture. Instead, Whitman made an amicable arrangement for the volume's printing with old friends Tom, Andrew, and James Rome, Scottish immigrants who operated a small printing office in Brooklyn specializing in legal books. During the late weeks of spring, Whitman walked daily from his Brooklyn home on Ryerson Street to the Rome brothers' print shop at the corner of Cranberry and Fulton Streets, composed at quick speed a long prose introduction to the volume, read that morning's copy of Horace Greeley's *New York Daily Tribune* (in which one of the poems, "Europe, The 72d and 73d Years of These States," had originally been printed as "Resurgemus" in 1850), and even took a hand at setting his lines in type. Once the work in the printing shop was done and a binder contracted with,

---

3   For a discussion of the notebooks, see **pp. 120–22.**

Whitman took an early bound copy across the river and registered it, as required by mid-century copyright law, at the courthouse of the Southern District of New York under his formal name of Walter. The initial notice of the work appeared in the 6 July issue of the *Tribune*, advertising it for sale at several sites in Manhattan and Brooklyn. Although it was also soon available for sale in one or two Boston bookstores, as well as through the mail, it lacked the kind of broad national distribution that would have been possible had the book not been self published.

"Song of Myself" was positioned in the 1855 *Leaves of Grass* after the just-composed prose manifesto as the volume's untitled lead poem, its forty-four-page length greater than that of the other eleven poems combined. The poem challenged poetic decorum even at eye level. Formal punctuation marks were kept to a minimum, individual verses were frequently so long that they ran on to the next line, stanzas varied wildly in length from several lines to several pages, and no system of names or numbers was used to organize the poem by stanza or section. Not entirely satisfied with the poem then or later, Whitman ceaselessly revised the text, sometimes in significantly altered fashion, for inclusion in each of the subsequent five American editions of *Leaves of Grass* published over the remaining thirty-seven years of his life. Among the many changes he introduced, he tried out a variety of titles, patterns of punctuation and spelling, alterations of language and structure, and internal organization – changes of such frequency and character as to render the poem unusually suitable for variorum treatment and hypertext archiving. Not surprisingly, literary critics and historians have for decades been embroiled in wide-ranging disagreement about the "best" choice of text, a debate not yet ended. They do broadly agree, though, that the main choice for definitive status is between the 1855 and 1881 editions (for a fuller exploration of those two editions, see the introduction to Key Passages and Full Text, **pp. 117–19**).

Its reception history – and that of *Leaves of Grass* – has been as complicated as its textual history. Readers and critics have generally agreed through the years on but one point: "Song of Myself," whether admired or reviled, represents the core of Whitman's poetic mission. That assessment of its centrality undoubtedly matches Whitman's own thinking in 1855; he not only gave it priority as the lead poem but saw its contents as interchangeable with that of the other poems. Generally speaking, the first edition of *Leaves of Grass* was far more widely reviewed than read. Leading national magazines and a fair number of daily newspapers reviewed it in the weeks and months following publication, but its roughly 800-copy first printing was more than sufficient to fill demand. Critical reception was uneven at best, and so it remained throughout the century. A small number of reviewers in 1855 praised it strongly, but even most of those who saw merit in the work typically complained about its flagrant violation of aesthetic and social decorum. Meanwhile, social conservatives denounced the book as flouting accepted norms of morality; literary critics for so undermining standards of verse that it was unrecognizable as poetry. Accolades such as Emerson's were in the minority, and praise was seldom unaccompanied by criticism. The major exception was Whitman himself, always his own strongest proponent, who engaged in anonymous self reviews immediately following publication and remained an unceasingly energetic, ingenious, even shameless self-promoter throughout his entire career.

A worse sign for Whitman, subsequent editions of *Leaves of Grass* received less formal attention, at least through the 1870s, while readership remained sharply limited. Whereas leading writers and critics of his time – Emerson, Henry David Thoreau, Henry Wadsworth Longfellow, Bayard Taylor, John Burroughs, Matthew Arnold, Alfred, Lord Tennyson, Algernon Swinburne, Oscar Wilde, John Addington Symonds – were well aware, if not uniformly admiring, of Whitman's verse, the reading public was generally apathetic or hostile. In 1882 that hostility took a legal turn, when the Boston district attorney threatened action against both the book (specifying numerous passages of "Song of Myself," as well as of other poems) and Whitman's publisher for violating the state's obscenity statutes. When his intimidated publisher, James Osgood, demanded compliance and Whitman refused, Osgood withdrew and passed the sheets and stereotype plates on to Whitman, who at first sold bound copies from his home in Camden, New Jersey, then made an arrangement with publishers across the Delaware River in Philadelphia for its distribution. Even at his life's end, Whitman's reputation more nearly approximated that of a poet's poet than that of the poet of the people, as he had represented himself in the 1855 frontispiece.

But if he did not have reputable fame, he had notoriety, which with changing standards of morality, aesthetics, and politics gradually became indistinguishable from fame. He remained optimistic to the end of his life about posterity's judgment, and he was soon proven correct. Newspaper coverage of Whitman was commonplace during his last decade, and by the time of his death he was a widely known, if hardly uniformly respected, poet in the United States and Great Britain, as well as to a lesser degree in Latin America and across the European Continent. Changing mores and aesthetics in *fin de siècle* America produced a cultural atmosphere far more accepting of Whitman's poetry. A clear sign of his altered status was the 1902 publication of a handsome ten-volume *Complete Writings of Walt Whitman* by a major New York publishing house, G. P. Putnam's Sons. By the time of the generation of literary modernism, Whitman was one of the several best-known American poets around the world – a writer who was as often as any other the standard invoked for good or for bad writing. By the 1920s, the growth of his reputation as a "standard" American writer paralleled the inchoate institutionalization of American literature as a body of letters and a field of study. Well aware of this development was the English writer D. H. Lawrence, who in his seminally influential *Studies in Classic American Literature* (1923) called Whitman the greatest of modern writers, the pathbreaking, advance scout for the twentieth century: "Whitman, the great poet, has meant so much to me. Whitman, the one man breaking a way ahead. Whitman the one pioneer. And only Whitman. No English pioneers, no French."[4] That claim might have been unconventional and idiosyncratic, but by the 1920s it was well prepared for.

During the last three generations of the twentieth century, Whitman became a core figure in the canon of American literature. Already in 1941 the Harvard literary scholar F. O. Matthiessen positioned Whitman alongside Emerson as the central figures in nineteenth-century American literature in his magisterial *Ameri-*

---

4   D. H. Lawrence, *Studies in Classic American Literature* (New York: Thomas Seltzer, 1923), p. 253. An excerpt from his assessment of Whitman can be found in Interpretations, p. 79–81.

can Renaissance, the most influential academic study during the mid-century decades of nineteenth-century American literature. Whitman's reputation also benefited from the fallout of the Second World War, as the post-war military and economic supremacy of the United States had analogous cultural ramifications repositioning American literature as, for the first time, an internationally respected body of letters. The great African-American poet Langston Hughes expressed the spirit of the period well in a 1946 essay entitled "The Ceaseless Rings of Walt Whitman": "In this atomic age of ours, when the ceaseless rings are multiplied a millionfold, the Whitman spiral is upward and outward toward a freer, better life for all, not narrowing downward toward death and destruction. Singing the greatness of the individual, Whitman also sings the greatness of unity, cooperation, and understanding."[5] Nevertheless, there remained a partial resistance to Whitman in many academic quarters, especially to the antiformalist elements conspicuous in "Song of Myself." As a result, that poem had a lesser stature to some critics than that of the more conventionally structured "Out of the Cradle Endlessly Rocking" and "When Lilacs Last in the Dooryard Bloom'd." Ironically, although the centenary of the publication of the first *Leaves of Grass* was marked by the publication of the first authoritative Whitman biography, *The Solitary Singer*, its author, Gay Wilson Allen, had difficulty comparable to Whitman's a century earlier in finding a commercial publisher.

During the past fifty years, Whitman's reputation has both solidified nationally and expanded worldwide. So, in particular, has that of "Song of Myself," whose relative stature has improved dramatically in a newly compatible cultural context of the past few decades, as the critical discourses of New Historicism, postmodernism, and cultural studies have gained broad acceptance.[6] If in the years following the Second World War "Song of Myself" came in for increasingly, if never consistently, reverential treatment as part of the literary canon, in our own generation it thrives, ironically, more considerably on its merits as a marginalized text at home in our decentralized literary culture. An earlier era's uneasiness with the poem's sprawling breadth, vast inclusiveness, experimental techniques, and blatant, unconventional sexuality has been transformed generally to praise. Furthermore, the turn in the last generation to an ideological criticism concerned with race, gender, sex and sexuality (including homosexuality), transgression, and globalism has led a new generation of critics to see "Song of Myself," even to a degree surpassing that of any other of Whitman's poems, as a stunningly rich analogue to its concerns.

---

5   The essay has been reprinted in Jim Perlman, Ed Folsom, and Dan Campion, eds., *Walt Whitman: The Measure of His Song* (Duluth, Minn.: Holy Cow! Press, 1998), p. 187. For a Langston Hughes poem written with Whitman in mind, see Interpretations, **pp. 81–82.**
6   "New Historicism" refers to a particular version of the scholarly "return to history" in literary studies common during the 1980s and 1990s with an emphasis on the dynamic relations between texts and the cultures in which they were produced and on the ways that authors (including scholars) and other historic agents interact with social and linguistic systems both past and present. "Postmodernism" refers to the combination of positions taken by artists and intellectuals in the various fields of arts and letters that since the 1960s attack unitary or unified notions of self, perspective, voice, and tradition in favor of an often socially or culturally activist position that stresses multiplicity, relativism, and contingency. "Cultural studies" refers to the multidisciplinary academic area, emergent in the 1990s, that explores issues of power, knowledge, discourse patterns, and disciplinarity in order to understand cultures and social practices of the past and present.

This does not mean that the poem currently finds universal approval or that it has lost its capacity to provoke and to incite controversy. Debate continues, centering in the past twenty years on the poem's political progressivism, as different ideological camps, for instance, within feminism and ethnic studies, have alternately found the poem's politics stifling or liberating. Just the same, there has been a broad consensus view that identifies "Song of Myself" as a core text of modern literature, and that judgment does not seem likely to change any time soon. Even in a revolutionary age of new communication technologies and challenges to the traditional definitions and understandings of culture, "Song of Myself" is and seems likely to remain one of the most pioneering, influential, and provocative poems of the current era.

This sourcebook is designed to bring all these issues – the poem's compositional history from manuscript to successive print editions, publication history, reception history, social and political engagement in its time and ours, and relation to its own cultural context – to the attention of the current generation of college and university students. It proceeds through a series of interrelated parts. The first part (Contexts) provides students with a variety of contexts for understanding "Song of Myself": the life of the poet and his society, the volatile political and social milieu in which he lived and wrote, and the cultural ambience of the print world in and through which the poem took physical form. The second part (Interpretations) reprints and comments on a wide array of important nineteenth- and twentieth-century reviews that raise prevailing aesthetic, critical, and ideological issues in Whitman criticism. The third part (Key Passages and Full Text) reproduces the full text of the poem in its "final" 1881 form as well as seven sections of the poem from its initial 1855 form that have been central to the critical debate on "Song of Myself." In addition, this part of the volume highlights the textual variations that occurred over the long compositional and recompositional life of the poem. The final part (Further Reading) assembles a compact annotated list of useful primary and secondary, print and online, sources for students interested in pursuing additional study of "Song of Myself" and Whitman.

One editorial practice followed throughout the volume needs to be made explicit. All references in the text and footnotes to line numbers or section numbers from "Song of Myself" correspond to the text of the 1881 edition reprinted in Key Passages and Full Text. Readers can thereby conveniently connect Whitman's text to the commentary about it.

1

Contexts

Contextual Overview

In a late, summary essay, "A Backward Glance o'er Travel'd Roads," Whitman made one of his strongest pronouncements about his life's work: " 'Leaves of Grass' indeed (I cannot too often reiterate) has mainly been the outcropping of my own emotional and other personal nature – an attempt, from first to last, to put *a Person*, a human being (myself, in the later half of the Nineteenth Century, in America) freely, fully and truly on record."[1] No Whitman poem accomplishes that feat more richly than "Song of Myself."

By the same token, no Whitman poem – and no other American poem of the nineteenth century – more comprehensively, inclusively, or creatively represents the fullness of life during that era. During the flurry of years that he worked on the poem, Whitman's receptors were so exquisitely sensitive and active that the poem incorporates a remarkable swath of contemporaneous Americana into itself. There is a large measure of truth to the gargantuan boast that he makes about the ideal American poet (that is, himself) in his Preface to the 1855 edition of *Leaves of Grass*: "His spirit responds to his country's spirit . . . . He incarnates its geography and natural life and rivers and lakes."[2] In this sense, one may fairly conceive of "Song of Myself" as a prodigious act of incarnation. Moreover, the poem's powerful rhetoric engages many of the most pressing social, political, and cultural issues of its time, an era of heated ideological debate and internal and sectional divisiveness that would explode six years after the poem's publication in civil war and a sequence of far-reaching social, political, economic, and legal changes that together constituted a second American revolution.

This section builds upon the poem's encyclopedic breadth to locate it in its local and national environment. It sets out to accomplish this task by setting Whitman and his work against a variety of the major contexts – political, social, and cultural – in the era in which he lived and wrote. Exceptionally self-conscious about that era, Whitman memorably tagged it "the middle range of the Nineteenth century in the New World; a strange, unloosen'd, wondrous time."[3] Whatever else it may be, "Song of Myself" is the exuberantly rich, imaginative, idiosyncratic record of that time.

1 In Justin Kaplan, ed., *Whitman, Poetry and Prose* (New York: Library of America, 1982), p. 671.
2 1855 Preface, in Kaplan, *Whitman, Poetry and Prose*, p. 7.
3 *Specimen Days*, in Kaplan, *Whitman, Poetry and Prose*, p. 690n.

Political and Social Context

The literary historian Betsy Erkkila has written that "the drama of identity" in the 1855 "Song of Myself" "is rooted in the political drama of a nation in crisis."[4] Whitman lived his formative years as a printer, journalist, newspaper editor, and poet during one of the most volatile periods in the history of the United States. The two-party political system he had known his entire life was disbanding by the time he wrote and published *Leaves of Grass*. Following his father's loyalties, he had grown up and reached maturity with an allegiance to the Democratic party of Thomas Jefferson and Andrew Jackson (presidents of the United States, serving 1801–09 and 1829–37 respectively).[5] When Whitman's father sent him out at age 12 to apprentice as a printer, it was for a local Brooklyn newspaper affiliated with the Democratic party, and years later he performed the longest continuous professional service of his life as the editor (1846–48) of the leading Democratic newspaper of Brooklyn, the *Daily Eagle*. But, under the pressure of the slavery issue, which increasingly dominated American politics throughout the 1850s and triggered the events leading to the outbreak of the Civil War in 1861, he had shifted his loyalties by 1848 to the new Free Soil party, which opposed the spread of slavery to the new territories of the Midwest and Southwest. That party was short lived, however, its place taken over largely by the antislavery Republican party founded in 1854. Meanwhile, the Democratic party, long a champion of union, persisted in weakened condition as an increasingly sectional party during the half-dozen years leading up to and throughout the Civil War.

The central – indeed, the predominant – issue of American politics during the 1850s was slavery, one that seemed increasingly likely as the decade transpired to split the nation in two along its north–south seam at the Mason Dixon line, the southern half slave-owning and the northern free. Tensions over the extent and regulation of slavery grew exacerbated by the physical transformation of the country, as the territorial United States expanded across the Rocky Mountains to the Pacific Coast following the victorious prosecution of the United States–Mexican War of 1846–48 and the 1846 border agreement with Great Britain ceding control of Oregon and Washington to the United States. The peace treaty with Mexico in particular, many contemporary observers anticipated, had the capacity to upset the delicate balance between North and South in the Senate, with each section fearing that the other might gain a numerical advantage in Congress as territories were admitted into the Union as slave or free states. In the mid 1850s that fear turned into actual skirmishing between proslavery and antislavery militias in the border territories of Kansas and Missouri.

Caught in the middle of this intense sectional agitation and rivalry were the slaves, their defenders, their masters, and, following the passage of the 1850 Fugitive Slave Act, the general public – all subject during the middle third of the century to the dictates of the federal government and, increasingly, the courts. Not surprisingly, the 1840s and 1850s witnessed the heyday of the antislavery

---

4   Betsy Erkkila, *Whitman the Political Poet* (New York: Oxford University Press, 1989), p. 95.
5   See Directory of Contextual Figures, pp. 30–33, for further information on key figures mentioned in the Contexts section.

and abolition movements, on which Whitman kept a close but guarded eye. His most outspoken poetic response to the slavery issue was the composition of "A Boston Ballad," a ferocious satire on the forced return in 1854 of the fugitive slave Anthony Burns to his master by the Boston authorities. Whitman included that poem the next year in *Leaves of Grass*, as well as a scene of a runaway slave in "Song of Myself" (see section 10) and of a slave at auction in (the later-titled) "I Sing the Body Electric."

But slavery was only the most conspicuous of the many issues facing Whitman's America during the mid-century years. The rights of many other groups, including immigrants, Native Americans, and women, became the subject of intense debate and agitation during this period. The middle decades of the century witnessed an unprecedented mass immigration, particularly of Roman Catholics from Ireland and the German states, to North America, for which the country was categorically unprepared. One major result was an intensification of religious strife and nativism (from which not even Whitman was immune at times in the 1840s), especially in the major cities of the Northeast. At the same time, considerable attention was given in Congress, the White House, and the press to the status of Native Americans, whose hold on their native grounds came into increasing conflict with the demands of a geographically and numerically expanding nation spouting an ideology of manifest destiny.[6] The result was the removal and displacement of some tribes and armed conflict with others. Heated debate also began over the status of women, particularly following the first women's-rights convention in July 1848 at Seneca Falls, New York, which culminated in a feminist Declaration of Sentiments proclaiming that "all men and women are created equal" and calling for female suffrage and other egalitarian measures.

Assessing the Seneca Falls convention and the times in general, a local newspaper opined accurately, "This is the age of reform."[7] Reform was pervasively in the air in this, the most vigorous era of social as well as political reform in nineteenth-century American history. Not only were the rights of black people, women, immigrants, and working people under debate but also the physical, sexual, mental, spiritual, and religious health of society. The era witnessed intense agitation over temperance reform, dietary and hygienic reform, religious revivalism, millennialism, free love, and communitarian living. All had their proponents and detractors, and many had their publishers (one of the most active in the fields of sexual, dietary, and other forms of personal reform was Fowler and Wells, the distributor of the first edition and publisher of the second edition of *Leaves of Grass*).

Even the physical shape and extent of the Union was changing dramatically as the country went through an unprecedented growth spurt. Whitman's hometown Brooklyn was transformed during his several decades' residence from a village into one of the largest cities in the United States, and Manhattan into the largest city in North America, while new cities were springing up along rivers all the way to, along, and across the Mississippi River. At the same time, railroad lines were

---

6   Manifest destiny, a term denoting a federal policy of westward continental expansion of the United States, became a popular political stance in the 1840s and was used to justify, among other federal activities, the United States–Mexican War and Indian removal.

7   *Oneida Whig*, 1 August 1848.

expanding north, east, and south, improving transportation and trade and facilitating the mobility of an already volatile population. Altogether, it was indeed, as Whitman tagged it, "a strange, unloosen'd, wondrous time."

Cultural Context

"In the four corners of the globe, who reads an American book? Or goes to an American play? or looks at an American picture or statue?" So wrote the sharp-tongued British essayist Sydney Smith in the respected *Edinburgh Review* in 1820, a remark that clearly struck a nerve in the nineteenth-century American psyche. Smith's timing was exquisitely bad. During the next generation, the United States experienced not only a prodigious expansion of the traditional institutions of culture, such as theater, opera, museums, art galleries, and bookstores, as well as of the producers and consumers of literature and the arts, but also a liberalization of the idea and forms of culture itself.

New York was the fast emerging cultural center of the country by the antebellum years and Whitman, a professional journalist and amateur enthusiast of the arts, took full advantage of the city's proliferating offerings. During the years leading up to the composition of *Leaves of Grass*, he visited the old and new forms of culture with such frequency that reports on his visits became a staple of his newspaper coverage. He heard popular European soprano Jenny Lind in solo concert in 1850 during her P. T. Barnum-arranged celebrity tour and in the early 1850s the great Italian opera performers who passed through New York City; attended performances by many of the era's leading actors, including Edwin Booth, Charles Kean, Ellen Tree, Fanny Kemble, and Edwin Forrest; visited the Egyptology museum on Broadway and the leading art galleries of both Manhattan and Brooklyn, toured the daguerreotype parlors of the leading photographers in the city (for some of whom he also sat, such as Mathew Brady); haunted the exhibitions of technology and art at the new Crystal Palace[8]; and listened to the antislavery lectures of the finest orators of the day, including Frederick Douglass, William Lloyd Garrison, Cassius Marcellus Clay, and Wendell Phillips. He also demonstrated a passion for a new American form of popular entertainment, minstrelsy, that was the cultural rage of the antebellum generation, going numerous times to see "the original 'Jim Crow' "[9] at the Park and other theaters in Manhattan and a variety of the leading minstrel groups of the day, such as the Christy Minstrels and the Ethiopian Serenaders.[10] Altogether, the future performance

---

8 The New York Crystal Palace was a monumentally sized domed structure of steel and glass built on a four-block plot of undeveloped land near 42nd Street and 5th Avenue. Built in imitation of and intended to rival the great Crystal Palace of London, it opened in July 1853 with a World's Fair but never attained the popularity anticipated by its designers and investors.

9 Jim Crow, a stereotypical rendering of blacks by whites in song and dance, was the stock figure of minstrelsy beginning in the 1830s, long before the term became associated with postbellum segregationist practices. The originating figure of minstrelsy to whom Whitman referred was the popular and pioneering white blackface actor Thomas "Daddy" Rice (1808–60).

10 Whitman reported on the local cultural scene regularly during his two-year editorships of the *Brooklyn Daily Eagle* (1846–48) and *Brooklyn Daily Times* (1857–59) as well as irregularly in a variety of other Manhattan and Brooklyn newspapers. He gave a particularly full account of his attendance at antebellum cultural events in his retrospective sketch "Old Actors, Singers, Shows, &C., in New York," in Kaplan, *Whitman, Poetry and Prose*, pp. 1288–293.

artist of "Song of Myself" and *Leaves of Grass* kept the closest eye on the profusion of performance arts of his own time.

The popularization of culture equally affected – indeed, transformed – the printing-related sector of the New York economy that Whitman had known first-hand from his days in the early 1830s as a printer's apprentice in small newspaper printing offices and later in 1841 as a compositor for the mass-circulation weekly magazine *New World*.[11] The gap between those two professional assignments accurately represents the changing scale and character of literary culture and cultural production in the city and nation. The small-scale, artisan-based craft economy Whitman knew in his early years and continued to venerate for much of his life quickly gave way in the 1840s and 1850s to a more impersonal, capitalistic model of economic activity employing improved technological methods and resulting in larger-scale production.

The ramifications for literary culture were great. The main roles of literary production were altered. Publishers replaced printers as the primary initiators and financiers of literary works, while printers increasingly became hired workers and in the process lost autonomy and status. Large, more heavily capitalized publishing houses assumed a central position in the production of books and magazines, which began to circulate more regularly on a national (sometimes even an international) basis by the 1840s. Printing technologies and processes improved dramatically during the antebellum years, print runs increased, prices of printed products fell, readership grew, and the commercial phenomenon of bestselling books and magazines as a phenomenon was born. In keeping with these changes in process and product, authorship likewise assumed a greater degree of professionalism.

Whitman attempted to find a flexible middle position for himself as a writer, and for *Leaves of Grass* as a representation of contemporary America, between inherited ideals and practices of the republic of letters, small-scale cultural production, and amateur authorship on the one hand and new emergent ideals and practices of commercialized culture, large-scale production techniques, and professionalized authorship on the other. In addition to negotiating the structural politics of culture, he also needed to address the growing split in the nation itself. To speak of America as an ideal, or even as a collective whole, as Whitman was to do obsessively in the 1855 *Leaves of Grass*, became increasingly difficult as the country was torn apart following the election of the Republican candidate, Abraham Lincoln, in the 1860 presidential election. How could a writer claim, in the dark days of secession and the darker days of armed conflict, as Whitman had in the 1855 Preface, "the genius of the United States is not best or most in its executives or legislatures, nor in its ambassadors or authors or colleges or churches or parlors, nor even in its newspapers or inventors . . . . but always most in the common people"?[12] The ambition to write to and on behalf of the supposed common people was a mission fraught with challenges, difficulties, and complications.

---

11 See Figure 1 (p. 15) for an example of a printing house that was a throwback to the earlier era of small-scale production. For an example of the new industrial scale mode of printing, see the model of the Harper and Brothers factory in lower New York in Ezra Greenspan, *Walt Whitman and the American Reader* (New York: Cambridge University Press, 1990), p. 130.

12 1855 Preface, in Kaplan, *Whitman, Poetry and Prose*, pp. 5–6.

A Life in Print, with Portraits

Whitman's life and career are traced in the Chronology on **pp. 18–23**, but his relationship with the rapidly developing cultures of print and photography is worth noting in more detail.

Whitman grew to maturity in a print environment that needs to be understood in both its immediate and its broad contexts. Understood as an immediate phenomenon, the printing office was in effect Whitman's substitute for the schoolroom. Once his formal education ended at age 11, he trained and later found employment in a succession of printing shops, then worked for most of the fifteen years preceding the publication of *Leaves of Grass* in proximity to printers and printing as a newspaper editor. The result was a visceral, practical experience in the culture of letters that remained with him his entire life. The "making" of poems, for Whitman, had a multiple dimension that found expression in his boast that he had taken a turn in setting the 1855 *Leaves of Grass* to press. By no coincidence, the central *double entendre* of his career, "*leaves* of grass," drew on this formal training: the leaves of his poems were simultaneously connected to the worlds of nature and printing (that is, paper). He was so sensitive to the tactile character of ink, press, and paper that it affected his poetic imagination. It is no exaggeration to say that Whitman composed his poems with a printer's awareness of the physical character of paper, the presence of margins, the look of typefaces. In composing the text of the 1881–82 edition of *Leaves of Grass*, he instructed the publisher to have the book printed from new types and justified the request: "the typographical show of my poems – how they shall show (negatively as well as absolutely) on the black and white page – is always in my idea in making them – I am printer enough for that."[13] Likewise, he proofread and made corrections to successive copies of text with a printer's trained eye and manner. In addition, he paid heed to the changing technologies that brought the printed word to a geographically broadening circle of readers with increasing speed and cost-efficiency. Only a writer obsessed with the physical mechanism of print-based communication could have issued the strange invitation – it is one of the strangest in all Whitman – to unmediated seduction that opened the untitled second poem of the 1855 *Leaves of Grass* (later titled "A Song for Occupations"):

Come closer to me,
Push close my lovers and take the best I possess,
Yield closer and closer and give me the best you possess.

This is unfinished business with me . . . . how is it with you?
I was chilled with the cold types and cylinder and wet paper
   between us.

I pass so poorly with paper and types . . . . I must pass with the
   contact of bodies and souls.

13 Edwin Haviland Miller, ed., *Walt Whitman: The Correspondence*, 6 vols. (New York: New York University Press, 1961–77), 3: 230.

At the same time, Whitman was a fascinated witness to the unprecedented proliferation of print that spread across New York City and that connected it to the rest of the country. The Great Fire of 1835 had gutted more than a dozen acres of lower Manhattan's prime commercial real estate, but the city recovered quickly and soon prepared for a huge expansion. So did the print sector, one of the largest in the city's economy. Whitman observed with heightened interest and sharp insight as New York City became the center of the nation's print and publishing trades and one of the most important centers of print-based industries in the world. At the time he set to work on his first edition the largest employer in the city was Harper and Brothers, which by the mid 1850s was printing nearly 5 million volumes a year, more than any other publisher in the world. The penny press was thriving, with city newspapers (several of which Whitman had edited) issuing in the hundreds of thousands each day. Likewise, leading monthly magazines such as *Harper's Monthly* (in which Whitman eventually published several poems) and weekly story papers such as the New York *Ledger* had a circulation surpassing a quarter of a million copies. More to the point, he not only saw the revolution in printing and publishing, he participated in it. As printer, journalist, editor, publisher, and – finally – author, he came to appreciate, even to count upon, the power that the medium of print had to reach and have an impact on the city and national reading public. As author of *Leaves of Grass*, he went one giant, imaginative step further: he tended to identify that reading public with the

Figure 1 **The 1855 *Leaves of Grass* was printed in a small printing house in Brooklyn, similar to this one on Hudson Street in lower Manhattan (Collection, New-York Historical Society)**

Figure 2 Whitman used this provocative workman's pose, taken a year earlier, as the frontispiece of the 1855 *Leaves of Grass* to embody its ideal of the modern poet as man of the people (Courtesy of University of South Carolina Library)

Figure 3 *Left* This romantic portrait, painted by his friend Charles Hine, was used by Whitman to embody his altered self-image for the 1860 *Leaves of Grass* (Courtesy of University of South Carolina Library)

Figure 4 *Right* This portrait of the aged Whitman, safely settled into the "good gray poet" image of his later years, was taken in 1880 in Philadelphia by the well-known photographer Frederick Gutekunst (Courtesy of University of South Carolina Library)

national corpus and, at some basic level, to imagine that New York's print network might serve as the carrier of his word to all parts of the country.

Whitman was also highly aware of the power of the image and utilized portraits expertly and ingeniously to craft his own image in his published works. With the possible exception of Mark Twain, he had no nineteenth-century equal among American writers as poseur and, like Twain, he was as adept at posing for the camera as for the seen or unseen public. He had an almost uncanny affinity for photography, befriended and sat for many of the leading photographers of his time, and kept their work close by his side to the end of his life.[14]

The most famous Whitman likeness is the one he used as the frontispiece of the 1855 (also the 1856, 1876, and 1881) *Leaves of Grass* (Figure 2). It was taken as a daguerreotype in July 1854 by his Brooklyn friend Gabriel Harrison, from which Samuel Hollyer made the steel engraving used in the volume. Deployed as the equivalent of the implied poet's signature, Whitman's pose as a workingman poet, dressed casually with his hat askew and his elbow akimbo, was deliberately provocative. It deviated as much from the formal painterly aesthetic of portraiture as did the volume's poems (and their author) from the then current aesthetic of verse.

Figure 3 comes from the frontispiece of the 1860 *Leaves of Grass*. It, too, is a steel engraving, although in this case made after a painting done in 1859 by his friend Charles Hine. Perhaps the most striking thing about this engraved likeness is how differently it presents the poet five years later: not just fleshier but more fashionable, almost to the point of dandyhood.

Figure 4 comes from the verso to p. 214 of the 1889 pocket edition of *Leaves of Grass*. The photograph was taken by Frederick Gutekunst, a fashionable studio photographer in Philadelphia. By then safely categorized as the "good gray poet" in the memorable phrase coined by his supporter William O'Connor, the chronically ill poet flaunted his aged appearance as readily as he had boasted his hale, hearty look in earlier years.

---

14 For the most comprehensive Whitman portrait gallery, see the online *Walt Whitman Archive*, Ed Folsom and Kenneth M. Price, eds.: <http://jefferson.village.virginia.edu/whitman/gallery/>.

Chronology

The chronology summarizes much information on Whitman's life and career and on important national events taking place as that life unfolded. For this reason it should be read through in its entirety, after which it might serve as a ready reference.

Bullet points are used to denote events in Whitman's life, and asterisks to denote national events.

1819
- Whitman born 31 May on a farm near Huntington, Long Island
* United States gains control of Florida through border treaty with Spain and begins seizing ships involved in the transatlantic importation of slaves

1823
- Family moves to the village of Brooklyn, New York
* Passage of Monroe Doctrine; first New York minstrel show closes

1825
- Attends public and Sunday schools, the former a novelty in Brooklyn
* Erie Canal opens; John Quincy Adams assumes presidency

1830
- His formal schooling ends; goes to work as an office boy to prominent local lawyers
* Church of Jesus Christ of Latter Day Saints founded by Joseph Smith at Fayette, New York

1831
- Begins apprenticeship as printer at newspaper office of *Long Island Patriot*, then moves the following year to the rival *Long Island Star*
* Alexis de Tocqueville begins the year-long tour of the United States that serves as the basis of his formative study of the United States, *Democracy in America*

1835
- Completes his apprenticeship and moves to New York City to work as compositor
- Lower New York City devastated by fires, a situation aggravated by a severe economic recession

1836
- Cannot find employment and rejoins his family, now situated in Hempstead, Long Island, and takes up rural teaching assignments
- Martin Van Buren reclaims presidency for Democrats, the Whitman family's party, as effects of recession spread

1838
- Begins publication of his short-lived weekly paper the *Long Islander*, but his main vocation remains teaching
- Cherokee nation, expelled by federal order from its native grounds in the Southeast, begins its "trail of tears" march to Oklahoma Territory

1840
- Publishes a number of conventional poems and a series of meditative essays, "Sun-Down Papers from the Desk of a School-Master," in the *Long Island Democrat*
- Decade of unprecedented waves of immigration to New York begins, chiefly from Ireland and Germany

1841
- Returns to Manhattan as printer for the *New World*, a popular magazine
- Whig candidate William Henry Harrison becomes ninth president in March but dies a month later; succeeded by John Tyler

1842
- Becomes editor of the two-penny daily *New York Aurora*; publishes *Franklin Evans*, a temperance novel, at request of former employer at *New World*
- Croton Reservoir opens, supplying New York City with fresh water

1845
- Returns to Brooklyn to live with his family, recently resettled in the booming city, and edits *Long Island Star*
- James Polk returns presidency to Democrats and implements expansionist territorial policies

1846
- Begins two-year stint as editor of Brooklyn's leading newspaper, the *Daily Eagle*
- Outbreak of Mexican–American War, whose outcome leads to annexation by the United States of a huge area of the Southwest; border treaty with Great Britain fixing international border at 49th parallel solidifies US territorial rights to Oregon and Washington

1848

- Quits the *Brooklyn Daily Eagle* and takes position as assistant editor of the *New Orleans Daily Crescent*; soon tires of that situation and returns home in June, then in September founds the *Brooklyn Freeman*, a short-lived Free Soil weekly reflecting his new political orientation
- * Revolutions spread across Europe; first women's-rights convention held, at Seneca Falls, New York; Associated Press formed in New York

1850

- Publishes free-verse polemical poems in the progressive New York newspapers of William Cullen Bryant (*New York Evening Post*) and Horace Greeley (*New York Daily Tribune*)
- * Passage of the Compromise of 1850, a component of which was the controversial Fugitive Slave Act; founding of *Harper's Monthly*, soon the most popular general magazine in the mid-century United States

1854

- Composes "A Boston Ballad" in angry response to the Anthony Burns fugitive slave trial but withholds publication
- * Passage of the Kansas–Nebraska Act, dividing the territory into two entities, one free and the other slave; Republican party founded soon afterward with an antislavery orientation

1855

- Self-publishes first edition of *Leaves of Grass* in July
- * Frederick Douglass publishes *My Bondage and My Freedom* in August, Henry Wadsworth Longfellow *Hiawatha* in November, and Herman Melville "Benito Cereno" in the October–December numbers of *Putnam's Monthly*

1856

- Publishes second edition of *Leaves of Grass*, with twenty additional poems
- * James Buchanan retains the White House for the Democrats in a bitter, sectionally and racially divided election

1857

- Tries unsuccessfully to find a publisher for planned new edition of *Leaves of Grass*; returns to journalism as editor of *Brooklyn Daily Times*
- * Severe recession contracts the US economy and cripples the publishing sector; founding of *Atlantic Monthly*

1859

- Quits the *Daily Times* and commits himself to the composition of new poems and the preparation of the delayed third edition of *Leaves of Grass*
- * John Brown attacks the federal arsenal at Harpers Ferry in October, hoping to provoke general insurrection; is tried and hanged within six weeks

1860
- Publishes the third edition of *Leaves of Grass* in Boston by invitation of Thayer and Eldridge, young abolitionist publishers
- Republican candidate Abraham Lincoln is elected president; South Carolina secedes from the Union in December

1861
- Whitman remains in Brooklyn, unsure of his role in wartime and stalled in his desire to bring out a sequel to the third edition following the bankruptcy of Thayer and Eldridge
- Outbreak of Civil War; first battle is fought 21 July at Bull Run in northern Virginia, 25 miles from Washington, DC

1862
- Goes down to Virginia in December to locate his wounded brother; delays return unexpectedly to Brooklyn
- Major Civil War battles fought at Shiloh, New Orleans, Malvern Hill, Second Bull Run, and Antietam; Preliminary Emancipation Proclamation issued in September, taking effect 1 January 1863

1863
- Stays on in Washington as self-appointed nurse in war hospitals; Washington remains primary residence until 1873
- Major Civil War battles fought at Chancellorsville, Gettysburg, Vicksburg, Chickamauga, and Chattanooga; anti-draft riots convulse New York City in July

1865
- Publishes *Drum-Taps* in New York in April, then *Sequel to Drum-Taps* in October (including "When Lilacs Last in the Dooryard Bloom'd"); fired from clerkship in Bureau of Indian Affairs by secretary of interior probably for supposed immorality of his poetry but soon afterward finds new position in attorney general's office; publication by Whitman's friend William O'Connor of hagiographic *The Good Gray Poet*
- Lincoln assassinated days before the end of the Civil War in April and succeeded by Andrew Johnson; slavery abolished by the thirteenth amendment

1867
- Publishes fourth edition of *Leaves of Grass*; John Burroughs publishes *Notes on Walt Whitman, as Poet and Person*, the first biography of the poet (who collaborated with Burroughs)
- Beginning of Reconstruction; United States purchases Alaska from Russia for $7,200,000

1868
- William Michael Rossetti brings out in London selected volume, *Poems*, the first non-American edition
- Impeachment trial of Andrew Johnson ends in acquittal; U. S. Grant is elected his successor

1870

- Completes composition of "Passage to India," which became part of the *Passage to India* annex to the fifth edition of *Leaves of Grass*
- * Beginning of construction of Brooklyn Bridge (opened in 1883); passage of the fifteenth amendment to the US Constitution expands suffrage to African Americans

1871

- Publishes new edition of *Leaves of Grass* in New York with J. S. Redfield, as well as *Democratic Vistas* in Washington
- * Indian Appropriation Act is passed, nullifying all treaties and rendering all Native Americans wards of the federal government; first US civil service commission established

1873

- Suffers stroke in Washington in January and in poor health travels in May to Camden, New Jersey, where he becomes a boarder in his brother George's house; lives remaining years in Camden
- * Panic of 1873 convulses American economy; Society for Suppression of Vice sponsors passage of act prohibiting sending of obscene literature through the mails

1876

- Self-publishes author's edition of *Leaves of Grass* in Camden, as well as *Two Rivulets* and *Memoranda During the War*
- * Rutherford B. Hayes wins contested presidential election; Centennial Exposition hosted in Philadelphia; founding of American Library Association

1879

- Makes his furthest trip west, traveling by train to Denver and stopping on the way back for a visit of several weeks with brother Jeff in St. Louis
- * Radcliffe College is established; Thomas Edison perfects electric light bulb

1881

- Publishes new, final edition of *Leaves of Grass* in Boston with James Osgood, who soon thereafter withdraws the book after the Boston district attorney threatens him with obscenity charges
- * James Garfield is inaugurated president, assassinated six months later, and succeeded by Chester Arthur; completion of last major elevated railroad in Manhattan

1882

- Takes back the sheets and plates *of Leaves of Grass* from Osgood and distributes the work from his house, then reaches an agreement with Rees, Welsh in Philadelphia for its publication; publishes *Specimen Days* with Rees, Welsh, which soon passes on Whitman's publications to David McKay, Whitman's publisher for the rest of the century

* Passage of Chinese Exclusion Act, prohibiting immigration of Chinese to the United States: deaths of Ralph Waldo Emerson, Henry Wadsworth Longfellow, and Charles Darwin

1884

- Buys house at 328 Mickle Street, Camden, New Jersey, his final residence
* Grover Cleveland is elected president; McClure's newspaper syndicate is founded

1888

- Publishes *Complete Poems and Prose* in 600-copy edition and *November Boughs*, both with David McKay in Philadelphia
* George Eastman perfects box-camera technology; construction of Boston Public Library begins

1891

- Publishes *Good-bye, My Fancy* with David McKay
* Congress passes the International Copyright Act; Thomas Edison files patent for first motion picture; Carnegie Hall opens in New York with all-Tchaikovsky program conducted by the composer

1892

- Publishes "deathbed" edition of *Leaves of Grass* with David McKay in Philadelphia; dies at home in Camden on 26 March
* Ellis Island opens as immigrant depot on 1 January; Columbia Exposition takes place in Chicago; Homestead Strike explodes in violence outside Pittsburgh

Contemporary Documents

Advertisement for *Leaves of Grass, New York Daily Tribune,*
7 July 1855

Small advertisements like this for *Leaves of Grass* began running in the *New York Daily Tribune* on 6 July. Whitman had a long-standing knowledge and appreciation of the paper; he had published a poem in it in 1850 and read it for years. Furthermore, he was personally acquainted with both the editor and the assistant editor of the paper, Horace Greeley and Charles Dana; the latter wrote one of the earliest and most positive reviews of *Leaves of Grass*, in the *Tribune* (it is reprinted in Interpretations, **pp. 39–43**). But the reason Whitman placed his advertisement in that paper was that he knew that it had the highest literary reputation among New York's morning newspapers and consequently was the one most favored by publishers and readers for the advertisement of books and magazines.

The advertisement was disproportionately modest for a volume whose prefatory essay, a strident, self-referential manifesto about the form and function of American national poetry, proclaimed that "The United States themselves are essentially the greatest poem" and concluded with the prophetic announcement "The proof of a poet is that his country absorbs him as affectionately as he has absorbed it."[1] Sale by just two retail outlets in the greater New York area hardly made possible the grand reception Whitman had in mind for his work of transcontinental, nation-making poetry (although Fowlers and Wells did distribute the work through its Boston outlet, as well).

But one can interpret the advertisement in a different way by reading it in juxtaposition with its immediate print context. The *Tribune* ran many other advertisements on its front page that day, as was its typical practice. *Leaves of Grass* found itself for sale in a commercial neighborhood that included not just a miscellany of positions for hire and properties for rent or sale but a broad cross-section of advertisements for New York's burgeoning art and cultural

---

1   1855 Preface, in Kaplan, *Whitman, Poetry and Prose*, pp. 5, 26.

scene, including productions of music, drama, and painting, as well as books and magazines. Among the books advertised that day were *Memoirs of James Gordon Bennett* (proprietor of the *New York Herald*, a scandalous daily that would merge with the *Tribune* in the twentieth century), a sensationalistic *Female Life among the Mormons*, and a Revolutionary War novel, *Glanmore; or, The Bandits of Saratoga*. But the most conspicuous title that day was prominent minister Henry Ward Beecher's *Star Papers*, a collection of journal essays reissued by New York City publisher J. C. Derby, who the following month published another popular book in Frederick Douglass' *My Bondage and My Freedom* (which outsold *Leaves of Grass* by more than twenty fold). Using a fairly new tactic, Derby saturated the front page that day with multiple advertisements for *Star Papers*, bringing it a degree of publicity that Whitman could not afford for his book.

Although books were the largest source, there were advertisements on the front page also for other kinds of cultural display. One was for a map of the ongoing siege of Sebastopol, the pivotal battle in the Crimean War. Another was for the popular Düsseldorf Gallery, whose paintings Whitman was familiar with. Master showman P. T. Barnum advertised his American Museum's newest performance, a bearded Swiss woman and a bearded infant (origin unstated), while other local theaters – the Broadway and the National – also ran advertisements for their current shows and Niblo's Garden for an operatic performance. The advance agent for the hugely popular French actress Rachel was also at work

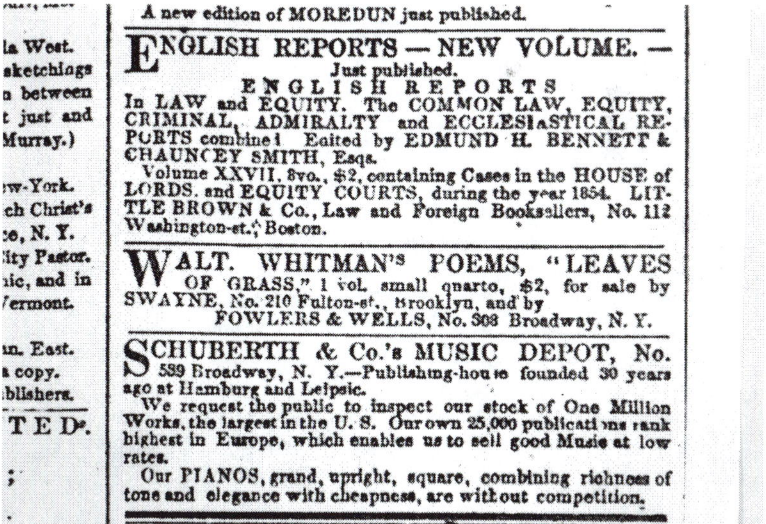
A new edition of MOREDUN just published.

ENGLISH REPORTS — NEW VOLUME. — Just published. ENGLISH REPORTS In LAW and EQUITY. The COMMON LAW, EQUITY, CRIMINAL, ADMIRALTY and ECCLESIASTICAL REPORTS combined. Edited by EDMUND H. BENNETT & CHAUNCEY SMITH, Esqs.

Volume XXVII, 8vo., $2, containing Cases in the HOUSE of LORDS, and EQUITY COURTS, during the year 1854. LITTLE BROWN & Co., Law and Foreign Booksellers, No. 112 Washington-st., Boston.

WALT. WHITMAN'S POEMS, "LEAVES OF GRASS," 1 vol. small quarto, $2, for sale by SWAYNE, No. 210 Fulton-st., Brooklyn, and by FOWLERS & WELLS, No. 308 Broadway, N. Y.

SCHUBERTH & Co.'s MUSIC DEPOT, No. 539 Broadway, N. Y.—Publishing-house founded 30 years ago at Hamburg and Leipsic.

We request the public to inspect our stock of One Million Works, the largest in the U. S. Our own 25,000 publications rank highest in Europe, which enables us to sell good Music at low rates.

Our PIANOS, grand, upright, square, combining richness of tone and elegance with cheapness, are without competition.

Figure 5 **First advertisement for 1855 *Leaves of Grass*, in *New York Daily Tribune*, one of the city's and country's leading antebellum newspapers (Courtesy of University of South Carolina Library)**

promoting her upcoming performance. A different kind of popular entertainment on Broadway was the George Christy and Wood's Minstrels (not the
same group as the Christy Minstrels, the most popular minstrelsy act in the
country then engaged in a ten-year run at the city's Mechanics Hall). Whitman
was well aware of the craze for minstrelsy (for more about his interest in it, see
p. 12). Indeed, he befriended the kinds of working-class white men who
constituted its primary audience, and there are references in "Song of Myself,"
such as to the "revolving eyes" of the runaway slave (section 10, l. 195), that bear
traces of minstrel stereotyping.

Advertisement for 1881 *Leaves of Grass, The Critic*
1 (13 August 1881): 221

The *Critic* was one of the few reputable, late-nineteenth-century literary
magazines not simply open to but partisan to Whitman. Years after his death,
editor Jeannette Gilder reminisced that "one of the things of which I am most
proud is that the *Critic* was the first publication of its class to invite Walt
Whitman to contribute to its pages."[2] Whitman was a frequent contributor,
as was Joel Chandler Harris, who submitted some of his earliest Uncle Remus
tales.

These two Whitman blurbs convey something of the major effort made in
1881 to promote his reputation. They were timed to coincide with the
forthcoming publication of a revised edition of *Leaves of Grass*, for which
Whitman had contracted with James Osgood of Boston. The second blurb
was factually accurate in one important regard: Osgood was the most
reputable publisher Whitman had ever persuaded to handle *Leaves of
Grass*. The high expectations both he and Whitman had for their collaboration,
however, quickly came to naught when early the next year the Boston
district attorney pressured Osgood to censor the book. Osgood appealed to
Whitman to make excisions and, when Whitman refused, terminated their
agreement.

The other blurb was typical of the gossipy pieces that Whitman and his
small circle of steadfast supporters frequently placed in newspapers and magazines in order to keep him as much as possible in the public eye. Dr. Richard
Maurice Bucke, a Canadian psychiatrist, became Whitman's strongest supporter in the last dozen years of the poet's life and by 1881 was planning a
biograpy – naturally, with Whitman's endorsement and help. Bucke's *Walt
Whitman* was published in 1883 by Whitman's own publisher, David McKay of
Philadelphia.

---

2   Quoted in Charles N. Elliot, ed., *Walt Whitman as Man, Poet, and Friend* (Boston: R. G. Badger,
      1915), p. 97.

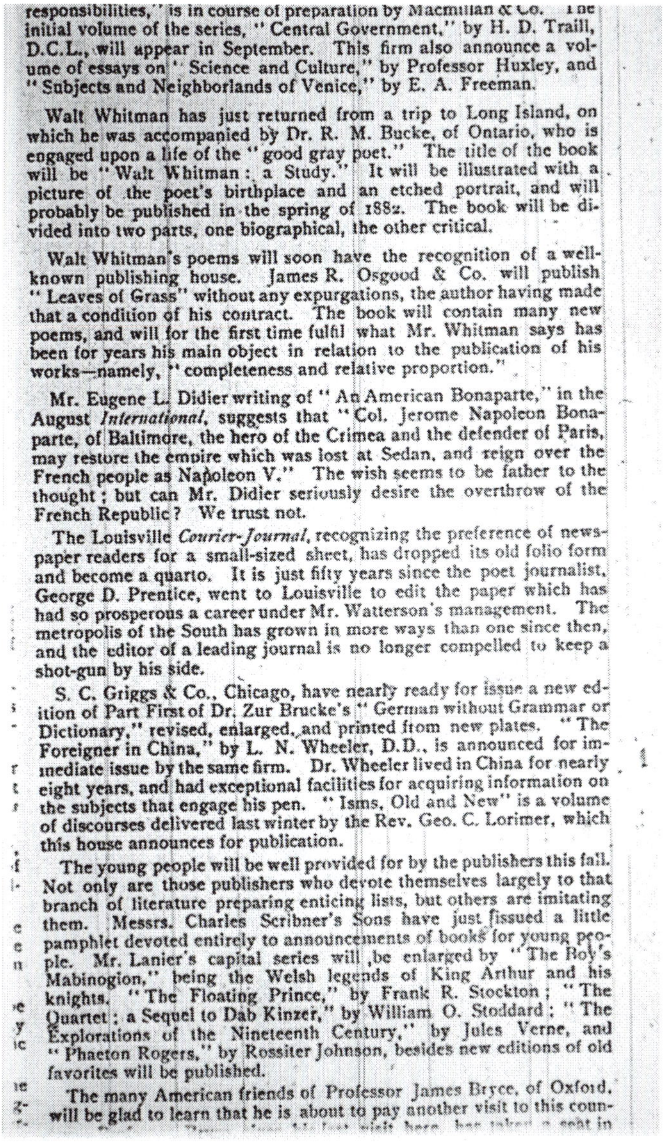

responsibilities," is in course of preparation by Macmillan & Co. The initial volume of the series, "Central Government," by H. D. Traill, D.C.L., will appear in September. This firm also announce a volume of essays on "Science and Culture," by Professor Huxley, and "Subjects and Neighborlands of Venice," by E. A. Freeman.

Walt Whitman has just returned from a trip to Long Island, on which he was accompanied by Dr. R. M. Bucke, of Ontario, who is engaged upon a life of the "good gray poet." The title of the book will be "Walt Whitman: a Study." It will be illustrated with a picture of the poet's birthplace and an etched portrait, and will probably be published in the spring of 1882. The book will be divided into two parts, one biographical, the other critical.

Walt Whitman's poems will soon have the recognition of a well-known publishing house. James R. Osgood & Co. will publish "Leaves of Grass" without any expurgations, the author having made that a condition of his contract. The book will contain many new poems, and will for the first time fulfil what Mr. Whitman says has been for years his main object in relation to the publication of his works—namely, "completeness and relative proportion."

Mr. Eugene L. Didier writing of "An American Bonaparte," in the August *International*, suggests that "Col. Jerome Napoleon Bonaparte, of Baltimore, the hero of the Crimea and the defender of Paris, may restore the empire which was lost at Sedan, and reign over the French people as Napoleon V." The wish seems to be father to the thought; but can Mr. Didier seriously desire the overthrow of the French Republic? We trust not.

The Louisville *Courier-Journal*, recognizing the preference of newspaper readers for a small-sized sheet, has dropped its old folio form and become a quarto. It is just fifty years since the poet journalist, George D. Prentice, went to Louisville to edit the paper which has had so prosperous a career under Mr. Watterson's management. The metropolis of the South has grown in more ways than one since then, and the editor of a leading journal is no longer compelled to keep a shot-gun by his side.

S. C. Griggs & Co., Chicago, have nearly ready for issue a new edition of Part First of Dr. Zur Brucke's "German without Grammar or Dictionary," revised, enlarged, and printed from new plates. "The Foreigner in China," by L. N. Wheeler, D.D., is announced for immediate issue by the same firm. Dr. Wheeler lived in China for nearly eight years, and had exceptional facilities for acquiring information on the subjects that engage his pen. "Isms, Old and New" is a volume of discourses delivered last winter by the Rev. Geo. C. Lorimer, which this house announces for publication.

The young people will be well provided for by the publishers this fall. Not only are these publishers who devote themselves largely to that branch of literature preparing enticing lists, but others are imitating them. Messrs. Charles Scribner's Sons have just issued a little pamphlet devoted entirely to announcements of books for young people. Mr. Lanier's capital series will be enlarged by "The Boy's Mabinogion," being the Welsh legends of King Arthur and his knights. "The Floating Prince," by Frank R. Stockton; "The Quartet: a Sequel to Dab Kinzer," by William O. Stoddard; "The Explorations of the Nineteenth Century," by Jules Verne, and "Phaeton Rogers," by Rossiter Johnson, besides new editions of old favorites will be published.

The many American friends of Professor James Bryce, of Oxford, will be glad to learn that he is about to pay another visit to this coun-

Figure 6 Advertisement for the 1881 Osborne edition of *Leaves of Grass*, soon thereafter threatened with censorship and withdrawn from the market (Courtesy of University of South Carolina Library)

"Counter-Jumps: A Poemettina, After Walt Whitman," *Vanity Fair* (17 March 1860): 183

By contrast with Emily Dickinson, Whitman was hardly an unknown poet during his lifetime. His career failure was one not of attracting attention but of earning approval. One sign of the attention he received was the frequency with which his verse was parodied, or worse.

This clever 1860 parody of "Song of Myself" was published in a humorous magazine friendly to Whitman at a time when his writing was receiving the most attention since the publication of the first *Leaves of Grass* nearly five years before. The immediate reason for the renewed publicity was the forthcoming appearance of the third edition, scheduled for publication in spring. For the first time in his career, Whitman had something of a publicity machine behind him. His publishers in Boston were doing everything they could to promote his name, as was his New York friend and crony Henry Clapp, publisher of a popular weekly magazine in which appeared various poems by Whitman, gossipy pieces about him, reviews and letters of support, and occasional parodies. (For more on Clapp and his weekly magazine, see **p. 72 n. 3.**) This particular parody should be understood in the context of renewed attention paid to Whitman.

The unknown author was well acquainted not only with Whitman's poetry but also with contemporary opinion. In fact, the author anticipated audience reaction by caricaturing what their contemporaries saw as the poem's egregious flaws: materialism, colloquialism, egotism, and − worst of all − anti-poetic subject and style. Following the line of Whitman's strongest opponents, it mocked any claim that "Song of Myself" could be recognizable as poetry. With a deft stroke, its closing line even rephrased perhaps the single most frequently derided verse not only in the poem (l. 1333) but in all of *Leaves of Grass.*

Whitman's reaction to this parody is unknown, but it is hard to believe that it would have given him much pause. He delighted in public attention and ingeniously created it himself when no one else took what he considered correct or sufficient regard of his work.

COUNTER-JUMPS

A POEMETTINA, − AFTER WALT WHITMAN

I am the Counter-jumper, weak and effeminate.
I love to loaf and lie about dry-goods.
I loaf and invite the Buyer.
I am the essence of retail. The sum and result of small profit and
    quick returns.
The Picayune is part of me, and so is the half cent, and the mill only
    arithmetically appreciable.
The shining, cheap, woven sarsnet is of me, and I am of it.
The white bobinet,
And the moiré antique, thickly webbed and strown with impossible
    flowers,

And the warm winter gloves lined with fur,
And the delicate summer gloves of silk threads,
And the intermediate ones built of the hide of the Swedish rat,
All these things are of me, and many more also.
For I am the shop, and the counter, and the till,
But particularly the last.
And I explore and rummage the till, and am at home in it.
And I am the shelves on which lie the damaged goods;
The damaged goods themselves I am,
And I ask what's the damage?
I am the crate, and the hamper, and the yard-wand, and the box of
    silks fresh from France.
And when I came into the world I paid duty,
And I never did my duty,
And never intend to do it,
For I am the creature of weak depravities;
I am the Counter-jumper;
I sound my feeble yelp over the roofs of the World.

Directory of Contextual Figures

This Directory provides information on figures mentioned in the Introduction, Contexts section, and headnotes to the Interpretations section.

Amos Bronson Alcott (1799–1888) was an unconventional educator and thinker known and widely derided for his mystical ideas and notions. At Emerson's urging, he came down to Brooklyn with Thoreau to make the acquaintance of Whitman in autumn 1856.

Matthew Arnold (1822–88) was a major English essayist, poet, and cultural arbiter. Arnold held a low opinion of Whitman, whom he derided for "trad[ing] merely on his own bottom" rather than incorporating the best of their common heritage into his work.

P(hineas) T(aylor) Barnum (1810–91), one part showman, the other part con man, was the premier impresario of his time in the United States.

Edwin Booth (1833–93) was a member of a great American acting family and was highly regarded in both the United States and Europe particularly for his classical roles. His brother John Wilkes was also a well-known actor, although the role that has perpetuated his name was as the assassin of Abraham Lincoln.

Mathew Brady (1823–96) was one of the leading daguerreotypists and photographers of mid-century America; he and his employees photographed many of the leading figures in politics and the arts, including Whitman, but he is perhaps better known today for the unprecedented exhibition he staged at his New York gallery in July 1862 of photographs of Civil War corpses taken by his corps of photographers at Antietam battlefield, a milestone in the history of war reportage.

John Burroughs (1837–1921), a prolific and popular nature writer, befriended Whitman in Washington in 1863 and wrote, with Whitman's active assistance, the first Whitman biography (*Notes on Walt Whitman, as Poet and Person*, 1867).

Abraham Cahan (1860–1951) was the leading Yiddish-language journalist in the United States and the author of the classic immigrant novel *The Rise of David Levinsky* (1917).

Cassius Marcellus Clay (1810–1903) was a flamboyant statesman who turned against his Kentucky slave-owning heritage to play a significant role in antislavery agitation in the 1840s and in the formation of the antislavery Republican party in 1854.

Stephen Crane (1871–1900), best known for *The Red Badge of Courage* (1895), was one of the leading short-story writers, novelists, and poets of his generation.

Emily Dickinson (1830–86) was one of the greatest lyrical poets of the nineteenth century and Whitman's nearest peer among American poets. The only known mention by her of Whitman's work was a possibly tongue-in-cheek response by letter (25 April 1862) to an inquiry: "You speak of Mr Whitman – I never read his Book – but was told that he was disgraceful."

Frederick Douglass (1817–1895), born to slavery in Maryland but escaped to freedom in 1838, was arguably the leading African American orator, journalist, and author of the antebellum generation and a lifelong leader of the struggle of black people and women for equal rights.

Ralph Waldo Emerson (1803–82), essayist, philosopher, and poet, was a seminal influence on nineteenth-century American culture generally, and on Whitman specifically.

Edwin Forrest (1806–72), renowned in particular for his flamboyant style of acting, was the most famous American tragedian of his generation.

Margaret Fuller (1810–50), author, critic, and reformer, was the editor of the Transcendentalist newspaper the *Dial*, and a pioneering feminist, in which cause she wrote the classic *Woman in the Nineteenth Century* (1845).

Hamlin Garland (1860–1940), a self-educated prose writer from Wisconsin, was a well-regarded novelist, story-teller, and essayist best known for his debunking stories of life on the American Plains.

William Lloyd Garrison (1805–79), the most dynamic white figure in the anti-slavery movement in the United States, was a founder of the New England Anti-slavery Society and American Antislavery Society and editor of the influential abolitionist journal *The Liberator*.

Horace Greeley (1811–72), founder and editor of the liberal *New York Daily Tribune*, was one of the most influential journalists in antebellum and Civil War America and an unsuccessful candidate for the presidency in 1872.

Joel Chandler Harris (1848–1908), born and raised in Georgia, was a popular American writer and journalist best known for his race-based, folksy stories set on pre-Civil War plantations, which responded to a widespread post-Reconstruction nostalgia for the lost South and simpler times.

Gabriel Harrison (1818–1902), a man of many talents, was a New York-based daguerreotypist, landscape painter, actor, and playwright who shot the well-known "carpenter" picture of his friend Whitman one hot summer day in 1854 (see Figure 2, **p. 16**).

Andrew Jackson (1767–1845) was the seventh president of the United States (serving 1829–37). Like Jefferson (see below), his policies were perceived as supporting the interests of the "common man," a category of great significance to Whitman.

Henry James (1843–1916), prolific American novelist, critic, and dramatist, is widely regarded as one of the masters of modern fiction. Throughout the twentieth century critics counterposed James and Whitman as opposing models of sophistication and "naturalness."

Thomas Jefferson (1743–1826) was the third president of the United States (serving 1801–09). (See entry on Jackson, above, for further information.)

Charles Kean (1811–68) was one of the leading actors of his time and was perhaps best known for his revivals of Shakespeare. (For further information, see entry on Ellen Tree.)

Fanny Kemble (1809–93) was one of the most dazzling English actors of her generation in both Great Britain and the United States, which she toured to acclaim in 1832–34; she later became an outspoken critic of slavery, despite her marriage to a wealthy plantation owner.

Abraham Lincoln (1809–65) was the sixteenth president of the United States (serving 1861–65). Whitman, who occasionally passed him by on the streets of Washington during the Civil War, came to idolize him and commemorated him shortly after Lincoln's assassination with one of his greatest poems ("When Lilacs Last in the Dooryard Bloom'd") as well as with one of his most popular poems ("O Captain! My Captain!").

Jenny Lind (1820–87), nicknamed in her own time the "Swedish Nightingale," was an enormously popular soprano in Europe who gained her American reputation chiefly during a successful countrywide tour of 1850–52.

Henry Wadsworth Longfellow (1807–82), the most famous American poet of his time, enjoyed a great popular and critical success in 1855 with *The Song of Hiawatha*, which dwarfed the popular and critical reception of *Leaves of Grass* that year.

Herman Melville (1819–91) was better known for his novels (chief among them, *Moby-Dick*), but he was also a poet of great power and has often been compared to Whitman. As far as we know, the two men never met or commented on each other's work.

James Osgood (1836–92) began his distinguished publishing career working his way up through the ranks of the prominent literary publishing firm of Ticknor and Fields, which he took over after the death of William Ticknor and the retirement of James Fields. One of the leading literary publishers in the country, Osgood published in 1881 not only a new edition of *Leaves of Grass* but also new works by Mark Twain and Henry James.

Wendell Phillips (1811–84), though born of Boston Brahmin ancestry, was a major figure along with Garrison (see above) in the antislavery movement, as well as an energetic advocate of other radical political causes such as women's rights and the abolition of capital punishment.

Edgar Allan Poe (1809–49), major American poet, short-story writer, and critic, was a figure with whom Whitman was often compared and contrasted during the latter's lifetime. Whitman attended the 1875 public reburial of Poe's remains in Baltimore but declined a request to speak.

Algernon Charles Swinburne (1837–1909) was a popular English poet who associated in the 1860s with the Pre-Raphaelites (one of whom, William Michael Rossetti, brought out the first English edition of Whitman's poems, in 1868). Swinburne at first supported Whitman's poetry and even composed an ode "To Walt Whitman in America" (1871), but later cooled in his enthusiasm.

John Addington Symonds (1840–93), English man of letters and pioneer writer on the taboo subject of homosexuality, was a vocal, early supporter of Whitman. When he tried to draw Whitman out about his sexual orientation, he received Whitman's now famous evasive response about youthful indiscretions resulting in "six children," which sent a generation of scholars looking for Whitman's supposed illegitimate offspring in New Orleans.

Bayard Taylor (1825–78) was a well-regarded American travel writer, poet, and novelist whom Whitman saw, as he did Longfellow, as a convention-bound, lesser writer than himself.

Alfred, Lord Tennyson (1809–92) was Poet Laureate of England (1850–92) and one of the most revered poets in both Britain and the United States during the Victorian era. Whitman corresponded with him late in life but was cool to his poetry.

Henry David Thoreau (1817–62) was a writer and naturalist best known for *Walden* (1854). He visited Whitman at his home in Brooklyn in 1856, the only time the two men met.

Horace Traubel (1858–1919) was a companion and amanuensis to Whitman and recorded in his multivolume *With Walt Whitman in Camden* a transcription of the disabled poet's wide-ranging conversation during his last years.

Ellen Tree (1805–80; also known as Ellen Tree Kean) was a premier figure of the English stage as well as co-manager with her husband Charles Kean of the Princess' Theatre in London.

Mark Twain (1835–1910) was one of the greatest American novelists and humorists of the nineteenth century. Comparisons between him and Whitman as American writers have been a commonplace since the early twentieth century.

Oscar Wilde (1854–1900) was the witty author of *The Importance of Being Earnest* and other satiric comedies. Wilde was a long-time admirer of Whitman (perhaps the man more than the poet or poetry), and visited him in Camden in 1882 during a lecture tour across the United States.

2

Interpretations

Introduction

Immediately following its July 1855 publication in *Leaves of Grass*, "Song of Myself" was singled out from the volume's other poems by critics, reviewers, and private readers for particular attention, and that has remained the pattern ever since. Even as critical taste has varied, "Song of Myself" has been held up as the exemplar of what is best and worst about Whitman's poetics. This has been the pattern not only among critics but also among parodists, imitators, and creative artists influenced by Whitman. Despite the continuities in the poem's reception, it is not only possible but useful to divide its reception into nineteenth and twentieth century components, for by the early twentieth century "Song of Myself," once widely reviled, was rapidly emerging as a world classic. Furthermore, social and critical norms operative in the nineteenth century quickly gave way with the coming of the early twentieth century modernist movement to a different set of norms.

One editorial practice operative in this section needs to be made explicit. Extended excerpts from "Song of Myself," which were more common in the nineteenth than in the twentieth century, have generally been omitted. The major exception is the very earliest reviews, where they are included in order to give the reader a sense of contemporary taste and reviewing practice (and, in the case of Whitman's self-review, a window on Whitman reading Whitman).

Nineteenth-Century Responses and Criticism

If Whitman had hoped in composing "Song of Myself" to write the great American poem of his time, the discrepancy between his ambition and the poem's actual reception was gaping. Quickly fearing or sensing this fact himself, he labored steadfastly from its initial publication until the end of his life to promote its acceptance. But the simple reality was that the poem's formal, intellectual, and philosophical radicalism so greatly challenged contemporary readers' expectations and values that popular acceptance proved nearly completely elusive and critical acceptance came only slowly and erratically. Indeed, the poem's assault on middle-class norms and values was so great that many readers found it difficult to see "Song of Myself" as art at all and in several instances the poem (and the volume) was formally censored.

Letter from Ralph Waldo Emerson to Walt Whitman, 21 July 1855

Emerson's personal letter to Whitman is today perhaps the most famous assessment by one American writer of another. In its own day it was anything but. Written almost immediately after reception of the 1855 *Leaves of Grass* as an unsolicited "gift" (in other words, review copy) and meant as a private tribute to what Emerson took to be a remarkable display of original genius, the letter was intended to express Emerson's pleasure and obligation strictly to the author. Emerson was so unsure about the identity of the unknown author that he posted the letter to the New York office of Fowlers and Wells, the book's distributor, which had advertised the book in the Boston and New York newspapers.

Whitman, for his part, was utterly delighted with Emerson's generous response. He had been considerably influenced by Emerson's cultural nationalism, and it seems safe to say that Emerson's opinion was, for Whitman, the single most important that could be delivered on the book's merits. Operating with a much looser standard of literary etiquette than Emerson's, Whitman gave the letter in October to his acquaintance Charles Dana, of the *New York Daily Tribune*, for publication in the newspaper. (For Dana's own review, see **pp. 39–43**.) As though that were not breach of etiquette enough, he had Emerson's words "I greet you at the beginning of a great career" and name printed without permission on the spine of the second edition of *Leaves of Grass*. Furthermore, he reprinted Emerson's letter and added his own open letter in response in an appendix following the poems.

Emerson could not have been pleased with such behavior, which was reported back to him through numerous private and public sources (for an example of which, see the review by Rufus Griswold on **pp. 54–56**). He declined, however, to complain to Whitman, whom he visited in New York in December 1855 and with whom he remained in touch, primarily through the mails, for many years.

Dear Sir,

I am not blind to the worth of the wonderful gift of "Leaves of Grass." I find it the most extraordinary piece of wit & wisdom that America has yet contributed. I am very happy in reading it, as great power makes us happy. It meets the demand I am always making of what seemed the sterile & stingy Nature, as if too much handiwork or too much lymph in the temperament were making our western wits fat & mean. I give you joy of your free & brave thought. I have great joy in it. I find incomparable things said incomparably well, as they must be. I find the courage of *treatment*, which so delights us, & which large perception only can inspire.

I greet you at the beginning of a great career, which yet must have had a long foreground somewhere for such a start. I rubbed my eyes a little to see if this sunbeam were no illusion; but the solid sense of the book is a sober certainty. It has the best merits, namely, of fortifying & encouraging.

I did not know until I, last night, saw the book advertised in a newspaper, that I could trust the name as real & available for a post-office. I wish to see my benefactor, & have felt much like striking my tasks, & visiting New York to pay you my respects.

R. W. Emerson.

Mr. Walter Whitman.

From Charles A. Dana, "New Publications: Leaves of Grass,"
New York Daily Tribune (23 July 1855): 3

This was apparently the first public review of *Leaves of Grass*. Whitman had more than a passing acquaintance with Dana and the newspaper, a leading daily in the city and nation and the one in which Whitman had placed the earliest advertisements for the book. Despite its mixed assessment, it must have pleased Whitman, who was keenly sensitive to the value of any publicity, good or bad.

One of the outstanding American journalists of the nineteenth century, Dana was in 1855 managing editor of the *Tribune*. Before joining its staff as city editor in 1847 he had been a stalwart figure at the Brook Farm utopian community. This communitarian farm in West Roxbury, Massachusetts, operated from 1841 to 1847 and was home to Dana, novelist Nathaniel Hawthorne (for a brief time) and a number of people associated with the Transcendentalist movement. Here Dana made the acquaintance not only of Hawthorne, but Emerson, as well as the author, critic, and feminist reformer Margaret Fuller and the educator and thinker Amos Bronson Alcott, to whose unconventional *Orphic Sayings* Dana compares *Leaves of Grass*. Even in his early years with the *Tribune*, he developed a tougher, less idealistic sensibility, though not fully at the expense of his earlier self. Both sides of his sensibility are in evidence here. (See the Directory of Contextual Figures, for more information on Fuller (**p. 31**) and Alcott (**p. 30**).)

This strongly ambivalent review anticipates several key aspects of nineteenth-century Whitman criticism: that there is an original genius on display in the poetry but that it violates the accepted norms of poetic and social decorum, that Whitman's poetry is comparable to the visionary work of Transcendentalists such as Emerson and Alcott, and that Whitman's poetry is an ideological verse intended to represent the nation (or, at least, a particular working-class ideal of the nation). The review also nicely exemplifies several practices common in nineteenth-century reviews. One is the heavy reliance on excerpts, a norm in the era's often subjective style of formal reviewing and freer circulation of both copyrighted and uncopyrighted texts than in our time. Another is an editorial license unacceptable by twentieth-century standards, evidenced here by Dana's heavy-handed policy of inserting his own titles to the verse excerpts from *Leaves*. His titles, which seem completely un-Whitmanlike, are instructive: "The Lover of Nature" (from section 21 of "Song of Myself"), "After a Sea-Fight" (from section 36 of "Song of Myself"), "Natural Idealism" (from "A Song for Occupations"), "The Last of Earth" (from "To Think of Time"), and "The Human Face Divine" (from "Faces"). The excerpts from poems other than "Song of Myself" have been omitted.

From the unique effigies of the anonymous author of this volume which graces the frontispiece, we may infer that he belongs to the exemplary class of society sometimes irreverently styled "loafers."[1] He is therein represented in a garb, half sailor's, half workman's, with no superfluous appendage of coat or waistcoat, a "wide-awake" perched jauntily on his head, one hand in his pocket and the other on his hip, with a certain air of mild defiance, and an expression of pensive insolence in his face which seems to betoken a consciousness of his mission as the "coming man." This view of the author is confirmed in the preface. He

---

1   Dana is referring to the daguerreotype engraving used as the frontispiece to the 1855 edition (see Figure 2, p. 16).

vouchsafes, before introducing us to his poetry, to enlighten our benighted minds as to the true function of the American poet. Evidently the original, which is embodied in the most extraordinary prose since the "Sayings" of the modern Orpheus,[2] was found in the "interior consciousness" of the writer. Of the materials afforded by this country for the operations of poetic art we have a lucid account.

A long excerpt from the 1855 Preface is cited.

With veins full of such poetical stuff, the United States, as we are kindly informed, "of all nations most needs poets, and will doubtless have the greatest and use them the greatest." Here is a full-length figure of the true poet:

Another long excerpt from the 1855 Preface is cited.

Of the nature of poetry the writer discourses in a somewhat too oracular strain, especially as he has been anticipated in his "utterances" by Emerson and other modern "prophets of the soul":

The poetic quality is not marshaled in rhyme or uniformity or abstract addresses to things, nor in melancholy complaints or good precepts, but is the life of these and much else and is in the soul. The profit of rhyme is that it drops seeds of a sweeter and more luxuriant rhyme, and of uniformity that it conveys itself into its own roots in the ground out of sight. The rhyme and uniformity of perfect poems show the free growth of metrical laws and bud from them as unerringly and loosely as lilacs or roses on a bush, and take shapes as compact as the shapes of chestnuts and oranges and melons and pears, and shed the perfume impalpable to form. The fluency and ornaments of the finest poems or music or orations or recitations are not independent but dependent. All beauty comes from beautiful blood and a beautiful brain. If the greatnesses are in conjunction in a man or woman it is enough. . . . the fact will prevail through the universe. . . . but the gaggery and gilt of a million years will not prevail. Who troubles himself about his ornaments or fluency is lost. This is what you shall do: Love the earth and sun and the animals, despise riches, give alms to every one that asks, stand up for the stupid and crazy, devote your income and labor to others, hate tyrants, argue not concerning God, have patience and indulgence toward the people, take off your hat to nothing known or unknown or to any man or number of men, go freely with powerful uneducated persons and with the young and with the mothers of families, read these leaves in the open air every season of every year of your life, reexamine all you have been

2   A spell-binding poet and musician in Greek mythology.

told at school or church or in any book, dismiss whatever insults your own
soul, and your very flesh shall be a great poem and have the richest fluency
not only in its words but in the silent lines of its lips and face and between
the lashes of your eyes and in every motion and joint of your body.

Such is the poetic theory of our nameless bard. He furnishes a severe standard
for the estimate of his own productions. His *Leaves of Grass* are doubtless
intended as an illustration of the natural poet. They are certainly original in their
external form, have been shaped on no pre-existent model out of the author's own
brain. Indeed, his independence often becomes coarse and defiant. His language is
too frequently reckless and indecent though this appears to arise from a naive
unconsciousness rather than from an impure mind. His words might have passed
between Adam and Eve in Paradise, before the want of fig-leaves brought no
shame; but they are quite out of place amid the decorum of modern society, and
will justly prevent his volume from free circulation in scrupulous circles. With
these glaring faults, the *Leaves of Grass* are not destitute of peculiar poetic merits,
which will awaken an interest in the lovers of literary curiosities. They are full of
bold, stirring thoughts—with occasional passages of effective description, betray-
ing a genuine intimacy with Nature and a keen appreciation of beauty—often
presenting a rare felicity of diction, but so disfigured with eccentric fancies as to
prevent a consecutive perusal without offense, though no impartial reader can fail
to be impressed with the vigor and quaint beauty of isolated portions. A few
specimens will suffice to give an idea of this odd genius.

THE LOVER OF NATURE

I am he that walks with the tender and growing night;
I call to the earth and sea half-held by the night.
Press close barebosomed night! Press close magnetic nourishing night!
Night of south winds! Night of the large few stars!
Still nodding night! Mad naked summer night!
Smile O voluptuous coolbreathed earth! Earth of the slumbering and
    liquid trees!
Earth of departed sunset! Earth of the mountains misty-topt!
Earth of the vitreous pour of the full moon just tinged with blue!
Earth of shine and dark mottling the tide of the river!
Earth of the limpid gray of clouds brighter and clearer for my sake!
Far-swooping elbowed earth! Rich apple-blossomed earth!
Smile, for your lover comes!

Prodigal! you have given me love!. . . . therefore I to you give love!
O unspeakable passionate love!
You sea! I resign myself to you also. . . . I guess what you mean,
I behold from the beach your crooked inviting fingers,
I believe you refuse to go back without feeling of me;
We must have a turn together. . . . I undress. . . . hurry me out of sight of
    the land,
Cushion me soft. . . . rock me in billowy drowse,
Dash me with amorous wet. . . . I can repay you.

Sea of stretched ground-swells!
Sea breathing broad and convulsive breaths!
Sea of the brine of life! Sea of unshoveled and always-ready graves!
Howler and scooper of storms! Capricious and dainty sea!
I am integral with you. . . . I too am of one phase and of all phases.

AFTER A SEA-FIGHT.

Stretched and still lay the midnight,
Two great hulls motionless on the breast of the
    darkness,
Our vessel riddled and slowly sinking . . . preparations to pass to the one
    we had conquered,
The captain on the quarter-deck coldly giving his orders through a
    countenance white as a sheet,
Near by the corpse of the child that served in the cabin,
The dead face of an old salt with long white hair and carefully curled
    whiskers,
The flames spite of all that could be done flickering aloft and below,
The husky voices of the two or three officers yet fit for duty,
Formless stacks of bodies and bodies by themselves . . . dabs of flesh
    upon the mass and spars,
The cut of cordage and dangle of rigging . . . . the slight shock of the
    soothe of waves,
Black and impassive guns, and litter of powder parcels, and the strong
    scent,
Delicate sniffs of the seabreeze . . . . smells of sedgy grass and fields by
    the shore. . . . death messages given in charge to survivors,
The hiss of the surgeon's knife and the gnawing teeth of his saw,
The wheeze, the cluck, the swash of falling blood. . . . the short wild
    scream, the long dull tapering groan,
These so . . . . these irretrievable!

Long citations from "A Song for Occupations," "To Think of Time," and "Faces"
follow.

The volume contains many more "Leaves of Grass" of similar quality, as well as
others which cannot be especially commended either for fragrance or form.
Whatever severity of criticism they may challenge for their rude ingenuousness,
and their frequent divergence into the domain of the fantastic, the taste of not
over dainty fastidiousness will discern much of the essential spirit of poetry
beneath an uncouth and grotesque embodiment.

Anonymous, "Leaves of Grass – an Extraordinary Book," *Brooklyn Daily Eagle* (15 September 1855): 2

The identity of the author of this spirited, generally sympathetic review is unknown, but it seems likely that he knew or knew of Whitman, a former editor of the newspaper in the late 1840s and long-time resident of Brooklyn. Perhaps for this reason his review dwells on personal matters: the frontispiece illustration ("a daguerreotype of his inner being"), its figure's pose as a common man, the author's freedom from convention, and the character of the ideal poet.

The reviewer's selection of passages for citation is interesting. No doubt his interest in the poet and his persona led him to read seriously the Preface, but he also highlighted several of the more lyrical passages, such as the opening stanza of section 6 of the child of nature and the whole of section 11 of the twenty-eight bathers, which also caught the attention of many other contemporary readers. (See discussion in Key Passages, **p. 135**.) This particular nineteenth-century reader might not have gotten the point of the twenty-ninth bather, but Boston district attorney Oliver Stevens did in 1882; in threatening to outlaw sale of the book, he demanded that the line about the "hand of the twenty-ninth bather" caressing the naked male bodies be removed, as well as many other phrases, lines, and passages of "Song of Myself" and other poems. (For a good account of the censorship of the 1881 Osgood edition, see Jerome Loving, *Walt Whitman: The Song of Himself* (Berkeley: University of California Press, 1999), pp. 413–17.)

Here we have a book which fairly staggers us. It sets all the ordinary rules of criticism at defiance. It is one of the strangest compounds of transcendentalism, bombast, philosophy, folly, wisdom, wit and dullness which it ever entered into the heart of man to conceive. Its author is Walter Whitman, and the book is a reproduction of the author. His name is not on the frontispiece, but his portrait, half length, is.[1] The contents of the book form a daguerreotype of his inner being, and the title page bears a representation of its physical tabernacle. It is a poem; but it conforms to none of the rules by which poetry has ever been judged. It is not an epic nor an ode, nor a lyric; nor does its verses move with the measured pace of poetical feet – of Iambic, Trochaic or Anapaestic, nor seek the aid of Amphibrach, of dactyl or Spondee, nor of final or cesural pause, except by accident. But we had better give Walt's own conception of what a poet of the age and country should be. We quote from the preface:

> "Other States indicate themselves in their deputies, but the genius of the
> United States is not best or most in executives or legislatures, nor in its
> ambassadors or authors, or colleges, or churches, or parlors, nor even in
> its newspapers or inventors; but always most in the common people,
> their manners, speech, dress, friendship – the friendship and candor of

---

1   His attention captured, as was that of many of his contemporaries, this reviewer is referring to the frontispiece illustration to the 1855 edition (see Figure 2, p. 16).

their physiognomy – the picturesque looseness of their carriage – their deathless attachment to freedom – their aversion to anything indecorous, or soft or mean, the practical acknowledgment of the citizens of all other States – the fierceness of their roused resentments – their curiosity and welcome of novelty – their self-esteem and wonderful sympathy – their susceptibility of a slight – the air they have of persons who never knew how it felt to stand in the presence of superiors – the fluency of their speech – their delight in music, the sure symptom of manly tenderness and native elegance of soul – their good temper and open handedness – the terrible significance of their elections – the President's taking off his hat to them, not they to him – these too are unrhymed poetry."[2]

But the poetry which the author contemplates must reflect the nation as well as the people themselves.

"His spirit responds to his country's spirit; he incarnates its geography and natural life, and rivers and lakes. Mississippi with annual freshets and changing chutes, Missouri, and Columbia, and Ohio, and the beautiful masculine Hudson, do not embouchure where they spend themselves more than they embouchure into him. The blue breadth over the inland sea of Virginia and Maryland, and the sea of Massachusetts and Maine, over Manhattan Bay, and over Champlain and Erie, and over Ontario and Huron, and Michigan and Superior, and over the Texan, and Mexican, and Floridian and Cuban seas, and over the seas of California and Oregon, is not tallied by the blue breadth of the waters below more than the breadth of above and below is tallied by him.

. . . "To him enter the essence of the real things, and past and present events – of the enormous diversity of temperature, and agriculture, and mines – the tribes of red aborigines – the weather-beaten vessels entering new ports or making landings on rocky coasts – the first settlement North and South – the rapid stature and muscle – the haughty defiance of '76, and the war, and peace, and formation of the constitution – the union surrounded by blatherers, and always impregnable – the perpetual coming of immigrants – the wharf-hemmed cities and superior marine – the unsurveyed interior – the log houses, and clearings, and wild animals, and hunters, and trappers – the free commerce, the fishing, and whaling, and gold digging – the endless gestation of new States – the convening of Congress every December, the members duly coming up from all climates and the uttermost parts – the noble character of the young mechanics, and of all free American workmen and workwomen – the general ardor, and friendliness, and enterprise – the perfect equality of the female with the male – the large amativeness – the fluid movement of the population," &c. . . .

---

2   As Dana did several months before, this critic is quoting here and below from the 1855 Preface.

"For such the expression of the American poet is to be transcendent and new."

And the poem seems to accord with the ideas here laid down. No drawing room poet is the author of the *Leaves of Grass*; he prates not of guitar thrumming under ladies' windows, nor deals in the extravagances of sentimentalism; no pretty conceits or polished fancies are tacked together "like orient pearls at random strung;"[3] but we have the free utterance of an untramelled spirit without the slightest regard to established models or fixed standards of taste. His scenery presents no shaven lawns or neatly trimmed arbors; no hot house conservatory, where delicate exotics odorise the air and enchant the eye. If we follow the poet we must scale unknown precipices and climb untrodden mountains; or we boat on nameless lakes, encountering probably rapids and waterfalls, and start wild fowls never classified by Wilson or Audubon;[4] or we wander among primeval forests, now pressing the yielding surface of velvet moss, and anon caught among thickets and brambles. He believes in the ancient philosophy that there is no more real beauty or merit in one particle of matter than another; he appreciates all; every thing is right that is in its place, and everything is wrong that is not in its place. He is guilty, not only of breaches of conventional decorum but treats with nonchalant defiance what goes by the name of refinement and delicacy of feeling and expression. Whatever is natural he takes to his heart; whatever is artificial (in the frivolous sense) he makes of no account. The following description of himself is more truthful than many self-drawn pictures:

"Apart from the pulling and hauling, stands what I am,
Stands amused, complacent, compassionating, idle, unitary,
Looks down, is erect, bends an arm on an impalpable certain rest,
Looks with its side-curved head curious, what will come next,
Both in and out of the game, and watching and wondering at it."[5]

As a poetic interpretation of nature, we believe the following is not surpassed in the range of poetry:

"A child said, What is grass! fetching it to me with full hands;
How could I answer the child! I do not know any more than he.
I guess it is the handkerchief of the Lord;
A scented gift and remembrancer, designedly dropped,
Bearing the owner's name someway on the corners, that we may see,
    and remark, and say, Whose?"[6]

We are afforded glimpses of half-formed pictures to tease and tantalize with their

---

3   The quotation is a line from Sir William Jones's (1746–94) "A Persian Song of Hafiz."
4   The reference is to two important American ornithologists: Alexander Wilson (1766–1813), author of *American Ornithology* (1808–13); and John James Audubon (1785–1851), author and artist of the nonpareil *Birds of America* (1827–38).
5   Ll. 75–79 of "Song of Myself."
6   The often quoted opening lines of section 6, "Song of Myself" – though very loosely and selectively quoted.

indistinctness: like a crimson cheek and flashing eye looking on us through the leaves of an arbor – mocking us for a moment, but vanishing before we can reach them. Here is an example:

> "Twenty-eight young men bathe by the shore;
> Twenty-eight young men, and all so friendly.
> Twenty-eight years of womanly life and all so lonesome.
> She owns the fine house by the rise of the bank;
> She hides handsome and richly drest aft the blinds of the window.
> Which of the young men does she like the best?
> Ah, the homeliest of them is beautiful to her.
> Dancing and laughing along the beach came the twenty-ninth bather;
> The rest did not see her, but she saw them, &c."[7]

Well, did the lady fall in love with the twenty-ninth bather, or *vice versa*? Our author scorns to gratify such puerile curiosity; the denouement which novel readers would expect is not hinted at.

In his philosophy justice attains its proper dimensions:

> "I play not a march for victors only: I play great marches for conquered
>   and slain persons.
> Have you heard that it was good to gain the day?
> I also say that it is good to fall – battles are lost in the same spirit in
>   which they are won.
> I sound triumphal drums for the dead – I fling thro' my embouchures the
>   loudest and gayest music for them.
> Vivas to those who have failed and to those whose war vessels sank in
>   the sea.
> And to those themselves who sank into the sea.
> And to all generals that lost engagements, and all overcome heroes and
>   the numberless unknown heroes equal to the greatest heroes
>   known."[8]

The triumphs of victors had been duly celebrated, but surely a poet was needed to sing the praises of the defeated whose cause was righteous, and the heroes who have been trampled under the hoofs of iniquity's onward march.

He does not pick and choose sentiments and expressions fit for general circulation – he gives a voice to whatever is, whatever we see, and hear, and think, and feel. He descends to grossness, which debars the poem from being read aloud in any mixed circle. We have said that the work defies criticism; we pronounce no judgment upon it; it is a work that will satisfy few upon a first perusal; it must be read

---

7   The often quoted opening lines of section 11, "Song of Myself."
8   See "Song of Myself," section 18. The text of this section would receive a number of minor
    alterations over the course of 1855–81, but hardly as many as this reviewer introduced, carelessly
    or otherwise, in regularizing punctuation and altering stanza breaks.

again and again, and then it will be to many unaccountable. All who read it will agree that it is an extraordinary book, full of beauties and blemishes, such as nature is to those who have only a half formed acquaintance with her mysteries.

[Walt Whitman], "Walt Whitman and His Poems," *United States Review* 5 (September 1855): 205–12

Enormously excited by his recent achievement, Whitman was taking no chances. Always something of an auto-impresario, he wrote and published altogether four anonymous self-reviews in the weeks following the publication of the 1855 *Leaves of Grass*. In this one he announces the arrival of "an American bard at last" with the same bravado with which his persona asserts his selfhood in the opening verse of "Song of Myself."

He took few pains to disguise his identity in this review. In fact, his repetitive invocation of his own name is nearly talismanic. A reasonably perceptive reader might well have noticed semantic and stylistic similarities between the Preface and this review. One person who did and who exposed his finding was the talented young journalist John Swinton, later a friend and defender of the poet. Swinton's review appeared in the *New York Times* (13 November 1856): 2. Whitman's reaction was characteristic; he was so unabashed that several years later he reprinted Swinton's notice in the pamphlet of reviews, *Leaves of Grass Imprints*, distributed by his publisher to publicize the 1860 *Leaves of Grass*.

This is arguably the most fascinating of Whitman's four self-reviews in most nearly approximating the style and manner and most closely matching the zeal of *Leaves of Grass* itself. One curiosity about it, as about any self-review, is its choice of passages for excerpting. His main text, not surprisingly, is "Song of Myself," although it is curious to see its three-line opening stanza here compressed into two lines.

An American bard at last! One of the roughs, large, proud, affectionate, eating, drinking, and breeding, his costume manly and free, his face sunburnt and bearded, his posture strong and erect, his voice bringing hope and prophecy to the generous races of young and old. We shall cease shamming and be what we really are. We shall start an athletic and defiant literature. We realize now how it is, and what was most lacking. The interior American republic shall also be declared free and independent.

For all our intellectual people, followed by their books, poems, novels, essays, editorials, lectures, tuitions, and criticism, dress by London and Paris modes, receive what is received there, obey the authorities, settle disputes by the old tests, keep out of rain and sun, retreat to the shelter of houses and schools, trim their hair, shave, touch not the earth barefoot, and enter not the sea except in a complete bathing-dress. One sees unmistakably genteel persons, travelled, college-learned, used to be served by servants, conversing without heat or vulgarity, supported on chairs, or walking through handsomely-carpeted parlors, or along shelves bearing well-bound volumes, and walls adorned with curtained and collared portraits, and china things, and nick-nacks. But where in American literature is the first show of America? Where are the gristle and beards, and broad breasts, and space and ruggedness and nonchalance that the souls of the people love? Where is the tremendous outdoors of these States? Where is the majesty of the federal mother, seated with more than antique grace, calm, just, indulgent to her brood of children, calling them around her regarding the little and the large and the younger and the older with perfect impartiality? Where is the vehement growth of our cities? Where is the spirit of the strong rich life of the American mechanic, farmer, sailor, hunter, and miner? Where is the huge composite of all other nations, cast in a fresher and brawnier matrix, passing adolescence, and needed this day, live and arrogant, to lead the marches of the world?

Self-reliant, with haughty eyes, assuming to himself all the attributes of his country, steps Walt Whitman into literature, talking like a man unaware that there was ever hitherto such a production as a book, or such a being as a writer. Every move of him has the free play of the muscle of one who never knew what it was to feel that he stood in the presence of a superior. Every word that falls from his mouth shows silent disdain and defiance of the old theories and forms. Every phrase announces new laws; not once do his lips unclose except in conformity with them. With light and rapid touch he first indicates in prose the principles of the foundation of a race of poets so deeply to spring from the American people, and become ingrained through them, that their Presidents shall not be the common referees so much as that great race of poets shall. He proceeds himself to exemplify this new school, and set models for their expression and range of subjects. He makes audacious and native use of his own body and soul. He must re-create poetry with the elements always at hand. He must imbue it with himself as he is, disorderly, fleshy, and sensual, a lover of things, yet a lover of men and women above the whole of the other objects of the universe. His work is to be achieved by unusual methods. Neither classic or romantic is he, nor a materialist any more than a spiritualist. Not a whisper comes out of him of the old stock talk and rhyme of poetry—not the first recognition of gods or goddesses, or Greece or Rome. No breath of Europe, or her monarchies, or priestly conventions, or her notions of gentlemen and ladies founded on the idea of caste, seems ever to have fanned his face or been inhaled into his lungs. But in their stead pour vast and fluid the fresh mentality of this mighty age, and the realities of this mighty continent, and the sciences and inventions and discoveries of the present world. Not geology, nor mathematics, nor chemistry, nor navigation, nor astronomy, nor anatomy, nor physiology, nor engineering, is more true to itself than Walt Whitman is true to them. They and the other sciences underlie his whole superstructure. In the beauty of the work of the poet, he affirms, are the tuft and final applause of science.

Affairs then are this man's poems. He will still inject nature through civilization. The movement of his verses is the sweeping movement of great currents of living people, with a general government, and state and municipal governments, courts, commerce, manufactures, arsenals, steamships, railroads, telegraphs, cities with paved streets, and aqueducts, and police and gas—myriads of travellers arriving and departing—newspapers, music, elections and all the features and processes of the nineteenth century in the wholesomest race and the only stable form of politics at present upon the earth. Along his words spread the broad impartialities of the United States. No innovations must be permitted on the stern

severities of our liberty and equality. Undecked also is this poet with sentimentalism, or jingle, or nice conceits or flowery similes. He appears in his poems surrounded by women and children, and by young men, and by common objects and
qualities. He gives to each just what belongs to it, neither more or less. The person
nearest him, that person he ushers hand in hand with himself. Duly take places in
his flowing procession, and step to the sounds of the newer and larger music, the
essences of American things, and past and present events—the enormous diversity
of temperature and agriculture and mines—the tribes of red aborigines—the
weather-beaten vessels entering new ports, or making landings on rocky coasts—
the first settlements north and south—the rapid stature and impatience of outside
control—the sturdy defiance of '76, and the war and peace, and the leadership of
Washington, and the formation of the Constitution—the Union always calm and
impregnable—the perpetual coming of immigrants—the wharf-hemmed cities and
superior marine—the unsurveyed interior—the log-house, and clearings, and wild
animals, and hunters, and trappers—the fisheries, and whaling, and gold-digging
—the endless gestation of new states—the convening of Congress every December,
the members coming up from all climates, and from the utter-most parts—the
noble character of the free American workman and workwoman—the fierceness of the people when well-roused—the ardor of their friendships—the large
amativeness—the Yankee swap—the New York fireman, and the target excursion—the southern plantation life—the character of the north-east, and of the
north-west and south-west—and the character of America and the American
people everywhere.[1] For these the old usages of poets afford Walt Whitman no
means sufficiently fit and free, and he rejects the old usages. The style of the bard
that is waited for is to be transcendent and new. It is to be indirect and not direct
or descriptive or epic. Its quality is to go through these to much more. Let the age
and wars (he says) of other nations be chanted, and their eras and characters be
illustrated, and that finish the verse. Not so (he continues) the great psalm of the
republic. Here the theme is creative and has vista. Here comes one among the
well-beloved stonecutters, and announces himself, and plans with decision and
science, and sees the solid and beautiful forms of the future where there are now
no solid forms.

The style of these poems, therefore, is simply their own style, new-born and red.
Nature may have given the hint to the author of the *Leaves of Grass*, but there
exists no book or fragment of a book, which can have given the hint to them. All
beauty, he says, comes from beautiful blood and a beautiful brain. His rhythm
and uniformity he will conceal in the roots of his verses, not to be seen of themselves, but to break forth loosely as lilies on a bush, and take shapes compact as
the shapes of melons, or chestnuts, or pears.

The poems of the *Leaves of Grass* are twelve in number. Walt Whitman at first
proceeds to put his own body and soul into the new versification:

> "I celebrate myself, And what I assume you shall assume,
> For every atom belonging to me, as good belongs to you."

---

1   This long cumulative sentence closely approximates in prose the cataloging device that character-
izes parts of "Song of Myself," especially sections 15 and 33.

He leaves houses and their shuttered rooms, for the open air. He drops disguise and ceremony, and walks forth with the confidence and gayety of a child. For the old decorums of writing he substitutes new decorums. The first glance out of his eyes electrifies him with love and delight. He will have the earth receive and return his affection; he will stay with it as the bride-groom stays with the bride. The cool-breathed ground, the slumbering and liquid trees, the just-gone sunset, the vitre-ous pour of the full moon, the tender and growing night, he salutes and touches, and they touch him. The sea supports him, and hurries him off with its powerful and crooked fingers. Dash me with amorous wet! then he says, I can repay you.

By this writer the rules of polite circles are dismissed with scorn. Your stale modesties, he says, are filthy to such a man as I.

> "I believe in the flesh and the appetites,
> Seeing, hearing, and feeling are miracles, and each part and tag of
>   me is a miracle.
> I do not press my finger across my mouth,
> I keep as delicate around the bowels as around the head and heart."[2]

No sniveller, or tea-drinking poet, no puny clawback or prude, is Walt Whitman. He will bring poems fit to fill the days and nights—fit for men and women with the attributes of throbbing blood and flesh. The body, he teaches, is beautiful. Sex is also beautiful. Are you to be put down, he seems to ask, to that shallow level of literature and conversation that stops a man's recognizing the delicious pleasure of his sex, or a woman hers? Nature he proclaims inherently pure. Sex will not be put aside; it is a great ordination of the universe. He works the muscle of the male and the teeming fibre of the female throughout his writings, as whole-some realities, impure only by deliberate intention and effort. To men and women he says: You can have healthy and powerful breeds of children on no less terms than these of mine. Follow me and there shall be taller and nobler crops of humanity on the earth.

In the *Leaves of Grass* are the facts of eternity and immortality, largely treated. Happiness is no dream, and perfection is no dream. Amelioration is my lesson, he says with calm voice, and progress is my lesson and the lesson of all things. Then his persuasion becomes a taunt, and his love bitter and compulsory. With strong and steady call he addresses men. Come, he seems to say, from the midst of all that you have been your whole life surrounding yourself with. Leave all the preaching and teaching of others, and mind only these words of mine.

> "Long enough have you dreamed contemptible dreams,
> Now I wash the gum from your eyes,
> You must habit yourself to the dazzle of the light and of every moment
>   of your life.
> Long have you timidly waded, holding a plank by the shore,
> Now I will you to be a bold swimmer,

---

2   Whitman is playing fast and loose with his own text. The first two lines correspond to ll. 522–23 of "Song of Myself"; the last two to ll. 519–20.

To jump off in the midst of the sea, and rise again and nod to me and
   shout, and laughingly dash with your hair.
I am the teacher of athletes,
He that by me spreads a wider breast than my own proves the width of
   my own,
He most honors my style who learns under it to destroy the teacher.
The boy I love, the same becomes a man not through derived power but
   in his own right,
Wicked, rather than virtuous out of conformity or fear,
Fond of his sweetheart, relishing well his steak,
Unrequited love or a slight cutting him worse than a wound cuts,
First rate to ride, to fight, to hit the bull's eye, to sail a skiff; to sing a
   song, or play on the banjo,
Preferring scars and faces pitted with small-pox over all latherers and
   those that keep out of the sun.

I teach straying from me, yet who can stray from me?
I follow you whoever you are from the present hour;
My words itch at your ears till you understand them.
I do not say these things for a dollar, or to fill up the time while I wait for
   a boat;
It is you talking just as much as myself—I act as the tongue of you.
It was tied in your mouth—in mine it begins to be loosened.

I swear I will never mention love or death inside a house,
And I swear I never will translate myself at all, only to him or her who
   privately stays with me in the open air."[3]

The eleven other poems have each distinct purposes, curiously veiled. Theirs is
no writer to be gone through with in a day or a month. Rather it is his pleasure to
elude you and provoke you for deliberate purposes of his own.

Doubtless in the scheme this man has built for himself the writing of poems is
but a proportionate part of the whole. It is plain that public and private performance, politics, love, friendship, behavior, the art of conversation, science, society,
the American people, the reception of the great novelties of city and country, all
have their equal call upon him and receive equal attention. In politics he could
enter with the freedom and reality he shows in poetry. His scope of life is the
amplest of any yet in philosophy. He is the true spiritualist. He recognizes no
annihilation, or death, or loss of identity. He is the largest lover and sympathizer
that has appeared in literature. He loves the earth and sun, and the animals. He
does not separate the learned from the unlearned, the Northerner from the Southerner, the white from the black, or the native from the immigrant just landed at
the wharf. Every one, he seems to say, appears excellent to me, every employment
is adorned, and every male and female glorious.

---

3 This citation comes from a continuous passage in the 1855 text of "Song of Myself" that corres-
   ponds, with some minor changes, to ll. 1228–251 of sections 46–47 of the 1881–82 text.

"The press of my foot to the earth springs a hundred affections,
They scorn the best I can do to relate them.

I am enamored of growing out-doors,
Of men that live among cattle or taste of the ocean or woods,
Of the builders and steerers of ships, of the wielders of axes and mauls,
    of the drivers of horses,
I can eat and sleep with them, week in and week out.

What is commonest and cheapest and nearest and easiest is Me,
Me going in for my chances, spending for vast returns,
Adorning myself to bestow myself on the first that will take me,
Not asking the sky to come down to my good will.
Scattering it freely for ever."[4]

If health were not his distinguishing attribute, this poet would be the very
harlot of persons. Right and left he flings his arms, drawing men and women with
undeniable love to his close embrace, loving the clasp of their hands, the touch of
their necks and breasts, and the sound of their voice. All else seems to burn up
under his fierce affection for persons. Politics, religion, institutions, art, quickly
fall aside before them. In the whole universe, he says, I see nothing more divine
than human souls.

"When the psalm sings instead of the singer,
When the script preaches instead of the preacher,
When the pulpit descends and goes instead of the carver that carved the
    supporting desk,
When the sacred vessels or the bits of the eucharist, or the lath and plast,
    procreate as effectually as the young silversmiths or bakers, or the
    masons in their overalls,
When a university course convinces like a slumbering woman and child
    convince,
When the minted gold in the vault smiles like the night-watchman's
    daughter,
When warrantee deeds loafe in chairs opposite, and are my friendly
    companions,
I intend to reach them my hand and make as much of them as I make of
    men and women."[5]

Who then is that insolent unknown? Who is it, praising himself as if others were
not fit to do it, and coming rough and unbidden among writers to unsettle what
was settled, and to revolutionize, in fact, our modern civilization? Walt Whitman
was born on Long-Island, on the hills about thirty miles from the greatest American city, on the last day of May, 1819, and has grown up in Brooklyn and New

4   Ll. 253–63 of "Song of Myself."
5   The closing lines of "A Song for Occupations," the second poem in the 1855 *Leaves of Grass*.

York to be thirty-six years old, to enjoy perfect health, and to understand his country and its spirit.[6]

Interrogations more than this, and that will not be put off unanswered, spring continually through the perusal of these Leaves of Grass.

If there were to be selected, out of the incalculable volumes of printed matter in existence, any single work to stand for America and her times, should this be the work?

Must not the true American poet indeed absorb all others, and present a new and far more ample and vigorous type?

Has not the time arrived for a school of live writing and tuition consistent with the principles of these poems? consistent with the free spirit of this age, and with the American truths of politics? consistent with geology, and astronomy, and all science and human physiology? consistent with the sublimity of immortality and the directness of common-sense?

If in this poem the United States have found their poetic voice, and taken measure and form, is it any more than a beginning? Walt Whitman himself disclaims singularity in his work, and announces the coming after him of great successions of poets, and that he but lifts his finger to give the signal.

Was he not needed? Has not literature been bred in and in long enough? Has it not become unbearably artificial?

Shall a man of faith and practice in the simplicity of real things be called eccentric, while the disciple of the fictitious school writes without question?

Shall it still be the amazement of the light and dark that freshness of expression is the rarest quality of all?

You have come in good time, Walt Whitman! In opinions, in manners, in costumes, in books, in the aims and occupancy of life, in associates, in poems, conformity to all unnatural and tainted customs passes without remark, while perfect naturalness, health, faith, self-reliance, and all primal expressions of the manliest love and friendship, subject one to the stare and controversy of the world.

Rufus W. Griswold, untitled review of *Leaves of Grass,* *Criterion* I (10 November 1855): 24

Griswold's name is most frequently linked to that of Edgar Allan Poe (see Directory of Contextual Figures, **p. 33**), whom he served as literary executor and whose reputation he savaged. But the dealings with Poe were only a small part of the literary activity of one of the most influential cultural arbiters of his generation. His anthologies *The Poets and Poetry of America, The Female Poets of America,* and *The Prose Writers of America* were standard-setting works at a time when no canon of American literature yet existed.

Given his cultural prominence and his conservative views, it is not surprising that he reviewed *Leaves of Grass* and skewered it. The antagonism was mutual: if

---

6   Whitman would often sketch his autobiography publicly, though seldom as accurately as he does here.

Whitman's aesthetic views and practices represented to Griswold everything bad about poetry (or "poetry," as he must have thought of it), Griswold's standards represented to Whitman everything false and constricted about current culture. Whitman's feeling was visceral; there were few things he more consistently or unwaveringly asserted over the full length of his career than his contempt for the literary establishment.

Griswold's mode of attack is revealing: from the opening words he conceives of literary culture as a club to which entrance should be restricted. Curiously, the club member whom he singles out as the person responsible for mediating Whitman's ingress was Emerson, whose reprinted letter he takes as public endorsement of *Leaves of Grass*. For that matter, his attack on Whitman also includes a double attack on Emerson as a supporter of Whitman and a like-minded proponent of a visionary, "inner-light" illuminated poetics.

Griswold's assault was not to be easily dismissed. It fairly expressed the hostility of social, religious, and cultural conservatives to Whitman's assault on their cathedral of taste and portended the depth and breadth of antagonism that *Leaves of Grass* would incite for the remainder of the nineteenth century.

An unconsidered letter of introduction has oftentimes procured the admittance of a scurvy fellow into good society, and our apology for permitting any allusion to the above volume in our columns is, that it has been unworthily recommended by a gentleman of wide repute, and might, on that account, obtain access to respectable people, unless its real character were exposed.

Mr. Ralph Waldo Emerson either recognises and accepts these 'leaves,' as the gratifying results of his own peculiar doctrines, or else he has hastily endorsed them, after a partial and superficial reading. If it is of any importance, he may extricate himself from the dilemma. We, however, believe that this book does express the bolder results of a certain transcendental kind of thinking, which some have styled philosophy.

As to the volume itself, we have only to remark, that it strongly fortifies the doctrines of the Metempsychosists,[1] for it is impossible to imagine how any man's fancy could have conceived such a mass of stupid filth, unless he were possessed of the soul of a sentimental donkey that had died of disappointed love. This *poet* (?) without wit, but with a certain vagrant wildness, just serves to show the energy which natural imbecility is occasionally capable of under strong excitement.

There are too many persons, who imagine they demonstrate their superiority to their fellows, by disregarding all the politenesses and decencies of life, and, therefore, justify themselves in indulging the vilest imaginings and shamefullest license. But nature, abhorring the abuse of the capacities she has given to man, retaliates upon him, by rendering extravagant indulgence in any direction followed by an insatiable, ever-consuming, and never to be appeased passion.

Thus, to these pitiful beings, virtue and honor are but names. Bloated with

---

1   Those who believe in the transmigration of the soul from one body into another at the time of death.

self-conceit, they strut abroad unabashed in the daylight, and expose to the world the festering sores that overlay them like a garment. Unless we admit this exhibition to be beautiful, we are at once set down for non-progressive conservatives, destitute of the "inner light," the far-seeingness which, of course, characterize those gifted individuals. Now, any one who has noticed the tendency of thought in these later years, must be aware that a quantity of this kind of nonsense is being constantly displayed. The immodesty of presumption exhibited by these *seers*; their arrogant pretentiousness; the complacent smile with which they listen to the echo of their own braying, should be, and we believe is, enough to disgust the great majority of sensible folks; but, unfortunately, there is a class that, mistaking sound for sense, attach some importance to all this rant and cant. These candid, these ingenuous, these honest "progressionists;" these human diamonds without flaws; these men that have *come*, detest furiously all shams; "to the pure, all things are pure;" they are pure, and, consequently, must thrust their reeking presence under every man's nose.

They seem to think that man has no instinctive delicacy; is not imbued with a conservative and preservative modesty, that acts as a restraint upon the violence of passions, which, for a wise purpose, have been made so strong. No! these fellows have no secrets, no disguises; no, indeed! But they do have, conceal it by whatever language they choose, a degrading, beastly sensuality, that is fast rotting the healthy core of all the social virtues.

There was a time when licentiousness laughed at reproval; now it writes essays and delivers lectures. Once it shunned the light; now it courts attention, writes books showing how grand and pure it is, and prophesies from its lecherous lips its own ultimate triumph.

Shall we argue with such men? Shall we admit them into our houses, that they may leave a foul odor, contaminate the pure, healthful air? Or shall they be placed in the same category with the comparatively innocent slave of poverty, ignorance and passion, that skulks along in the shadows of by-ways; even in her deep degradation possessing some sparks of the Divine light, the germ of good that reveals itself by a sense of shame?

Thus, then, we leave this gathering of muck to the laws which, certainly, if they fulfil their intent, must have power to suppress such gross obscenity. As it is entirely destitute of wit, there is no probability that any one would, after this exposure, read it in the hope of finding that; and we trust no one will require further evidence—for, indeed, we do not believe there is a newspaper so vile that would print confirmatory extracts.

In our allusions to this book, we have found it impossible to convey any, even the most faint idea of its style and contents, and of our disgust and detestation of them, without employing language that cannot be pleasing to ears polite; but it does seem that some one should, under circumstances like these, undertake a most disagreeable, yet stern duty. The records of crime show that many monsters have gone on in impunity, because the exposure of their vileness was attended with too great indelicacy. "*Peccatum illud horribile, inter Christianos non nominandum.*"[2]

---

2   "That horrible sin that should not be named among Christians" (from Latin).

Fanny Fern, "Fresh Fern Leaves: Leaves of Grass," *New York Ledger* (10 May 1856): 4

Fanny Fern, pseudonym of Sara Willis Parton, was one of the most popular mid-century writers in the United States. A sign of her status, she was a featured writer paid an unprecedented salary for her contributions (of which this was one) to the *New York Ledger*, the most popular story paper in the country. A lively essayist with a keen sense of audience, she made her reputation with the publication of *Fern Leaves from Fanny's Portfolio* in 1853 and, a year later, a second series of *Fern Leaves* and her somewhat scandalous, autobiographical *roman-à-clef, Ruth Hall.*

Fern violated numerous norms of middle-class female propriety. She was divorced from her second husband, she exposed in print her male relatives' uncharitable behavior to her, and she spoke her mind in print freely and vociferously about numerous issues relating to the status of women. Given her reputation and views, it is especially fitting that she was the first woman to address *Leaves of Grass* in public. She and her new husband, the talented biographer James Parton, were well acquainted with Whitman as fellow residents of Brooklyn, but her purpose in taking up the book in public had less to do with Whitman than with his message.

Her review follows the customary mid-nineteenth-century practice of first-person commentary, *ad hominem* interpretation, and extensive citation, but her views are decidedly unconventional. What registered on many conservative reviewers as indelicate struck her as liberating. In fact, she reads *Leaves of Grass* as a rallying call to Americans but in particular to women to free themselves from social bonds.

Well baptized: fresh, hardy, and grown for the masses. Not more welcome is their natural type to the winter-bound, bed-ridden, and spring-emancipated invalid. *Leaves of Grass* thou art unspeakably delicious, after the forced, stiff, Parnassian[1] exotics for which our admiration has been vainly challenged.

Walt Whitman, the effeminate world needed thee. The timidest soul whose wings ever drooped with discouragement, could not choose but rise on thy strong pinions.

> "Undrape—you are not guilty to me, nor stale nor discarded;
> I see through the broadcloth and gingham whether or no."[2]

> "O despairer, here is my neck,
> You shall *not* go down! Hang your whole weight upon me."[3]

---

1   Parnassus was the mountain in Greece sacred to Apollo and the Muses and therefore often associated with poetry.
2   Ll. 145–46 of "Song of Myself."
3   Ll. 1012–13 of "Song of Myself."

Walt Whitman, the world needed a "Native American" of thorough, out and out breed—enamored of *women* not *ladies*, *men* not *gentlemen*; something beside a mere Catholic-hating Know-Nothing;[4] it needed a man who dared speak out his strong, honest thoughts, in the face of pusillanimous, toadeying, republican aristocracy; dictionary-men, hypocrites, cliques and creeds; it needed a large-hearted, untainted, self-reliant, fearless son of the Stars and Stripes, who disdains to sell his birthright for a mess of pottage; who does

> "Not call one greater or one smaller,
> That which fills its period and place being equal to any;"[5]

who will

> "Accept nothing which all cannot have their counterpart of on the same terms."[6]

Fresh *Leaves of Grass!* not submitted by the self-reliant author to the fingering of any publisher's critic, to be arranged, rearranged and disarranged to his circumscribed liking, till they hung limp, tame, spiritless, and scentless. No. It were a spectacle worth seeing, this glorious Native American, who, when the daily labor of chisel and plane was over, himself, with toil-hardened fingers, handled the types to print the pages which wise and good men have since delighted to endorse and to honor. Small critics, whose contracted vision could see no beauty, strength, or grace, in these *Leaves*, have long ago repented that they so hastily wrote themselves down shallow by such a premature confession. Where an Emerson, and a Howitt[7] have commended, my woman's voice of praise may not avail; but happiness was born a twin, and so I would fain share with others the unmingled delight which these "Leaves" have given me.

I say unmingled; I am not unaware that the charge of coarseness and sensuality has been affixed to them. My moral constitution may be hopelessly tainted or—too sound to be tainted, as the critic wills, but I confess that I extract no poison from these *Leaves*—to me they have brought only healing. Let him who can do so, shroud the eyes of the nursing babe lest it should see its mother's breast. Let him look carefully between the gilded covers of books, backed by high-sounding names, and endorsed by parson and priest, lying unrebuked upon his own family table; where the asp of sensuality lies coiled amid rhetorical flowers. Let him examine well the paper dropped weekly at his door, in which virtue and religion are rendered disgusting, save when they walk in satin slippers, or, clothed in purple and fine linen, kneel on a damask *"prie-dieu."*

Sensual!—No—the moral assassin looks you not boldly in the eye by broad daylight; but Borgia-like takes you treacherously by the hand, while from the

---

4   The Know-Nothings were a nativist political party that rose to prominence during the 1840s and 1850s in reaction against the unprecedented waves of mass immigration (mostly from Roman Catholic Ireland and Germany) to the United States.
5   Ll. 1142–143 of "Song of Myself."
6   L. 507 of "Song of Myself."
7   William Howitt (1792–1879), English man of letters, gave the 1855 *Leaves of Grass* a fairly favorable review in the *London Weekly Dispatch* (9 March 1856): 6.

glittering ring on his finger he distils through your veins the subtle and deadly poison.

Sensual? The artist who would inflame, paints you not nude Nature, but stealing Virtue's veil, with artful artlessness now conceals, now exposes, the ripe and swelling proportions.

Sensual? Let him who would affix this stigma upon *Leaves of Grass*, write upon his heart, in letters of fire, these noble words of its author:

> "In woman I see the bearer of the great fruit, which is
>   immortality. . . the good thereof is not tasted by *roues*, and never can
>   be.[8]

> Who degrades or defiles the living human body is cursed,
> Who degrades or defiles the body of the dead is not more cursed."[9]

Were I an artist I would like no more suggestive subjects for my easel than Walt Whitman's pen has furnished.

> "The little one sleeps in its cradle,
> I lift the gauze and look a long time, and silently brush away flies with
>   my hand.
> The farmer stops by the bars of a Sunday and looks at the oats and rye.[10]

> Earth of the slumbering and liquid trees!
> Earth of departed Sunset,
> Earth of the mountains misty-topt!
> Earth of the vitreous pour of the full moon just tinged with blue!
> Earth of shine and dark mottling the tide of the river!
> Earth of the limpid grey of clouds brighter and clearer for my sake!
> Far swooping elbowed earth! Rich apple-blossomed earth!
> Smile, for your lover comes!"[11]

I quote at random, the following passages which appeal to me:

> "A morning glory at my window, satisfies me more than the metaphysics
>   of books.[12]

---

8   She is quoting loosely from "I Sing the Body Electric."
9   The closing lines of "I Sing the Body Electric."
10 She is taking the liberty of joining ll. 148–49 and l. 272 of "Song of Myself."
11 Ll. 439–45 of "Song of Myself."
12 L. 549 of "Song of Myself."

Logic and sermons never convince.
The damp of the night drives deeper into my soul."[13]

Speaking of animals, he says:

"I stand and look at them sometimes half the day long.
They do not make me sick, discussing their duty to God.[14]

.   .   .   .

—Whoever walks a furlong without sympathy, walks to his own
funeral dressed in his shroud.[15]

.   .   .   .

I hate him that oppresses me,
I will either destroy him, or he shall release me.[16]

.   .   .   .

I find letters from God dropped in the street, and every one is signed
   by God's name,
And I leave them where they are, for I know that others will punctually
   come forever and ever.[17]

.   .   .   .

——Under Niagara, *the cataract falling like a veil over my
countenance.*"[18]

Of the grass he says:

"It seems to me *the beautiful uncut hair of graves.*"[19]

I close the extracts from these *Leaves*, which it were easy to multiply, for one
is more puzzled what to leave unculled, than what to gather, with the following
sentiments; for which, and for all the good things included between the covers
of his book Mr. Whitman will please accept the cordial grasp of a woman's
hand:

13 Ll. 653–54 of "Song of Myself."
14 She is joining l. 685 to l. 688 of "Song of Myself."
15 L. 1272 of "Song of Myself."
16 She is quoting from "The Sleepers."
17 Ll. 1286–288 of "Song of Myself."
18 L. 749 of "Song of Myself."
19 L. 110 of "Song of Myself."

"The wife—and she is not one jot less than the husband,
The daughter—and she is just as good as the son,
The mother—and she is every bit as much as the father."[20]

Anonymous, "Whitman's *Leaves of Grass*," [New York] *Critic* 1 (5 November 1881): 302–03

A small-circulation literary magazine founded the year of this review, the *Critic* was from its inception a strong, steady supporter of Whitman's poetry. This review was timed to the appearance of the 1881 "final" edition of *Leaves of Grass*, which Whitman and his supporters hoped would be a monumental event in spreading and solidifying his reputation.

The reviewer was well aware of the complicated printing and reception history of *Leaves of Grass*, which he/she can comment on with a measure of perspective. A generation has clearly made a difference: it is now possible to refer to "Song of Myself" as a "famous" poem, to take stock of the striking discrepancy between Whitman's avowed goal of speaking to and for the masses and of his being "caviare to the multitude," and to reconcile his spirit of experimentation with the aesthetics of a later generation. But perhaps the most interesting insight expressed here is the linkage between Whitman and Poe (another long neglected or vilified figure) as the most original American writers of their century and the corresponding prediction that Whitman's reputation will soon rise to general prominence. (For Poe, see Directory of Contextual Figures, **p. 33**.)

Practically, but not actually, this is the first time that Mr. Whitman has issued his poems through a publishing house instead of at his private cost. The two volumes called *Leaves of Grass* and the *Two Rivulets*, which he had printed and himself sold at Camden, N. J., are now issued in one, under the former title, without special accretions of new work, but not without a good deal of re-arrangement in the sequence of the poems.[1] Pieces that were evidently written later, and intended to be eventually put under *Leaves of Grass* now find their place; some that apparently did well enough where they were have been shifted to other departments. On the whole, however, the changes have been in the direction of greater clearness as regards their relation to the sub-titles. It is not apparent, however, that the new book is greatly superior to the old in typography, although undeniably the fault of the privately printed volumes, a variation in types used, is no longer met with. The margins are narrower, and the look of the page more commonplace. The famous poem called 'Walt Whitman' is now the 'Song of Myself.' It still maintains:

20 She is quoting from "A Song for Occupations."

1 The writer, who clearly was well acquainted with Whitman's career, is referring to the two-volume format that Whitman brought out of his prose (primarily contained in *Two Rivulets*) and poetry (primarily contained in a new issue of *Leaves of Grass*) in the centennial year of 1876.

I too am not a bit tamed,
I too am untranslatable;
I sound my barbaric yawp over the roofs of the world.[2]

It still has the portrait of Whitman when younger, standing in a loose flannel shirt and slouched hat, with one hand on his hip, the other in his pocket.[3] 'Eidolons' has been taken from the second volume and placed, for good reasons that the reader may not be ready to understand, among the first pieces gathered under the sub-title 'Inscriptions.'[4] It ends with the 'Songs of Parting,'[5] under which the last is 'So Long,' a title that a foreigner and perhaps many an American might easily consider quite as untranslatable as Mr. Whitman proclaims himself to be. The motive for the publication seems to be to take advantage of that wider popularity which is coming somewhat late in life to him whom his admirers like to call 'the good gray poet.'

One great anomaly of Whitman's case has been that while he is an aggressive champion of democracy and of the working-man, in a broad sense of the term working-man, his admirers have been almost exclusively of a class the farthest possibly removed from that which labors for daily bread by manual work. Whitman has always been truly caviare to the multitude. It was only those that knew much of poetry and loved it greatly who penetrated the singular shell of his verses and rejoiced in the rich, pulpy kernel. Even with connoisseurs, Whitman has been somewhat of an acquired taste, and it has always been amusing to note the readiness with which persons who would not or could not read him, raised a cry of affectation against those who did. This phenomenon is too well known in other departments of taste to need further remark; but it may be added that Mr. Whitman has both gained by it and lost. He has gained a vigorousness of support on the part of his admirers that probably more than outbalances the acrid attacks of those who consider his work synonymous with all that is vicious in poetical technique, and wicked from the point of morals. As to the latter, it must be confessed that, according to present standards of social relations, the doctrines taught by Whitman might readily be construed, by the overhasty or unscrupulous, into excuses for foul living: for such persons do not look below the surface, nor can they grasp the whole idea of Whitman's treatment of love. However fervid his expressions may be, and however scornful he is of the miserable hypocrisies that fetter but also protect the evilly disposed, it is plain that the idea he has at heart is that universal love which leaves no room for wickedness because it leaves no room for doing or saying unkind, uncharitable, unjust things to his fellow-man. With an exuberance of thought that would supply the mental outfit of ten ordinary poets, and with a rush of words that is by no means reckless, but

---

2   These verses (ll.1332–333 of "Song of Myself") had been widely cited from the time of the poem's first publication. The author has taken the liberty of rearranging as three lines the two-line construction that Whitman gave these verses in all editions.

3   The reference, of course, is to the engraving (see Figure 2, **p. 16**) with which Whitman introduced the 1855 *Leaves of Grass*. Its celebrity was growing along with that of Whitman and *Leaves of Grass*.

4   "Inscriptions" is the cluster of mostly short poems that Whitman placed at the beginning of all editions of *Leaves of Grass* beginning in 1871.

5   "Songs of Parting" is the cluster of poems (concluding with "So Long!") that Whitman placed at the end of all editions of *Leaves of Grass* beginning in 1871.

intensely and grandly labored, Whitman hurls his view of the world at the heads of his readers with a vigor and boldness that takes away one's breath.

This century is getting noted among centuries for singular departures in art and literature. Among them all, there is none bolder or more original than that of Whitman. Perhaps Poe in his own line might be cited as an equal. It is strange, and yet it is not strange, that he should have waited so long for recognition, and that by many thousands of people of no little culture his claims to being a poet at all are either frankly scouted or else held in abeyance. Literature here has remarkably held aloof from the vital thoughts and hopes of the country. It seems as if the very crudity of the struggle here drove people into a petty dilettante atmosphere of prettiness in art and literature as an escape from the dust and cinders of daily life. Hence our national love for 'slicked up' pictures, for instance, by which it is often claimed in Europe that promising geniuses in painting, there, have been ruined for higher work. Hence our patronage of poets that have all the polish of a cymbal, but all a cymbal's dry note and hollowness. Hence, at one time, our admiration for orators that were ornate to the verge of inanity. Into this hot-house air of literature Walt Whitman bounded, with the vigor and suppleness of a clown at a funeral. Dire were the grimaces of the mourners in high places, and dire are their grimaces still.

There were plenty of criticisms to make, even after one had finished crying Oh! at the frank sensuality, the unbelievable nakedness of Walt. Everything that decent folk covered up, Walt exhibited, and boasted of exhibiting! He was proud of his nakedness and sensuality. He cried, Look here, you pampered rogues of literature, what are you squirming about, when you know, and everybody knows, that things are just like this, always have been, always will be? But it must be remembered that this was what he wrote, and that he did with a plan, and by order from his genius. It has never been heard of him that he was disgusting in talk or vile in private life, while it has been known that poets celebrated for the lofty tone of their morality, for the strictness of their Christianity, the purity of their cabinet hymns, can condescend in private life to wallow in all that is base. That is the other great anomaly of Whitman. He rhapsodizes of things seldom seen in print with the enthusiasm of a surgeon enamoured of the wonderful mechanism of the body. But he does not soil his conversation with lewdness. If evil is in him, it is in his book.

Whitman's strength and Whitman's weakness lie in his lack of taste. As a mere external sign, look at his privately printed volumes. For a printer and typesetter, reporter and editor, they do not show taste in the selection and arrangement of the type. A cardinal sin in the eyes of most critics is the use of French, Spanish, and American-Spanish words[6] which are scattered here and there, as if Whitman had picked them up, sometimes slightly incorrectly, from wandering minstrels, Cubans, or fugitives from one of Walker's raids.[7] He shows crudely the American way of incorporating into the language a handy or a high-sounding word without elaborate examination of its original meaning, just as we absorb the different

---

6   For a similar complaint, see the twentieth-century extract from Randall Jarrell, **pp. 86–91.**
7   The reference is to William Walker (1824–60), an adventurer who led various mercenary raids into Mexico, Honduras, and, most notoriously, Nicaragua, where he managed to overthrow the government and install himself briefly as president (1856–57).

nationalities that crowd over from Europe. His thought and his mode of expression is immense, often flat, very often monotonous, like our great sprawling cities with their endless scattering of suburbs. Yet when one gets the "hang" of it, there is a colossal grandeur in conception and execution that must finally convince whoever will be patient enough to look for it. His rhythm, so much burlesqued, is all of a part with the man and his ideas. It is apparently confused; really most carefully schemed; certainly to a high degree original. It has what to the present writer is the finest thing in the music of Wagner[8]—a great booming movement or undertone, like the noise of heavy surf. His crowded adjectives are like the mediæval writers of Irish, those extraordinary poets who sang the old Irish heroes and their own contemporaries, the chiefs of their clans. No Irishman of to-day has written a nobler lament for Ireland, or a more hopeful, or a more truthful, than has Walt Whitman. Yet it is not said that he has Irish blood. Nor is there to be found in our literature another original piece of prose so valuable to future historians as his notes on the war. Nor is there a poet of the war-time extant who has so struck the note of that day of conflict as Whitman has in 'Drum Taps.'[9] He makes the flesh creep. His verses are like the march of the long lines of volunteers, and then again like the bugles of distant cavalry. But these are parts of him. As he stands complete in *Leaves of Grass*, in spite of all the things that regard for the decencies of drawing-rooms and families may wish away, he certainly represents, as no other writer in the world, the struggling, blundering, sound-hearted, somewhat coarse, but still magnificent vanguard of Western civilization that is encamped in the United States of America. He avoids the cultured few. He wants to represent, and does in his own strange way represent, the lower middle stratum of humanity. But, so far, it is not evident that his chosen constituency cares for, or has even recognized him. Wide readers are beginning to guess his proportions.

Anonymous, "Walt Whitman's Poems," *Literary World* 12
(19 November 1881): 411–12

This review of the new Osgood edition articulates the continuing resistance to Whitman's poetry among many mainstream organs. It lacks the fury of an earlier generation's first response to a work of brazen irreverence, even subversion, but it nevertheless judges the poetics and the content unacceptable. Few contemporaries practiced a religion or aesthetics that featured – to use this critic's memorable phrase – the "apotheosis of the Phallus." The poem once again chiefly cited is "Song of Myself." One of the few poems that the reviewer approves of – it was the one most frequently approved of throughout the last third of the century – was the uncharacteristically conventional "O Captain! My Captain!"

---

8   Richard Wagner (1813–83), one of the greatest German composers of the nineteenth century, was renowned in particular for his lavishly romantic, nationalistic operas.
9   *Drum-Taps* was Whitman's volume of mostly Civil War poetry. Originally published as a slim volume in 1865, it was subsequently incorporated, with changes, as a cluster into post-war editions of *Leaves of Grass*. It is today seen as the finest collection of poems to emerge from the Civil War, but it had little reputation in its own day.

The familiar indictment is the work's indecency. The reviewer's charge that the book is "guilty of an act of indecent exposure" proved prescient; a few months later the Boston district attorney formalized the charge and threatened to have its circulation prohibited unless the volume was considerably expurgated.

This is the collected and revised poetry of Walt Whitman, who, some will have it, is by preeminence of art and nature our representative American poet. It will be noticed that at last he has found a publisher other than himself. What this nation may become it might not be wise to prophesy; but we may at the start humbly entertain the hope, at least, that at this present writing our nationality, in root and fiber, is something else than what Mr. Whitman sings. His book is one of courage, most downright in its dogmatics, and says its say apparently without the slightest consideration for the fact that much it says must cross and shock the deepest ethical instincts of a great multitude—we should certainly hope the vast majority of those American men and women who by any misfortune are led to read him. For these poems are of that breed that they force the honest critic into a corner where he must either speak plain words, or step down and out from his judgment-seat. This is a book which makes not only war upon nearly all traditional theories of true poetry, but in many places a very brutal assault upon our fixed ideas of human decency and purity. For instance, it has long been held that poetry is not merely the prose of any philosophy, history, geography, anthropology, or, we might add, anatomy or sexual physiology; but must have some sort of inherent rhythm and melody—the heartbeats and spiritual pulsations of the poet. This, for want of a better term, we call the *form* of poetry. Tennyson, for example, is a master of poetic form. The poems under review, as to form, run to a chaos of monotonies. It is not the chaotic diversity of the wild woods, or the sea waves, or the autumn leaves, or the sand grains in a gravel-pit, in all which there is the articulated beauty and inbred virtue of nature obedient to the Great Craftsman. The chaos of Mr. Whitman's verse, to compare great with small, reminds us of the gray clay bluffs of Truro Beach.[1] Would it were as clean! In form he reminds us of Martin Farquhar Tupper.[2]

There is vastly more to be said as to his substance. First of all, and gladly, this: that he has, in his nigh four hundred pages, spurts and flashes of some things which say: "This could and should have been a noble creature." He has a quick, sharp sight for the surfaces of natural scenery, as when he speaks of the "heart-shaped" leaf of the lilac;[3] but somehow he seems incapable of grasping the inner spiritual lessons of field and flood, or a spiritual analogy. The best instance of the opposite we have found on a careful search is this:

---

1   Truro is an expansive, sandy beach near the northern tip of Massachusetts' Cape Cod.
2   Martin Farquhar Tupper (1810–89), an immensely popular English writer in the mid-century years, was best known for his moralizing, blank verse *Proverbial Philosophy* (1838), to which *Leaves of Grass* was frequently compared. By the late nineteenth century, however, when Tupper's critical reputation, never firm, was in serious decline, a comparison with him was no compliment.
3   From section 3 of "When Lilacs Last in the Dooryard Bloom'd."

I believe a leaf of grass is no less than the journey work of the stars.[4]

His grasp of the detail of an event, but not of its ethical quality, is shown in his description of a sea-fight.[5] Somehow he never shows us the soul of anything. We may ask even, "Does he believe there is any such thing as a soul?" American he is, of the ruder and more barbaric type, a prairie cow boy in a buffalo robe, with a voice of the east wind, shouting prophecies and incantations about what he thinks he sees and knows. But from civilized speech or melody he seems strangely remote. Egotism, if a virtue, is certainly an unfragrant one, and Walt Whitman's egotism, grotesque as it is, is perhaps less grotesque than gigantic. He describes himself well enough in the lines,

> I am not a bit tamed, I too am untranslatable—
> I sound my barbaric yawp over the roofs of the world.[6]

Mr. Whitman's religion is no doubt to him a serious matter, and it is a somewhat serious matter to discover what in the world it is. He often discourses eloquently of God, as when he says:

> I find letters from God dropt in the street and every one is signed by
>   God's name,
> And I leave them where they are for I know that wheresoever I go
> Others will punctually come forever and ever.[7]

Yet the prevalent tone of his verses is curiously Asiatic, as though he were an incarnation of Brahma, and a pantheist. He says:

> Clear and sweet is my soul, and clear and sweet is all that is not my
>   soul.[8]

(A cess-pool, for instance).

In fact, he declares himself to be all that the universe is, even to being at the same moment each of two exactly opposite things, as though a man at any given instant were and were not. Indeed, it is this rapt but noisy mysticism which makes it rather hard to finger Mr. Whitman and touch his quality. Not that true poetry does not allow mysticism, or that mystics are not often poets. Indeed, high poetry is often a blessed hint, and only a hint, of a vaster world within the veil of the unreachable and the non-measurable. Uhland's[9] ballad, "The Two Locks of Hair," for instance, hints at the draped and veiled world of sorrow, whose mysteries are only revealed to the mourners after here. Mr. Whitman's mysticism is a fog-bank that cloaks all, even the possible hint itself. Add to this his all-pervading

---

4   Ll. 1332–333 of "Song of Myself."
5   In sections 35–36, "Song of Myself."
6   Ll. 633–34 of "Song of Myself."
7   Ll. 1286–288 of "Song of Myself."
8   L. 52 of "Song of Myself."
9   Ludwid Uhland (1789–1862) was a popular German romantic poet well known for his lyrics and ballads.

oracularity of speech, and he is certainly a man hard to be "understood" of common folk. And yet there are gleams in his book, not only of great things, but of possibly magnificent ones. His tribute to Abraham Lincoln, beginning "O Captain! my Captain!" is a weird and rare performance. "The Singer in the Prison"[10] beginning

> O sight of pity, shame and dole
> O fearful thought—a convict soul,

is full of tenderness and pathos.

The ethical quality of Mr. Whitman's poems remains to be examined. Here, in all honesty, it is hard to know what to say or what to leave unsaid. Gray hairs have their rights, and ought to be a shield against taunt and bitterness; but woman's purity and human society have their rights also, and there are little children growing up into the arena of the world's toil and trial who have their rights as well. We go now upon the assumption that there are certain elements of decency which pervade all human society, heathen and otherwise, and that the world is not too old to blush. We say that there are passages in this book that never ought to have been written, much less published; passages which sound like a lecture on the obstetrics of lust and (may we say it with all deference to our well-bred readers) the apotheosis of the Phallus. It is hard to overstate this matter. When a man with such physical imagery of shame summons the very wind to be assistant in a poetical concubinage as realistic as a French invisible card, and the salt sea also, it is certainly time for us common mortals who have still some respect for the seventh commandment to stay in doors from the elements, or, if at sea, to make all speed for the shore. The offense in this wise is not all-pervading, but it is very acute and deep.

His apologists will say of him that he is only another Adam in the Garden,[11] naked and not ashamed. We say of him, and of all who have assisted in the making of his book, that they are guilty of an act of indecent exposure.

For the rest, what Mr. Whitman might have been in poetry we have tried to fairly state. We can only add that if in these *Leaves of Grass* he has shown himself to be a poet, then the great and shining ones whom the English-speaking race have been wont to honor with this high title, are not.

Thomas Wentworth Higginson, "Recent Poetry," *Nation* 33 (15 December 1881): 476–77

Higginson took serious issue with Whitman the man and poet, attacking him repeatedly, even obsessively, in print over the course of the 1880s and 1890s. Given the fact that he was in many ways an exemplar of progressive values in his

---

10 A minor Whitman poem first published on Christmas 1869 in the Washington *Saturday Evening Visitor* and later incorporated into *Leaves of Grass*.

11 In fact, Adam in the Garden was, as the critic might or might not have known, exactly the setting for Whitman's programmatic poem "To the Garden the World," first published in 1860.

and Whitman's heyday before retreating into a calcified conservatism, his views on Whitman are particularly interesting. They are for other reasons, as well. As a commanding officer during the Civil War, he spoke with considerable assurance on the subjects of manliness and patriotism. As a radical abolitionist who supported John Brown and as commander of the first African American regiment to serve in the war, he had pronounced views on racial relations; likewise, as a liberal Unitarian clergyman, on progressive religion. And as a highly respected, widely published author with numerous ties to the world of letters and publishing, he passed readily for a man of letters.

The residual power of *Leaves of Grass* to draw the most visceral reactions – ranging from euphoria to contempt – from its readers is evident here. Higginson's outright dismissal of *Leaves of Grass* is as vitriolic as was that of Rufus Griswold a generation (and five editions) earlier. His contempt toward Whitman and *Leaves of Grass* is both personal and professional – personal, as regards a man he considers a slacker for failing to register for combat; professional, as regards a poet he considers operating outside the rules and bounds of true poetry. The only poem he recognizes as poetry is, predictably, "O Captain! My Captain!" That judgment is particularly remarkable as the verdict of the man who since 1862 had been unofficially serving as "mentor" to Emily Dickinson.

We have read anew, from a sense of duty, the original and unexpurgated *Leaves of Grass*, by Walt Whitman, as now reprinted, with some milder additions. It cannot be said of them, as Sir Charles Pomander, in "Christie Johnstone,"[1] says of his broken statues, that "time has impaired their indelicacy." This somewhat nauseating quality remains in full force, and we see no good in their publication except to abate the outcries of the Liberal League against Mr. Anthony Comstock[2] and his laws respecting obscene publications. So long as *Leaves of Grass* may be sent through the mails, the country is safe from over-prudery, at least. Mr. Whitman is often ranked with the "fleshly school," and his circle of English admirers is almost identical with the coterie whose apostles are Swinburne and Wilde. But the erotic poems of these authors are to those of Whitman as rose-water to vitriol. The English poets have at their worst some thin veneering of personal emotion; with Whitman there seems no gleam of anything personal, much less of that simple, generous impulse which makes almost every young man throw some halo of ideal charm about the object of his adoration. Whitman's love, if such it can be called, is the sheer animal longing of sex for sex—the impulse of the savage, who knocks down the first woman he sees, and drags her to his cave. On the whole, the condition of the savage seems the more wholesome, for he simply gratifies his brute lust and writes no resounding lines about it.

Leaving this disagreeable aspect of the matter, we are impressed anew, on

1   A popular Victorian novel (first published in 1853) by the English writer and dramatist Charles Reade (1814–84).
2   Anthony Comstock (1844–1915) was a founder of the New York Society for the Suppression of Vice (1873), a force behind the passage of legislation prohibiting the mailing of obscene literature through the mails, and an incessant crusader against abortion and obscenity in art and literature.

reading these poems, by a certain quality of hollowness, which is nowhere more felt than in the strains called "Drum-Taps." It would be scarcely worth while to bring these strains to any personal test, perhaps, did not Mr. Whitman's admirers so constantly intrude his personality upon us; but we cannot quite forget what Emerson says, that "it makes a great difference to a sentence whether there be a man behind it or no." When Mr. Whitman speaks with utter contempt of the "civilian," and claps the soldier on the back as "camerado," we cannot help thinking of Thackeray's burly and peaceful Jos. Sedley[3] at Brussels, just before the battle of Waterloo, striding and swaggering between two military officers, and looking far more warlike than either. One can be aroused to some enthusiasm over the pallid shop-boy or the bookish undergraduate who knew no better than to shoulder his musket and march to the front in the war for the Union; but it is difficult to awaken any such emotion for a stalwart poet, who—with the finest physique in America, as his friends asserted, and claiming an unbounded influence over the "roughs" of New York—preferred to pass by the recruiting-office and take service in the hospital with the non-combatants.

When we come to purely intellectual traits, it is a curious fact that Mr. Whitman, by the production of one fine poem, has overthrown his whole poetic theory. Dozens of pages of his rhythmic prose are not worth "My Captain," which among all his compositions comes the nearest to accepting the restraints of ordinary rhyme. His success in this shows that he too may yet be compelled to recognize form as an element in poetic power. The discovery may have come too late, but unless he can regard its lessons he is likely to leave scarcely a complete work that will be remembered; only here and there a phrase, an epithet, a fine note—as when the midnight tolling for General Garfield is called "The sobbing of the bells."[4] These are the passages which his especial admirers style "Homeric," but which we should rather call Ossianic.[5] The shadowy Gaelic bard rejected the restraints of verse, like Whitman, and reiterated his peculiar images with wearisome diffuseness and minuteness. To be sure, he was not an egotist, and he kept within the limits of decency; but he gave fine glimpses and pictures, while there was always a certain large, free atmosphere about all his works. They were translated into all languages; he was ranked with Homer and Virgil; Goethe and Napoleon Bonaparte were his warm admirers—and the collections of English poetry do not now include a line of his composing. If Whitman, after the same length of time, proves more fortunate, it will be because he wrote "My Captain."

---

3 The reference is to a comic character in the popular Victorian novel *Vanity Fair* (1848), by William Makepeace Thackeray (1811–63), one of the most acclaimed English satirists and novelists.
4 James Garfield (1831–81), who rose to the rank of general during the Civil War, was the twentieth president of the United States. Whitman had a casual friendship with him in Washington and dedicated a poem to his memory following his assassination in 1881.
5 Ossian was a legendary Irish poet brought back to modern life in supposed "translations" of James McPherson (1736–96) that were influential in many quarters (though suspect in others) during the nineteenth century. The comparison between Whitman's lyricism and Ossian's mysticism is not complimentary.

From Thomas W. Higginson, *Cheerful Yesterdays* (Boston: Houghton, Mifflin, 1898)

Higginson first encountered Whitman in Boston in 1860, as he recalls in this excerpt from his memoir, at the offices of Thayer and Eldridge, a major local address for abolitionist publications. They had recently published a biography of abolitionist John Brown and contracted to publish Harriet Jacobs' *Incidents in the Life of a Slave Girl*. At that moment, however, they were excited about the prospects of publishing a new edition of *Leaves of Grass*, whose production Whitman had come to Boston to oversee. If Higginson disliked the "unsavoriness" of the poetry of an earlier edition, it is not hard to imagine that he would have been disgusted with the new "Calamus" and "Enfans d'Adam" clusters of the Boston edition, composed of intensely homosexual and heterosexual poems.

But his criticism of Whitman in this excerpt is more particularly about the quality of his "manliness." From the moment of their first meeting – or, more precisely, the recollection of that encounter – Higginson eyed the big man opposite him up and down, taking the measure of his physique and manner. Whether he was judging Whitman against a presupposed correspondence with the persona of *Drum-Taps* and *Leaves of Grass* or simply against his own standards goes unstated. His subsequent deprecation of Whitman's manliness, however, is explicitly stated as a reaction to Whitman's published boasts of his service as male nurse to the Union war effort. Those boasts and the larger tag attaching to Whitman as "wound dresser" clearly antagonized a war veteran who had been wounded on the field of action and who publicly derided the conduct of able-bodied men who had absented themselves from military service.

In February, 1860, after urgent appeals from Mrs. Rebecca Spring,[1] of New York, who had visited these men, I made up my mind to use for their relief a portion of certain funds placed in my hands for the benefit of the Brown family;[2] first, of course, consulting Mrs. Brown, who fully approved. Thayer and Eldridge, two young publishers in Boston, also took an interest in raising funds for this purpose; and the fact is fixed in my memory by the circumstance that, on visiting their shop one day, during the negotiations, I met for the first and only time Walt Whitman. He was there to consult them about the publication of his poems, and I saw before me, sitting on the counter, a handsome, burly man, heavily built, and not looking, to my gymnasium-trained eye, in really good condition for athletic work. I perhaps felt a little prejudiced against him from having read his "Leaves of Grass" on a voyage, in the early stages of seasickness,—a fact which doubtless increased for me the intrinsic unsavoriness of certain passages. But the personal impression

1   Rebecca Buffon Spring (1811–1911) was a progressive educator and vigorous supporter of the abolition movement.
2   John Brown led a group of twenty-one men, including several of his sons, on an October 1859 attack on the federal arsenal at Harper's Ferry, Virginia, in the hope of distributing weapons among slaves and provoking a large-scale revolt. The attack was quickly stymied by federal troops, and Brown was speedily tried, convicted, and hanged.

made on me by the poet was not so much of manliness as of Boweriness,[3] if I may coin the phrase; indeed rather suggesting Sidney Lanier's[4] subsequent vigorous phrase, "a dandy roustabout." This passing impression did not hinder me from thinking of Whitman with hope and satisfaction at a later day when regiments were to be raised for the war, when the Bowery seemed the very place to enlist them, and even "Billy Wilson's Zouaves"[5] were hailed with delight. When, however, after waiting a year or more, Whitman decided that the proper post for him was hospital service, I confess to feeling a reaction, which was rather increased than diminished by his profuse celebration of his own labors in that direction. Hospital attendance is a fine thing, no doubt, yet if all men, South and North, had taken the same view of their duty that Whitman held, there would have been no occasion for hospitals on either side.

From William Dean Howells, *Literary Friends and Acquaintance: A Personal Retrospect of American Authorship* (New York: Harper and Brothers, 1900)

Howells' late-life recollection of Whitman provides a nice foil to Higginson's. He, too, first encountered Whitman in the early 1860s, then in 1881 when Whitman came to Boston to superintend production of the Osgood edition of *Leaves of Grass*. That initial encounter took place at Pfaff's, a popular subterranean saloon on Broadway frequented by Whitman and his friends. A fair number of those friends moved in the orbit of the *New York Saturday Press*, which itself at the time revolved around Whitman.

Howells's reminiscence is more charitable than was his rather negative verdict on *Drum-Taps* in 1865. A man of catholic taste and generous spirit, Howells had recently encouraged and supported the work of such writers as Mark Twain, Henry James, Hamlin Garland, Abraham Cahan, and Stephen Crane (see Directory, **pp. 30–33**), though never Whitman. His praise falls, rather, into the cult of personality that Whitman and his supporters created and that peaked following Whitman's death. His regard for Whitman's poetry was never great.

He was often at Pfaff's with them, and the night of my visit he was the chief fact of my experience. I did not know he was there till I was on my way out, for he did not sit at the table under the pavement, but at the head of one farther into the room. There, as I passed, some amiable fellow stopped me and named me to him, and I remember how he leaned back in his chair, and reached out his great hand to me, as if he were going to give it me for good and all. He had a fine head, with a

---

3   The Bowery was a rough and tumble section of Manhattan associated in the mid nineteenth century with the multiethnic "b'hoy" street culture which Whitman knew well and sometimes associated himself with (as Higginson does here).
4   Sidney Lanier (1842–81) was a popular Southern postbellum poet, far more highly regarded in his own day (though never appreciated by Whitman) than today.
5   Zouaves were flamboyantly dressed, highly skilled soldiers from North Africa incorporated into the French colonial army beginning in the 1830s, then into the Union army during the Civil War. In both countries they earned a reputation for extraordinary bravery.

cloud of Jovian hair upon it, and a branching beard and mustache, and gentle eyes that looked most kindly into mine, and seemed to wish the liking which I instantly gave him, though we hardly passed a word, and our acquaintance was summed up in that glance and the grasp of his mighty fist upon my hand.[1] I doubt if he had any notion who or what I was beyond the fact that I was a young poet of some sort, but he may possibly have remembered seeing my name printed after some very Heinesque[2] verses in the *Press*.[3] I did not meet him again for twenty years, and then I had only a moment with him when he was reading the proofs of his poems in Boston.[4] Some years later I saw him for the last time, one day after his lecture on Lincoln, in that city, when he came down from the platform to speak with some hand-shaking friends who gathered about him.[5] Then and always he gave me the sense of a sweet and true soul, and I felt in him a spiritual dignity which I will not try to reconcile with his printing in the forefront of his book a passage from a private letter of Emerson's,[6] though I believe he would not have seen such a thing as most other men would, or thought ill of it in another. The spiritual purity which I felt in him no less than the dignity is something that I will no more try to reconcile with what denies it in his page; but such things we may well leave to the adjustment of finer balances than we have at hand. I will make sure only of the greatest benignity in the presence of the man. The apostle of the rough, the uncouth, was the gentlest person; his barbaric yawp, translated into the terms of social encounter, was an address of singular quiet, delivered in a voice of winning and endearing friendliness.

Hamlin Garland, "A Tribute of Grasses," *Prairie Songs* (Cambridge, Mass.: Stone and Kimball, 1893)

Garland was one of the rising new writers of the 1890s. He had made a national reputation in 1891 with the publication of *Main-Travelled Roads*, a collection of short stories about life on the Great Plains. William Dean Howells and other major critics in the 1890s had acclaimed his form of gritty, small-town writing and widely regarded Garland as the leading practitioner of Midwestern realism. A year following this review, Garland articulated in *Crumbling Idols* his own

---

1 Howells's sketch is one of the finest we have of Whitman's casual look and manner captured in an unguarded moment – a not surprising outcome given the fact that Howells, an accomplished novelist, was one of the finest verbal sketch artists of his generation.

2 After the manner of the great German poet Heinrich Heine (1797–1856), whose poems were famous for their lyrical beauty and often outlandish and wicked humor.

3 The *New York Saturday Press* (1858–66) was a leading literary weekly that published, among other distinguished works, Whitman's "Out of the Cradle Endlessly Rocking" (first titled "A Child's Reminiscence") and Twain's "The Notorious Jumping Frog of Calaveras County." Its founding editor, Henry Clapp, was a friend of Whitman's who used the paper to promote and support him.

4 That is, when he was reading the proofs of the 1881–82 Osgood edition of *Leaves of Grass*.

5 Whitman delivered a lecture on Abraham Lincoln in Boston's St. Botolph Club on 15 April 1881, one of many he gave in his later years on the anniversary of the assassination. The *Boston Herald* reported: "Many of the leading literati were at his lecture, and among them Mr. Howells was most cordial in his greeting" (quoted in Gay Wilson Allen, *The Solitary Singer: A Critical Biography of Walt Whitman* [New York: New York University Press, 1967], p. 491).

6 For the full text of the letter, see p. 39.

aesthetic of an American literature true to the specific conditions of American regional life.

One of his primary literary forebearers, he recognized, was Whitman, whom he addresses in this poem on the common grounds of their respective aesthetics – grass to grass, in Garland's figuration. The trope invoked is one that Garland consciously borrowed from Whitman's poetry of the tendered gift of grass (or flowers), in "Song of Myself" and other poems. As in Whitman, the intent is to span great divides, including the physical divide presented by the expanse of the United States, which Garland conceives of as an east–west continuum across which Whitman and he converge from opposite ends.

To W. W.

Serene, vast head, with silver cloud of hair
Lined on the purple dusk of death,
A stern medallion, velvet set—
Old Norseman, throned, not chained upon thy chair,
Thy grasp of hand, thy hearty breath
   Of welcome thrills me yet
   As when I faced thee there!

Loving my plain as thou thy sea,
Facing the East as thou the West,
I bring a handful of grass to thee—
The prairie grasses I know the best;
Type of the wealth and width of the plain,
Strong of the strength of the wind and sleet,
Fragrant with sunlight and cool with rain,
I bring it and lay it low at thy feet,
   Here by the eastern sea.

Twentieth-Century Responses and Criticism

Though still shunned or mocked in some circles early in the century, "Song of Myself" became over the course of the twentieth century one of the world's most widely recognized, influential poems. Broad acceptance, however, did not lead to broad agreement about its meaning. On the contrary, the poem has generated an extraordinary breadth of interpretations and opinions, a result no doubt of its experimental poetics, unconventional views, yawning comprehensiveness, and sheer length and breadth. For this reason, it has become a virtually nonpareil touchstone for registering the full variety of twentieth-century critical schools and opinions.

Ezra Pound, "A Pact," *Personae, Collected Shorter Poems* (New York: New Directions, 1915)

Proponent and practitioner of literary modernism, Pound was a major innovative figure in twentieth-century American poetry. Unlike Whitman, he looked primarily east for subject and inspiration. He was one of the first writers of his generation definitively to turn his back on the provincialism of the United States; from 1908 he made his home in England, where he conducted his search for a more cosmopolitan form of art.

This poem portrays his still unresolved fight with his American past. Shortly before writing this poem, he addressed a short poem to a fellow American expatriate artist, "To Whistler, American," which ends, "You and Abe Lincoln from that mass of dolts/ Show us there's chance at least of winning through." In the age of the iconoclastic journalist H. L. Mencken and satiric novelist Sinclair Lewis, that kind of unattractive self-depiction of the United States was not uncommon, though few carried it as far as Pound. His disdain for both Whitman and American culture was long-standing. In fact, he tended to equate them, as in the claim "He *is* America," which he made in his 1909 essay "What I Feel About Walt Whitman." In this poem, however, he sought a kind of reconciliation – if not of son with father(land), at least of younger rebel with older one engaging in a kind of "commerce."

In subsequent years, Pound went further than many of his contemporaries – such as experimental prose and poetry writer Gertrude Stein, short-story writer and novelist Ernest Hemingway, and even the major poet and critic T. S. Eliot – in cutting himself off from his American roots. He moved to Italy in 1921, became a vocal supporter of Mussolini, and during the Second World War made a series of anti-American, English-language propaganda broadcasts. When he finally returned to the United States in November 1945 it was in custody as a traitor.

I make a pact with you, Walt Whitman—
I have detested you long enough.
I come to you as a grown child
Who has had a pig-headed father;
I am old enough now to make friends.
It was you that broke the new wood,
Now is a time for carving.
We have one sap and one root—
Let there be commerce between us.

From Carl Sandburg, Introduction to Modern Library edition of *Leaves of Grass* (New York: Modern Library, 1921)

The Modern Library edition of *Leaves of Grass*, with Sandburg's championing Introduction, was an important event in the history of the work's reception. Although there were a variety of other editions of the work then in print in the United States, most, by contrast with this $0.95 edition, were too expensive to be available to the general reading public. The major exception was the famous J. M. Dent's Everyman edition (1912), published in England and distributed in the United States by Dutton in an edition that would be frequently reprinted throughout that decade and the next. Like the Everyman, the Modern Library edition had the effect of canonizing the work; the series title, "the modern library of the world's best books," indicates the status that Whitman's book achieved by the 1920s. Such inexpensive, small-sized, cloth-bound editions distributed on a national and international scale must have more nearly approximated Whitman's idealized notion of audience reception for *Leaves of Grass* than anything that had yet been published.

Sandburg was the logical choice to mediate the work's appearance in this format. Poet, journalist, biographer, political activist, and cultural popularizer, Sandburg exhibited a profile reminiscent of Whitman's. Like an increasing number of readers who had adopted Whitman's own logic, Sandburg identified Whitman with America; in fact, he tended to equate himself with both, as well, sometimes via his identification with Whitman.

His introduction presumes and pronounces Whitman's greatness – his singular greatness, in fact, among American writers – as though in the manner of a formal acclamation. It reprises the compositional history and critical reception of *Leaves of Grass* in a narrative comprised of equal parts fact, anecdote, legend, and outright error. That introduction and edition stand in contradistinction to the more scholarly text of *Leaves of Grass* edited by the early Whitman scholar Emory Holloway and brought out by Doubleday in 1924.

In Certain Particulars Walt Whitman's book, "*Leaves of Grass*," stands by itself and is the most peculiar and noteworthy monument amid the work of American literature.

First, as to style. In a large and growing circle of readers and critics, it is regarded as the most original book, the most decisively individual, the most sublimely personal creation in American literary art.

Second, as to handling by critics and commentators. It is the most highly praised and the most deeply damned book that ever came from an American printing press as the work of an American writer; no other book can compete with it in the number of bouquets handed it by distinguished bystanders on one side of the street and in the number of hostile and nasty brickbats flung by equally distinguished bystanders on the other side of the street.

Third, as to personality. It is the most intensely personal book in American literature, living grandly to its promissory line, "who touches this touches a man,"[1] spilling its multitude of confessions with the bravery of a first-rate autobiography.

Fourth, as to scope of life work. It packs within its covers, does "*Leaves of Grass*," the life and thought and feeling of one man; it was first published when the author was 36 years of age and he actually never wrote another book even though he lived to be 73 years of age; what he did all the rest of his life after publishing the first edition of "*Leaves of Grass*," was to rewrite and extend the first book.

Fifth, as to literary rank abroad. No other American poet, except Poe, has the name, the persistent audiences across decades of time, and the pervasive influence, credited to Walt Whitman as an American writer, an American force in Europe, Asia, Africa, Australia, and the archipelagoes of the sea.

Sixth, as to influence in America. No other American book has so persistent a crowd of friends, advocates and sponsors as that which from decade to decade carries on the ballyhoo for "*Leaves of Grass*"; in Chicago, as an instance, Walt Whitman is the only dead or living American author whose memory is kept by an informal organization that memorializes its hero with an annual dinner.

Seventh, as to Americanism. "*Leaves of Grass*" is the most wildly keyed solemn oath that America means something and is going somewhere that has ever been written; it is America's most classic advertisement of itself as having purpose, destiny, banners and beacon-fires.

---

1   A famous line from the closing poem of *Leaves of Grass*, "So Long!" "This" refers to the physical text of the book.

Therefore—because of the foregoing seven itemized points—and because there are further points into which the annals might be lengthened—and because still furthermore there are great and mystic points of contact that cannot be captured in itemized information—therefore *"Leaves of Grass"* is a book to be owned, kept, loaned, fought over, and read till it is dog-eared and dirty all over.

It was in 1855 that Whitman offered the American public its first chance at his poetry. Because no publisher of that day cared to undertake publication of the book, *"Leaves of Grass,"* the poet was his own publisher. That is, he invited himself to take a header into literature, accepted the invitation, and went to the party unabashed, in his shirtsleeves and in a slouch hat.

There has been mention on occasion of American "shirtsleeve diplomacy." Whitman is the commanding instance in shirtsleeve literature. A second edition of *"Leaves of Grass"* came out in 1856. And the poet published as a frontispiece a picture of himself in shirtsleeves, knockabout clothes, the left hand in the pants pocket, the right hand on the hip akimbo, the hat tossed at a slant, and the head and general disposition of the cosmos indicating a statement and an inquiry, "Well, here we are; it looks good to us; and while it isn't important, how do you like us?"[2]

On the cover of the book were the words gilded on a green background: "I greet you at the beginning of a great career—R. W. Emerson." The generally accredited foremost reputable figure of American letters and philosophy had written those words to Whitman the year before.

And in order to let everybody in and give free speech full play, there was printed as the last thing in the book, a criticism by a reviewer in the Boston *Intelligencer* of May 3, 1856, closing with this paragraph: "This book should find no place where humanity urges any claim to respect, and the author should be kicked from all decent society as below the level of the brute. There is neither wit nor method in his disjointed babbling, and it seems to us he must be some escaped lunatic, raving in pitiable delirium."

That was a beginning. It isn't over yet. The controversy yet rises and subsides.

The best loved figure in American literature—by those who loved him—he is counted also the most heartily damned figure—by those who damned him.

The most highly praised and the most roundly excoriated book America has produced—that is Walt Whitman's *"Leaves of Grass."*

"He is the poet who brought the slop-pail into the parlor," wrote one critic. "He is one of the sublime figures of all human annals, one to be set for companionship with Confucius, Socrates, and the teachers of high and sacred living," wrote another critic.

"The man was mad, mad beyond the cavil of a doubt," wrote Max Nordau.[3] Another European critic, Gabriel Sarrazin,[4] wrote: "He is the apostle of the idea that man is an indivisible fragment of the universal Divinity."

Walt Whitman is the only established epic poet of America. He is the single

---

2   The reference is to the illustration that Whitman used in the 1855 edition (see Figure 2, **p. 16**).
3   Max Nordau (1849–1923) was a Hungarian-born writer and medical doctor, as well as pioneering Zionist, whose works include a controversial study of madness, *Degeneration* (1893).
4   Gabriel Sarrazin (b. 1853) was a French poet and translator with an appreciation for nineteenth-century English and American poets (among the latter, especially for Whitman and Poe).

American figure that both American and European artists and critics most often put in a class or throw into a category with Shakespeare, Dante, Homer. He is the one American writer that Emerson, Burroughs,[5] John Muir,[6] Edward Carpenter,[7] and similar observers enter in their lists as having a size in history and an importance of utterance that places him with Socrates, Confucius, Lao Tse, and the silver-grey men of the half-worlds who left the Bhagavad Gita and writings known most often as sacred.

In stature, pride, stride, and scope of personality, he is a challenger. He warns us to come with good teeth if we are to join in his menu—to bring along our rough weather clothes. He is likely any time to tip us out of the boat to see whether we swim or sink. And there are blanks to be filled in among his writings where he seems to have whispered, "I am going away now and I leave you alone to work it out for yourself—you came alone and you will have to go away alone."

Walt Whitman wrote his vital passages at the height of America's most stormily human period of history. "We live in the midst of alarms; anxiety beclouds the future; we expect some new disaster with each newspaper we read," said Abraham Lincoln in the famous "Lost Speech" delivered the same year Walt Whitman's "*Leaves of Grass*" was first published.

"Blood will flow . . . and brother's hand will be raised against brother!" was the passionate outcry of that same speech, which because of its tenor of violence was withheld from publication and distribution by its orator.

In the same decade, Charles A. Dana, managing editor of the *New York Tribune*, was writing: "It may be that the day of revolutions is past, but, if so, why are they there in such abundance? . . . Let others give aid and comfort to despots. Be it ours to stand for Liberty and Justice, nor fear to lock arms with those who are called hotheads and demagogues."[8] The luminous fringes of romance attaching to those abstractions, "Liberty and Justice," as a result of the American and French revolutions, were still in the air. Dana wrote friendly explanations of just what the Frenchman, Proudhon,[9] meant by his thesis, "Property is Robbery." Thoreau was writing an essay, "On the Duty of Civil Disobedience." John Brown was stealing horses, running slaves by the underground railroad from slave to free soil, stocking arsenals, praying over strange, new projects. These all have their significance in showing the tint of the time spirit. Brook Farm, and its Utopian socialist outlooks, Fourier[10] and his phalanxes of workmen, the 1848 revolutions, these were hot topics of the time. The far-reaching tides and backwashes of thought and emotion resulting from the French and American revolutions, and all

---

5 For Emerson and Burroughs, see Directory of Contextual Figures, pp. 30–33.

6 John Muir (1838–1914) was a pioneering explorer, naturalist, and conservationist. His major accomplishments include leading the campaign to establish Yosemite and Sequoia as national parks (accomplished in 1890) and serving as the founding president of the Sierra Club (1892).

7 Edward Carpenter (1844–1929) was an ardent English socialist who credited his reading of *Leaves of Grass* as a young man with setting him on a path to reform society. He visited Whitman in Philadelphia in 1877 and wrote one of the nineteenth-century's most perceptive books about him.

8 This was the same Charles Dana who wrote the first review of *Leaves of Grass* (see pp. 39–43).

9 Pierre-Joseph Proudhon (1809–65) was a radical French philosopher and social theoretician and author of the influential attack on private property, *What Is Property?*, to which Sandburg is referring.

10 Charles Fourier (1773–1837) was a radical French social theoretician whose ideas of a workers' "phalanx" influenced utopian and practical social experiments throughout the nineteenth century and up to the kibbutz movement in early-twentieth-century Palestine.

that weave of circumstance touching the secession rights of states of the Union with its ramifications into chattel slavery, besides the swirl of events riding into that epic upheaval, the sectional war—these things, tangibles and intangibles, were in the air and the breath of men in the years when Walt Whitman was bringing his book to focus, getting ready to launch *"Leaves of Grass."* [. . .]

· · · · ·

"Song of Myself," which in the earliest editions was titled, "Poem of Walt Whitman, An American," is a specimen of the massive masterpiece. "I do not ask who you are, that is not important to me," he declares in one line, and, "I wear my hat as I please indoors and out," in another line.[11] Such lines are easily understood even by those who question whether it should classify as poetry. "What is a man anyhow? What am I? What are you?" or "I do not call one greater and one smaller," or "These are really the thoughts of all men in all ages, they are not original with me," or "I launch all men and women forward with me into the Unknown," these are further instances of the understandable.[12]

It is among the inarticulates of the primitive, the abysmal, on the borders where time, mystic dimensions, and the sphinxes of Nowhere ask their riddles, it is in this territory that Walt Whitman gives some people a grand everlasting thrill, while still other people get only a headache and a revulsion. "Rise after rise bow the phantoms behind me, Afar down I see the huge first Nothing, I know I was even there," he murmurs in "Song of Myself," "Long I was hugg'd close—long and long."[13]

From D. H. Lawrence, *Studies in Classic American Literature*
(New York: Thomas Seltzer, 1923), pp. 253–54, 259–60

These excerpts come from "Whitman," the concluding chapter in Lawrence's magisterial reading of pre-Civil War American writing. One of the greatest English novelists, poets, and critics of his time, Lawrence had admiringly been reading the imaginative works of American writers since childhood. James Fenimore Cooper, Ralph Waldo Emerson, Edgar Allan Poe, Nathaniel Hawthorne, and Herman Melville were all well known to him as he wrote his book, but Whitman represented to him, as to an increasing number of the cultural commentators of the 1920s, the writer indispensable to a reckoning with American life and writing.

Lawrence saw Whitman as the nonpareil "pioneer" not just of American but also of modern literature. At the same time, he was unsparingly judgmental. Although Whitman pointed the way down "the open road" (a partial title of a major *Leaves of Grass* poem central to Lawrence's interpretation of Whitman as an inspirational leader), Lawrence criticized him for failing to lead by his own

---

11 The quotations come, respectively, from ll. 1001 and 397.
12 The quotations come, respectively, from ll. 391, 1142, 355, and 1136.
13 The quotations come, respectively, from ll. 1152–153 and 1156.

example. Instead of exemplifying modern individualism in his own person (and persona), Lawrence charges, Whitman gives his imaginative powers over to a false sympathy in which he sacrifices the integrity of his own self to that of the "other."

One of the particular examples of identification cited by Lawrence, that of the slave in "Song of Myself," became in late-twentieth-century criticism a point of intense debate. (For a differing position from Lawrence's, see the excerpt from Karen Sánchez-Eppler, pp. 106–11.) Was Whitman a liberating presence who articulated a progressive, antislavery position and gave voice to the thoughts of enslaved African Americans? Or was he himself an unwitting collaborator in the usurpation of the voice and expression of the people he claimed to speak for? Whichever the case, it was remote from Lawrence's defense of individualism from encroachment by anything or anyone external to the integrity of selfhood.

Whitman, the great poet, has meant so much to me. Whitman, the one man breaking a way ahead. Whitman, the one pioneer. And only Whitman. No English pioneers, no French. No European pioneer-poets. In Europe the would-be pioneers are mere innovators. The same in America. Ahead of Whitman, nothing. Ahead of all poets, pioneering into the wilderness of unopened life, Whitman. Beyond him, none. His wide, strange camp at the end of the great high-road. And lots of new little poets camping on Whitman's camping ground now. But none going really beyond. Because Whitman's camp is at the end of the road, and on the edge of a great precipice. Over the precipice, blue distances, and the blue hollow of the future. But there is no way down. It is a dead end.

Pisgah. Pisgah sights. And Death. Whitman like a strange, modern, American Moses.[1] Fearfully mistaken. And yet the great leader.

The essential function of art is moral. Not aesthetic, not decorative, not pastime and recreation. But moral. The essential function of art is moral.

But a passionate, implicit morality, not didactic. A morality which changes the blood, rather than the mind. Changes the blood first. The mind follows later, in the wake.

Now Whitman was a great moralist. He was a great leader. He was a great changer of the blood in the veins of men.

[. . .]

Whitman's essential message was the Open Road. The leaving of the soul free unto herself, the leaving of his fate to her and to the loom of the open road. Which is the bravest doctrine man has ever proposed to himself.

Alas, he didn't quite carry it out. He couldn't quite break the old maddening bond of the love-compulsion; he couldn't quite get out of the rut of the charity habit—for Love and Charity have degenerated now into habit: a bad habit.

---

1   Moses climbs to the top of Pisgah, a peak east of the Jordan River and opposite Jericho, to look westward across to the Promised Land, which God has informed him he will not live to enter (Deuteronomy 34:1).

Whitman said Sympathy. If only he had stuck to it! Because Sympathy means feeling with, not feeling for. He kept on having a passionate feeling *for* the negro slave, or the prostitute, or the syphilitic—which is merging. A sinking of Walt Whitman's soul in the souls of these others.

He wasn't keeping to his open road. He was forcing his soul down an old rut. He wasn't leaving her free. He was forcing her into other people's circumstances.

Supposing he had felt true sympathy with the negro slave?[2] He would have felt *with* the negro slave. Sympathy—compassion—which is partaking of the passion which was in the soul of the negro slave.

What was the feeling in the negro's soul?

"Ah, I am a slave! Ah, it is bad to be a slave! I must free myself. My soul will die unless she frees herself. My soul says I must free myself."

Whitman came along, and saw the slave, and said to himself: "That negro slave is a man like myself. We share the same identity. And he is bleeding with wounds. Oh, oh, is it not myself who am also bleeding with wounds?"

This was not *sympathy*. It was merging and self-sacrifice. "Bear ye one another's burdens": "Love thy neighbour as thyself": "Whatsoever ye do unto him, ye do unto me."[3]

If Whitman had truly *sympathized*, he would have said: "That negro slave suffers from slavery. He wants to free himself. His soul wants to free him. He has wounds, but they are the price of freedom. The soul has a long journey from slavery to freedom. If I can help him I will: I will not take over his wounds and his slavery to myself. But I will help him fight the power that enslaves him when he wants to be free, if he wants my help, since I see in his face that he needs to be free. But even when he is free, his soul has many journeys down the open road, before it is a free soul."

Langston Hughes, "I, Too," *The Collected Poems*, ed. Arnold Rampersad and David Roessel (New York: Vintage, 1924)

The leading African American poet of his generation, Hughes had Whitman's poetry at his fingertips. He wrote this poem antiphonally in response to, or reaction against, such Whitman "songs" as "Song of Myself" and "I Hear America Singing." But the purpose and direction of Hughes's poem are distinctly different from Whitman's.

The circumstances of the poem's composition may partially explain the difference. At the time he wrote the poem, Hughes was down and out in Genoa, Italy, during a long excursion to Europe that had left him stranded without friends or funds. The loneliness of the poem, however, cannot be explained by those circumstances alone. Hughes was making as strong a declarative statement as Whitman of his claim to representative status as an American citizen and poet and was finding a language and style in which to make that statement on behalf of his people.

2   Lawrence has in mind the "hounded slave" episode in section 33 of "Song of Myself."
3   Biblical quotations from, respectively, Galatians 6:2, Leviticus 19:18 (and Matthew 19:19), and Matthew 25:40.

I, too, sing America.

I am the darker brother.
They send me to eat in the kitchen
When company comes,
But I laugh,
And eat well,
And grow strong.
Tomorrow,
I'll sit at the table
When company comes.
Nobody'll dare
Say to me,
"Eat in the kitchen,"
Then.

Besides,
They'll see how beautiful I am
And be ashamed—

I, too, am America.

Michael Gold, "Ode to Walt Whitman," *New Masses* 27 (5 November 1935): 21

Gold was a proletarian writer who deeply identified – and is himself today identified – with the grim urban reality and class conflict of depression-era America. One of the most polemical writers of an ideological decade and the long-time editor of the activist journal *New Masses*, in which he published this poem, Gold associated himself with the Communist program and critique of his time. But he also associated himself with Whitman, no friend of socialism himself but a poet taken up by socialists and Marxists from around the world in the first half of the twentieth century.

Gold could as readily declare himself "a son of Manhattan" (and of Walt Whitman) as Whitman could call himself "Walt Whitman, a kosmos, of Manhattan the son" (l. 497 of "Song of Myself"). The author of a vivid, still powerful chronicle of the poor, working-class neighborhoods of the city (*Jews Without Money*, 1930), Gold knew his native New York City as well as Whitman had known his several generations earlier and identified with it no less. Gold's New York would have been both recognizable and unrecognizable to his father figure: a vast, crude, heterogeneous, fast-paced commercial cityscape populated by names ("greenbaum" and "kelly") and groups perhaps alien to Whitman and placarded with ideologies remote to him (Leninism) – but all in all sensually and rhythmically familiar. At the same time, this poem conveys little of Whitman's powerful optimism. Instead, Gold's ode communicates a jaded reaction to the great city's and nation's squandered promise of greatness, beauty, and love.

Gold's identification with Whitman foreshadows the more famous alliance made a generation later by Allen Ginsberg. In fact, Gold's "Ode" anticipates Ginsberg's signature 1950s poem, "Howl," as a kind of Whitmanesque anthem in which New York City figured as the focal point of American life. For Ginsberg's own poetic address to Whitman, see **pp. 92–93**.

1.

Walt Whitman loafed under the trees[1]
Leaned on his cane and observed
In a slow and sunburned Manhattan—
But now they've killed his God
His love and horsecars and old trees—
Hear the shriek of the killer babbitts[2]
God is the smash of two taxis in a hurry
God is a skyscraper house of money
Where crazy little benitos murder love
And ring cash registers all day—
God is hate dollars chromium speed—
And no lilacs bloom,[3] Walt Whitman—
No hope no grass no quiet
Nothing to love but Coney Island[4]
Your ocean now a garbage dump
Where millions of young greenbaums sport
And must swallow colon germs B
Americanoes at twelve a week—

2.

And me a son of Walt Whitman
A son of Manhattan the bitch
Born on Rat and Louse street
Near Tuberculosis avenue—
In my unfortunate cradle
A tenement fell on my head
A double-crossing rotten Tammany[5] tenement
A shylock[6] tenement that devoured dreams—

---

1   A reference to the second stanza of "Song of Myself."
2   "Babbitt," a word taken from the title character of Sinclair Lewis' bestselling 1922 novel, quickly became a common American term for mindless mediocrity and conformity.
3   The reference is to Whitman's Civil War-era poem, "When Lilacs Last in the Dooryard Bloom'd."
4   A seaside neighborhood of Brooklyn, which, following the 1920 subway link to Manhattan and the opening of its beaches to the public three years later, became the recreational center for New York City's immigrant masses.
5   A district of lower Manhattan and a powerful Democratic political machine long associated in the nineteenth and twentieth centuries with cronyism and corruption.
6   A common term for cold-hearted, avaricious behavior, usually connected to money loaning, drawn from the name and figure of Shakespeare's character in *The Merchant of Venice*.

People tramped the hospital streets
Sick with the dysentery of life
Cowards without a flag—
And me a son of Walt Whitman
Kicked into a basement to die—
Eddie Greenbaum, skinny shipping clerk—
Americano at twelve a week—
Nietzsche[7] packing pink lady's underwear—
Pale, goofy young poet of hardware—
Department store intellectual dope—
Soaring with Keats[8] above the gum-chewers—
Doped by a priest named Walt Whitman—
Why did I mistake you for the sun?

3.

Love love love on the Bronx Express
Ten seconds to gain and a world to lose
O sweet unfortunate Baby
Phoney in five and dime jade and rayon
Constipated under the woolworth roses and lilies
You smelled bad, poor girl
Of swollen feet, rouge and cash registers—
My chest touched your little breasts—
The subway crush married us—
I dreamed among the gum-chewers—
"I sang the body electric"—[9]
You were the kind and lovely woman I had sought
In my long, long Walt Whitman dreams—
But you divorced me with loathing
At the Simpson Street subway station—
Why didn't I shoot myself
Goofy young Greenbaum rooting for love
In the garbage of my New York—
And yours, Walt Whitman—

4.

O Pioneers,[10] our foreman was a nervous little rat—
And all day like a third degree
Down in the basement hell with democracy
Commercial madhouse from 8 to 6

---

7 Friedrich Nietzsche (1844–1900), German philosopher and author of many seminal works, had a
   profound influence on the emergence of many strands and schools of twentieth-century thought,
   including existentialism.
8 John Keats (1795–1821) was one of England's and the world's greatest Romantic poets.
9 The title (slightly altered) of one of Whitman's most famous poems.
10 A reference to Whitman's influential poem "Pioneers! O Pioneers!"

I knew the clatter speedup and gangrened air
Electric bulb sweat and coffin fears—
Above us the macy gimbel[11] millionaires
Plotted bargains in young greenbaums and kelleys—[12]
Hell hell hell and low wages
And little salesgirls puked among the rayon—
Such was our life, O Pioneers—[13]
Until I gagged at Walt Whitman
His son of the open road and splendid silent sun—[14]
Lies, lies, a lazy poet's lies on a printed page
Meant for rich college boys—
No winds blow, no sun shines, America is my prison,
Don't mock me with your tales of the free,
Give me time, I want real love and fresh air,
Poetry is the cruelest bunk,
A trade union is better than all your dreams—

5.

So on April 14th we struck
A miracle like your lilacs, Walt Whitman—
Spring, spring, Rocky Mountain spring and democracy
Out of the basement greenbaums and kelleys—
And me, the dope, the factory fodder and jailbird,
Actually singing on a picket line—
Cops sneered and slugged and the millionaires went nuts—
But my heart glowed with proud happiness—
And Lenin[15] said, scorn not the dream—
See, see new skyscrapers for Manhattan
Communist factories for human love—
A pure ocean, and sunlit homes not tenements—
Streets for sun and friendship
And no more Tuberculosis avenues—
And no more hell in a basement—
Son of Walt Whitman, to strike is to dream!

6.

O Pioneers we build your dream America—
O Walt Whitman, they buried you in the filth
The clatter speedup of a department store basement
But you rose from the grave to march with us
On the picket line of democracy—

11 Macy's and Gimbel's were two of New York City's most fashionable department stores.
12 Greenbaums and Kellys were generic names (Jewish and Irish, respectively) of immigrants at a time
    when New York City was still absorbing the largest mass immigration to date to the United States.
13 Another reference to Whitman's poem "Pioneers! O Pioneers!"
14 A reference to Whitman's poem "Song of the Open Road."
15 Vladimir Ilyich Lenin (1870–1924) was the leader of the 1917 Bolshevik revolution and the first
    leader of the new Communist government of the Soviet Union.

Sing sing O new pioneers with Father Walt
Of a strong and beautiful America
Of the thrushes and oceans we shall win
Of sun, of moon, of Communism and joy in the wind
Of the free mountain boys and girls—
It will come! It will come! The strikes foretell it!
The Lenin dreams of the kelleys and greenbaums
Deep in the gangrened basements
Where Walt Whitman's America
Aches, to be born—

From Randall Jarrell, "Some Lines from Whitman," *Poetry and the Age* (New York: Knopf, 1953) pp. 112–32

Jarrell was one of the outstanding lyrical poets of the post-Second World War generation. He was also one of its clearest-eyed literary critics. His vivid appreciation of Whitman, from which these paragraphs are excerpted, constituted one chapter in his fiercely articulate defense of culture (but especially poetry) in the nuclear era, *Poetry and the Age*.

The words he applied to Whitman also apply to him: Jarrell had his nerve. His delight in its display was hardly less basic to his writing than it was to Whitman's. His nerve in this essay was his brazenly self-conscious act of challenging established critical taste. In a generation dominated by the formalist tenets of the New Criticism, two of whose leading proponents (Robert Penn Warren and John Crowe Ransom) he not only knew but had studied with at Vanderbilt University, Jarrell resisted the diminution common in academic circles of Whitman as a literary barbarian, a view by then a century old. The deprecation of Whitman as a literary barbarian had begun with the earliest reviews of *Leaves of Grass* in 1855, but the term became formalized in the 1900 essay "The Poetry of Barbarism" by the Harvard philosopher and critic George Santayana, which took Whitman as a prime specimen (and which also expressed a grudging admiration). To combat that view and to portray Whitman as, just the opposite, a poet's poet, Jarrell compiled a litany of Whitman's "biggest hits," citing a hodgepodge of phrases, lines, and stanzas and assuming that their power, beauty, and singularity would prove persuasive. In the end, however, Jarrell's defense of Whitman's poetry rests more nearly on the formalists' grounds of beauty, delicacy, and verbal singularity than on the post-Vietnam War generation's commitment to extra-literary issues and values.

WHITMAN, Dickinson, and Melville seem to me the best poets of the 19th Century here in America. Melville's poetry has been grotesquely underestimated, but of course it is only in the last four or five years that it has been much read; in the long run, in spite of the awkwardness and amateurishness of so much of it, it will surely be thought well of. (In the short run it will probably be thought entirely too well of. Melville is a great poet only in the prose of *Moby Dick*.) Dickinson's poetry has been thoroughly read, and well though undifferentiatingly loved—after a few decades or centuries almost everybody will be able to see through Dickinson to her poems. But something odd has happened to the living changing part of Whitman's reputation: nowadays it is people who are not particularly interested in poetry, people who say that they read a poem for what it says, not for how it says it, who admire Whitman most. Whitman is often written about, either approvingly or disapprovingly, as if he were the Thomas Wolfe[1] of 19th Century democracy, the hero of a de Mille[2] movie about Walt Whitman. (People even talk about a war in which Walt Whitman and Henry James chose up sides, to begin with, and in which you and I will go on fighting till the day we die.) All this sort of thing, and all the bad poetry that there of course is in Whitman—for any poet has written enough bad poetry to scare away anybody —has helped to scare away from Whitman most "serious readers of modern poetry." They do not talk of his poems, as a rule, with any real liking or know-ledge. Serious readers, people who are ashamed of not knowing all Hopkins[3] by heart, are not at all ashamed to say, "I don't really know Whitman very well." This may harm Whitman in your eyes, they know, but that is a chance that poets have to take. Yet "their" Hopkins, that good critic and great poet, wrote about Whitman, after seeing five or six of his poems in a newspaper review: "I may as well say what I should not otherwise have said, that I always knew in my heart Walt Whitman's mind to be more like my own than any other man's living. As he is a very great scoundrel this is not a very pleasant confession" [. . .]

To show Whitman for what he is one does not need to praise or explain or argue, one needs simply to quote.[4] He himself said, "I and mine do not convince by arguments, similes, rhymes,/ We convince by our presence." Even a few of his phrases are enough to show us that Whitman was no sweeping rhetorician, but a poet of the greatest and oddest delicacy and originality and sensitivity, so far as words are concerned. This is, after all, the poet who said, "Blind loving wrestling touch, sheath'd hooded sharp-tooth'd touch"; who said, "Smartly attired, coun-tenance smiling, form upright, death under the breast-bones, hell under the skull-bones"; who said, "Agonies are one of my changes of garments"; who saw grass as the "flag of my disposition," saw "the sharp-peak'd farmhouse, with its scal-lop'd scum and slender shoots from the gutters," heard a plane's "wild ascending lisp," and saw and heard how at the amputation "what is removed drops horribly in a pail." This is the poet for whom the sea was "howler and scooper of storms," reaching out to us with "crooked inviting fingers"; who went "leaping chasms with a pike-pointed staff, clinging to topples of brittle and blue"; who, a runaway slave, saw how "my gore dribs, thinn'd with the ooze of my skin"; who went "lithographing Kronos . . . buying drafts of Osiris"; who stared out at the "little plentiful mannikins skipping around in collars and tail'd coats,/ I am aware who

1   Thomas Wolfe (1900–38) was a prolific novelist known for his romantic sensibility and lavish prose. His omnivorous subjectivity and expansive style have made comparisons with Whitman commonplace.
2   Cecil B. de Mille (1881–1959) was one of the most influential and powerful directors during the early years of Hollywood and had a reputation in particular for his lavish productions.
3   Gerard Manley Hopkins (1844–89), English poet, academic, and Jesuit, is often compared to Whitman because of their common interest in experimental rhythms and colloquial language.
4   Because Jarrell proceeds to argue his case largely by quoting prolifically, it is impractical to anno-tate all his citations. Suffice it to say that he quotes particularly heavily from "Song of Myself," as well as from a medley of other *Leaves of Grass* poems.

they are, (they are positively not worms or fleas)." For he is, at his best, beautifully witty: he says gravely, "I find I incorporate gneiss, coals, long-threaded
moss, fruits, grain, esculent roots,/ And am stucco'd with quadrupeds and birds
all over"; and of these quadrupeds and birds "not one is respectable or unhappy
over the whole earth." He calls advice: "Unscrew the locks from the doors!
Unscrew the doors from their jambs!" He publishes the results of research:
"Having pried through the strata, analyz'd to a hair, counsel'd with doctors and
calculated close,/ I find no sweeter fat than sticks to my own bones." Everybody
remembers how he told the Muse to "cross out please those immensely overpaid
accounts,/ That matter of Troy and Achilles' wrath, and Aeneas', Odysseus' wan-
derings,"[5] but his account of the arrival of the "illustrious emigré" here in the
New World is even better: "Bluff'd not a bit by drainpipe, gasometer, artificial
fertilizers,/ Smiling and pleas'd with palpable intent to stay,/ She's here, installed
amid the kitchenware." Or he sees, like another Breughel,[6] "the mechanic's wife
with the babe at her nipple interceding for every person born,/ Three scythes at
harvest whizzing in a row from three lusty angels with shirts bagg'd out at their
waists,/ The snag-toothed hostler with red hair redeeming sins past and to come"
—the passage has enough wit not only (in Johnson's phrase) to keep it sweet, but
enough to make it believable. He says:

I project my hat, sit shame-faced, and beg.

Enough! Enough! Enough!
Somehow I have been stunn'd. Stand back!
Give me a little time beyond my cuff'd head, slumbers, dreams, gaping,
I discover myself on the verge of a usual mistake.[7]

There is in such changes of tone as these the essence of wit. And Whitman is even
more far-fetched than he is witty; he can say about Doubters, in the most improb-
able and explosive of juxtapositions: "I know every one of you, I know the sea of
torment, doubt, despair and unbelief./ How the flukes splash! How they contort
rapid as lightning, with splashes and spouts of blood!" Who else would have said
about God: "As the hugging and loving bed-fellow sleeps at my side through the
night, and withdraws at the break of day with stealthy tread,/ Leaving me baskets
cover'd with white towels, swelling the house with their plenty"?—the Psalmist
himself, his cup running over, would have looked at Whitman with dazzled eyes.
(Whitman was persuaded by friends to hide the fact that it was God he was
talking about.) He says, "Flaunt of the sunshine I need not your bask—lie over!"
This unusual employment of verbs is usual enough in participle-loving Whitman,
who also asks you to "look in my face while I snuff the sidle of evening," or tells
you, "I effuse my flesh in eddies, and drift it in lacy jags." Here are some typical
beginnings of poems: "City of orgies, walks, and joys. . . . Not heaving from my
ribb'd breast only. . . . O take my hand Walt Whitman! Such gliding wonders!

5   The references are to the classical epics of the ancient Greek poet Homer (the *Odyssey* and *Iliad*)
    and the ancient Roman poet Virgil (the *Aeneid*).
6   Pieter Breughel (1525–69) was one of the greatest Dutch genre and landscape painters; his vivid
    peasant scenes are well known.
7   Ll. 958–62 of "Song of Myself."

Such sights and sounds! Such join'd unended links. . . ." He says to the objects of the world, "You have waited, you always wait, you dumb, beautiful ministers"; sees "the sun and stars that float in the open air,/ The apple-shaped earth"; says, "O suns— O grass of graves— O perpetual transfers and promotions,/ If you do not say anything how can I say anything?" Not many poets have written better, in queerer and more convincing and more individual language, about the world's *gliding wonders:* the phrase seems particularly right for Whitman. He speaks of those "circling rivers the breath," of the "savage old mother incessantly crying,/ To the boy's soul's questions sullenly timing, some drown'd secret hissing"— ends a poem, once, "We have voided all but freedom and our own joy." How can one quote enough? If the reader thinks that all this is like Thomas Wolfe he *is* Thomas Wolfe; nothing else could explain it. Poetry like this is as far as possible from the work of any ordinary rhetorician, whose phrases cascade over us like suds of the oldest and most-advertised detergent.

The interesting thing about Whitman's worst language (for, just as few poets have ever written better, few poets have ever written worse) is how unusually absurd, how really ingeniously bad, such language is. I will quote none of the most famous examples; but even a line like *O culpable! I acknowledge. I exposé!* is not anything that you and I could do—only a man with the most extraordinary feel for language, or none whatsoever, could have cooked up Whitman's worst messes. For instance: what other man in all the history of this planet would have said, "I am a habitan of Vienna"? (One has an immediate vision of him as a sort of French-Canadian halfbreed to whom the Viennese are offering, with trepidation, through the bars of a zoological garden, little mounds of whipped cream.) And *enclaircise*—why, it's as bad as *explicate*! We are right to resent his having made up his own horrors, instead of sticking to the ones that we ourselves employ. But when Whitman says, "I dote on myself, there is that lot of me and all so luscious," we should realize that we are not the only ones who are amused. And the queerly bad and merely queer and queerly good will often change into one another without warning: "Hefts of the moving world, at innocent gambols silently rising, freshly exuding,/ Scooting obliquely high and low"—not good, but *queer!* – suddenly becomes, "Something I cannot see puts up libidinous prongs,/ Seas of bright juice suffuse heaven," and it is sunrise.

[. . .]

Sometimes Whitman will take what would generally be considered an unpromising subject (in this case, a woman peeping at men in bathing naked) and treat it with such tenderness and subtlety and understanding that we are ashamed of ourselves for having thought it unpromising, and murmur that Chekhov[8] himself couldn't have treated it better:

Section 11 is cited in its entirety.

---

8   Anton Chekhov (1860–1904), Russian short-story writer and dramatist, is known for his acute psychological depictions and unsparing realism.

And in the same poem (that "Song of Myself" in which one finds half his best work) the writer can say of a sea-fight:

Section 36 is cited in its entirety.

There are faults in this passage, and they *do not matter*: the serious truth, the complete realization of these last lines make us remember that few poets have shown more of the tears of things, and the joy of things, and of the reality beneath either tears or joy. Even Whitman's most general or political statements sometimes are good: everybody knows his "When liberty goes out of a place it is not the first to go, nor the second or third to go,/ It waits for all the rest to go, it is the last" [. . .]

[. . .]

[. . .] In some like sense Whitman is a world, a waste with, here and there, systems blazing at random out of the darkness. Only an innocent and rigidly methodical mind will reject it for this disorganization, particularly since there are in it, here and there, little systems as beautifully and astonishingly organized as the rings and satellites of Saturn:

Ll. 822–32, section 33, are cited.

In the last lines of this quotation Whitman has reached—as great writers always reach—a point at which criticism seems not only unnecessary but absurd: these lines are so good that even admiration feels like insolence, and one is ashamed of anything that one can find to say about them. How anyone can dismiss or accept patronizingly the man who wrote them, I do not understand.

The enormous and apparent advantages of form, of omission and selection, of the highest degree of organization, are accompanied by important disadvantages —and there are far greater works than *Leaves of Grass* to make us realize this. But if we compare Whitman with that very beautiful poet Alfred Tennyson, the most skillful of all Whitman's contemporaries, we are at once aware of how limiting Tennyson's forms have been, of how much Tennyson has had to leave out, even in those discursive poems where he is trying to put everything in. Whitman's poems *represent* his world and himself much more satisfactorily than Tennyson's do his. In the past a few poets have both formed and represented, each in the highest degree; but in modern times what controlling, organizing, selecting poet has created a world with as much in it as Whitman's, a world that so plainly *is* the world? Of all modern poets he has, quantitatively speaking, "the most comprehensive soul"—and, qualitatively, a most comprehensive and comprehending one, with charities and concessions and qualifications that are rare in any time.

[. . .]

They might have put on his tombstone WALT WHITMAN: HE HAD HIS

NERVE. He is the rashest, the most inexplicable and unlikely—the most impossible, one wants to say—of poets. He somehow *is* in a class by himself, so that one compares him with other poets about as readily as one compares *Alice* with other books. (Even his free verse has a completely different effect from anybody else's.) Who would think of comparing him with Tennyson or Browning or Arnold or Baudelaire?[9]—it is Homer, or the sagas, or something far away and long ago, that comes to one's mind only to be dismissed; for sometimes Whitman *is* epic, just as *Moby Dick* is, and it surprises us to be able to use truthfully this word that we have misused so many times. Whitman *is* grand, and elevated, and comprehensive, and real with an astonishing reality, and many other things—the critic points at his qualities in despair and wonder, all method failing, and simply calls them by their names. And the range of these qualities is the most extraordinary thing of all. We can surely say about him, "He was a man, take him for all in all. I shall not look upon his like again"[10]—and wish that people had seen this and not tried to be his like: one Whitman is miracle enough, and when he comes again it will be the end of the world.

I have said so little about Whitman's faults because they are so plain: baby critics who have barely learned to complain of the lack of ambiguity in *Peter Rabbit* can tell you all that is wrong with *Leaves of Grass*. But a good many of my readers must have felt that it is ridiculous to write an essay about the obvious fact that Whitman is a great poet. It is ridiculous—just as, in 1851, it would have been ridiculous for anyone to write an essay about the obvious fact that Pope[11] was no "classic of our prose" but a great poet. Critics have to spend half their time reiterating whatever ridiculously obvious things their age or the critics of their age have found it necessary to forget: they say despairingly, at parties, that Wordsworth[12] is a great poet, and *won't* bore you, and tell Mr. Leavis that Milton[13] is a great poet whose deposition *hasn't* been accomplished with astonishing ease by a few words from Eliot. . . .[14] There is something essentially ridiculous about critics, anyway: what is good is good without our saying so, and beneath all our majesty we know this.

Let me finish by mentioning another quality of Whitman's—a quality, delightful to me, that I have said nothing of. If some day a tourist notices, among the ruins of New York City, a copy of *Leaves of Grass*, and stops and picks it up and reads some lines in it, she will be able to say to herself: "How very American! If he and his country had not existed, it would have been impossible to imagine them."

9 Alfred, Lord Tennyson (1809–92), Robert Browning (1812–89), Matthew Arnold (1822–88), and Charles Baudelaire (1821–67), were four of Whitman's great contemporary poets.

10 *Hamlet* (Act 1, Scene 2) – Hamlet's description of his murdered father, whose ghost he will shortly see.

11 Alexander Pope (1688–1744) was one of the greatest and most influential English poets and critics of the eighteenth century.

12 William Wordsworth (1770–1850), poet and critic, was one of the leading figures of the Romantic movement in England.

13 John Milton (1608–74), one of England's greatest poets, is best known for his incomparable Protestant epic *Paradise Lost*.

14 F. R. Leavis (1895–1978), English literary critic, and T. S. Eliot (1888–1965), American poet, essayist, and critic, were Anglo-American cultural arbiters at the height of their influence around mid century.

Allen Ginsberg, "A Supermarket in California," [1955], *Howl, and other Poems* (San Francisco: City Lights, 1956)

Allen Ginsberg (1926–97), a major American poet of the Beatnik generation who made his reputation with *Howl, and Other Poems* (1956), saw himself as in a tradition of prophetic poetry running through William Blake and Whitman. He published the following poem as a tribute to Whitman, with full awareness, in the centennial year of the first edition of *Leaves of Grass*. Ginsberg was arguably the greatest devoté of Whitman among his generation of poets, and Whitman remained his touchstone throughout his own distinguished, nearly fifty-year career as a twentieth-century poet dedicated to personal and poetic experimentation.

Whitmanesque characteristics are conspicuous in this poem: long, supple lines that blur the boundary between prose and verse; playful affection for the material sheen of life; erotic plays of words and images (and, most particularly, those of a homoerotic nature) – all in service to a passionate search for America. But Ginsberg's America departs from as much as it follows the trail of Whitman's America in its bittersweet summoning of Whitman as "lonely old courage teacher" for an odyssey through post-war American affluence, suburbanization, and normalcy.

What thoughts I have of you tonight, Walt Whitman, for I walked down the sidestreets under the trees with a headache self-conscious looking at the full moon.

In my hungry fatigue, and shopping for images, I went into the neon fruit supermarket, dreaming of your enumerations!

What peaches and what penumbras! Whole families shopping at night! Aisles full of husbands! Wives in the avocados, babies in the tomatoes!—and you, García Lorca,[1] what were you doing down by the watermelons?

I saw you, Walt Whitman, childless, lonely old grubber, poking among the meats in the refrigerator and eyeing the grocery boys.

I heard you asking questions of each: Who killed the pork chops? What price bananas? Are you my Angel?

I wandered in and out of the brilliant stacks of cans following you, and followed in my imagination by the store detective.

We strode down the open corridors together in our solitary fancy tasting artichokes, possessing every frozen delicacy, and never passing the cashier.

Where are we going, Walt Whitman? The doors close in an hour. Which way does your beard point tonight?

(I touch your book and dream of our odyssey in the supermarket and feel absurd.)

Will we walk all night through solitary streets? The trees add shade to shade, lights out in the houses, we'll both be lonely.

---

1 Federico García Lorca (1898–1936) was a major Spanish poet and dramatist whose work was characterized by surrealistic and homoerotic effects.

Will we stroll dreaming of the lost America of love past blue automobiles in driveways, home to our silent cottage?

Ah, dear father, graybeard, lonely old courage-teacher, what America did you have when Charon quit poling his ferry and you got out on a smoking bank and stood watching the boat disappear on the black waters of Lethe?[2]

Berkeley, 1955

Pablo Neruda, "We Live in a Whitmanesque Age (A Speech to P.E.N.)," *New York Times* (14 April 1972): 37

Neruda, one of the leading Spanish-language poets of his generation, gave this speech just months after accepting the Nobel Prize for literature and a year before his death. Like many of his Chilean and South American peers, he was a writer fully engaged with the politics of his native country and continent.

The assignment of the complimentary term "totalitarian poet" to Whitman as a poet of liberation by a man long associated with the Communist Party and with the political Left's critique of the injustices and inequalities of capitalism is as strikingly paradoxical as is his conflation of Whitman's strident nationalism with universalism. For that matter, he conceives of Whitman as a trans-American colossus whose voice spoke to and addressed Americans across the north–south continental divide. Though conspicuously idiosyncratic, Neruda's appreciation of Whitman eloquently conveys the capacity of Whitman's poetry to reach and influence readers all around the globe, and Neruda's sense of living in "a Whitmanesque age" has resonated with both his postcolonial generation and ours.

I think I could turn and live with animals, they are so placid and self-
    contain'd,
I stand and look at them long and long.
They do not sweat and whine about their condition,
They do not lie awake in the dark and weep for their sins,
They do not make me sick discussing their duty to God,
Not one is dissatisfied, not one is demented with the mania of owning
    things,
Not one kneels to another, nor to his kind that lived thousands of years
    ago,
Not one is respectable or unhappy over the whole earth.
                                        (from Section 32, "Song of Myself")

IN THIS HALF CENTURY, men have reached the moon, complete with penicillin and with television. In the field of warfare, napalm has been invented, to render democratic by means of its purifying fire the ashes of a number of the

---

2   In Greek mythology, Charon was the ferryman of the dead in the underworld; Lethe was the place (often, the river) of oblivion.

inhabitants of our planet. In spite of half a century of intellectual understanding, relations between rich and poor—between nations which lend some crumbs of comfort and others which go hungry—continue to be a complex mixture of anguish and pride, injustice and the right to live.

It is important that we should all recognize what it is that we owe to each other. We must continually keep renegotiating the 'internal debt' which weighs upon writers everywhere. Each one of us owes much to his own intellectual heritage and much to that which we have drawn from the cultural treasury of all the world. The writers from the southern half of this continent, like myself, have grown up knowing and admiring—despite the difference of tongues—the vast growth of the world of letters in its northern half. We have been particularly impressed by the amazing awakening of the novel which, from the days of Dreiser[1] to the present time, has displayed a new strength—a convulsive and constructive strength—whose greatness and fierceness has no match in the literatures of the present age, unless it be among your own playwrights.

Your books, often cruel books, have exhibited the singular testimony of great and noble writers, faced with the conflicts involved in the vertiginous growth of your capitalist structure. In those exemplary works, none of the truth was concealed: the souls of multitudes and individuals, of the powerful and the weak, in city or in suburb, were laid bare—the drops of the very lifeblood of your 'body politic,' of your collective and your solitary lives.

For my part, I, who am now nearing seventy, discovered Walt Whitman when I was just fifteen, and I hold him to be my greatest creditor. I stand before you feeling that I bear with me always this great and wonderful debt which has helped me to exist.

I must start by acknowledging myself to be the humble servant of a poet who strode the earth with long, slow paces, pausing everywhere to love, to examine, to learn, to teach and to admire. The fact of the matter is that this great man, this lyric moralist, chose a hard path for himself: he was both a torrential and a didactic singer—qualities which appear opposed, seeming also more appropriate to a leader than to a writer. But what really counts is that Walt Whitman was not afraid to teach—which means to learn at the hands of life and undertake the responsibility of passing on the lesson! To speak frankly: he had no fear of either moralizing or immoralizing, nor did he seek to separate the fields of pure and impure poetry. He was the first totalitarian poet: his intention was not just to sing, but to impose on others his own total and wide-ranging vision of the relationships of men and nations. In this sense, his patent nationalism forms part of a total and organic universal vision: he held himself to be the debtor of happiness and sorrow alike, and also of both the advanced cultures and more primitive societies.

There are many kinds of greatness, but let me say (though I be a poet of the Spanish tongue) that Walt Whitman has taught me more than Spain's Cervantes:[2] in Walt Whitman's work one never finds the ignorant being humbled, nor is the human condition ever found offended.

---

1   Theodore Dreiser (1871–1945), American novelist and polemicist, wrote powerfully about social conditions in modern society.
2   Miguel de Cervantes (1547–1616), one of the earliest and greatest masters of fiction, was the author of *Don Quixote*.

We continue to live in a Whitmanesque age, seeing how new men and new societies rise and grow, despite their birth-pangs. Walt Whitman was the protagonist of a truly geographical personality: the first man in history to speak with a truly continental American voice, to bear a truly American name. The colonies of the most brilliant countries have left a legacy of centuries of silence: colonialism seems to slay fertility and stultify the power of creation.

In this age, we see how other new nations, other new literatures and new flags, are coming into being with what one hopes is the total extinction of colonialism in Africa and Asia.[3] Almost overnight, the capitals of the world are studded with the banners of people we had never heard of, seeking self-expression with the unpolished and pain-laden voice of birth. Black writers of Africa and America begin to give us the true pulse of the luckless races which had hitherto been silent. Man's liberation may often require bloodshed, but it always requires song—and the song of mankind grows richer day by day, in this age of sufferings and liberation.

From Lawrence W. Levine, *Highbrow/Lowbrow: The Emergence of Cultural Hierarchy in America* (Cambridge: Harvard University Press, 1988), pp. 223–26

Levine's seminal study of the late-nineteenth-century bifurcation of culture positions Whitman in resistance to a process increasingly dividing American democracy into distinct economic and cultural groups. Whitman's objection was highly principled: he viscerally rejected the hierarchical segmentation of culture and of society. In later years he remembered with great fondness his attendance during the years leading up to the composition of *Leaves of Grass* at opera houses, concert halls, and theaters in which class lines were blurred and attendance was general. That was no longer possible in the society of his old age, when in an era of mounting class, ethnic, and racial conflict institutions of high culture increasingly separated themselves from those serving the masses.

Whitman's originating ideal of a fit audience for *Leaves of Grass* was one that transcended class divisions. As he stated vociferously in a late manifesto, "No one will get at my verses who insists upon viewing them as a literary performance, or attempt at such performance, or as aiming mainly toward art or aestheticism."[1] He had resisted that misreading of his poetry as art ever since 1855, but the need to state it with finality intensified in his last years.

Levine's analysis has equally powerful ramifications for the study of culture today. It stands in the vanguard of recent academic redefinitions of culture along more inclusive, comprehensive lines that accommodate not only a late-twentieth-century multicultural model but also Whitman's own ideal of culture as open and available to the masses.

3   Neruda is referring to the rapid demise of colonialism in the decades following the Second World War and to the concomitant rise to national and international prominence of the cultures of the emergent polities.

1   Whitman, "A Backward Glance O'er Travel'd Roads" (1889), in Kaplan, *Whitman: Poetry and Prose*, p. 671.

Increasingly, in the closing decades of the nineteenth century, as public life became everywhere more fragmented, the concept of culture took on hierarchical connotations along the lines of Matthew Arnold's[2] definition of culture—"the best that has been thought and known in the world . . . the study and pursuit of perfection." The Englishman Arnold, whose critical writings preceded his trips to America in 1883 and 1886, did not discover a *tabula rasa* in America; he found many eager constituents here from the very beginning. Two years before Arnold's *Culture and Anarchy* was published, *Harper's* maintained that certain authors were "not only tests of taste but even of character." If a man gave himself to Shakespeare or Chaucer, "we have a clew to the man."

> The man who among all Operas prefers Don Giovanni, or Fidelio, or the Barber of Seville, or Robert le Diable, involuntarily unveils himself as he makes his preference known. He rises or falls, he is near or far in our regard just as he instinctively likes or rejects what you feel to be best.

Nevertheless, Arnold was perhaps the single most significant disseminator of such attitudes and had an enormous influence in the United States. The Arnold important to America was not Arnold the critic, Arnold the poet, Arnold the religious thinker, but Arnold the Apostle of Culture. "I shall not go so far as to say of Mr. Arnold that he invented" the concept of culture, Henry James commented in 1884, "but he made it more definite than it had been before—he vivified and lighted it up." Arnold had his detractors. Walt Whitman dismissed him as "one of the dudes of literature," and complained to Horace Traubel that Arnold brought to the world what the world already had a surfeit of—"delicacy, refinement, elegance, prettiness, propriety, criticism, analysis: all of them things which threaten to overwhelm us." Whitman was in the minority. More typical was William H. Dawson, who proclaimed in 1904, sixteen years after Arnold's death, "There is today a cult of Matthew Arnold; it is growing; it must grow. It will grow." "Why does nobody any more mention Arnold's name?" Ludwig Lewisohn[3] asked in 1927 and replied that it was because Arnold's views had become completely absorbed in the mainstream of American thought.

The ubiquitous discussion of the meaning and nature of culture, informed by Arnold's views, was one in which adjectives were used liberally. "High," "low," "rude," "lesser," "higher," "lower," "beautiful," "modern," "legitimate," "vulgar," "popular," "true," "pure," "highbrow," "lowbrow" were applied to such nouns as "arts" or "culture" almost *ad infinitum*. Though plentiful, the adjectives were not random. They clustered around a congeries of values, a set of categories that defined and distinguished culture vertically, that created hierarchies which were to remain meaningful for much of this century. That they are categories which to this day we have difficulty defining with any precision does not negate their influence. Central terms like "culture" changed their meaning, or at least their emphasis, in the second half of the nineteenth century. In early nineteenth-century editions of Webster's dictionary the primary definition of *culture* was

---

2   For Arnold, see Directory of Contextual Figures, p. 30.
3   Ludwig Lewisohn (1882–1955) was a leading academic better known for his scholarly and critical writings on literature and culture than for his fiction.

agricultural: "The act of tilling and preparing the earth for crops; cultivation; . . . The application of labor or other means in producing; as the *culture* of corn, or grass." By the second half of the nineteenth century, while the agricultural definitions held, *culture* was defined as "the state of being cultivated . . . refinement of mind or manners." Words like "enlightenment," "discipline," "mental and moral training," and "civilization," cropped up freely in the definitions. The word *cultivate*, in addition to its agricultural meaning, was defined as "to civilize; as to *cultivate* the untamed savage." In 1898 *The People's Webster Pronouncing Dictionary and Spelling Guide*, a pocket dictionary of 23,000 words with single-word definitions, defined "culture" simply as "refinement." By 1919 *Webster's Army and Navy Dictionary* and an elementary school edition of *Webster's New Standard Dictionary* armed American servicemen and school children with precisely the same succinct definition.

It was this concept of culture that Henry James had in mind when, some thirty years after the Astor Place Riot,[4] he pronounced it a manifestation of the "instinctive hostility of barbarism to culture." The new meanings that became attached to such words as "art," "aesthetics," and "culture" in the second half of the nineteenth century symbolized the consciousness that conceived of the fine, the worthy, and the beautiful as existing apart from ordinary society. In 1894 Hiram M. Stanley defined the "masses" as those whose sole delight rested in "eating, drinking, smoking, society of the other sex, with dancing, music of a noisy and lively character, spectacular shows, and athletic exhibitions." Anyone demonstrating "a permanent taste for higher pleasures," Stanley argued, "ceases, *ipso facto*, to belong to the 'masses.'" This practice of distinguishing "culture" from lesser forms of expression became so common that by 1915 Van Wyck Brooks[5] concluded that between the highbrow and the lowbrow "there is no community, no genial middle ground." "What side of American life is not touched by this antithesis?" Brooks asked. "What explanation of American life is more central or more illuminating?" The process that had seen the noun "class" take on a series of hierarchical adjectives—"lower," "middle," "upper," "working"—in the late eighteenth and early nineteenth centuries was operative for the noun "culture" a hundred years later. Just as the former development mirrored the economic changes brought about by the Industrial Revolution in England so the latter reflected the cultural consequences of modernization.

Walt Whitman consistently fought this new cultural hierarchy. He insisted that culture should not be "restricted by conditions ineligible to the masses," should not be created "for a single class alone, or for the parlors or lecture-rooms," and

4   The riot was the final act in a long-simmering class drama between the supporters of two popular rival actors: the American Edwin Forrest (about whom, see Directory of Contextual Figures, p. 31), championed by the working class; and the Englishman William Macready, championed by the elite. On the night of 10 May 1849, a rowdy crowd of Forrest supporters numbering in the thousands stood outside New York City's Astor Place Opera House, where Macready was appearing in *Macbeth*. A small portion of them began hurling bricks at the police force stationed around the theater and at the windows of the theater itself, then charged into the regiments of soldiers called in to secure the building. The soldiers eventually fired with live ammunition, killing several dozen rioters. The riot, the worst of its kind in New York before the Civil War draft riots, was widely seen at the time as an act of class conflict.

5   Van Wyck Brooks (1886–1963), one of the leading literary critics of his time, wrote prodigiously about American literature and culture. His influential *America's Coming-of-Age* is a precursor of Levine's analysis.

placed his hopes for the creation of a classless, democratic culture in the leader-ship of the new "middling" groups—"men and women with occupations, well-off owners of houses and acres, and with cash in the bank." The groups to which Whitman turned were neither willing nor able to fulfill his expectations. The emergence of the new middle and upper-middle classes, created by rapid indus-trialization in the nineteenth century, seems to have accelerated rather than inhibited the growing distinctions between elite and mass culture. When, in the waning years of the century, Thorstein Veblen[6] constructed his concept of con-spicuous consumption, he included not only the obvious material possessions but also "immaterial" goods—"the knowledge of dead languages and the occult sciences; of correct spelling; of syntax and prosody; of the various forms of domestic music . . . of the latest proprieties of dress, furniture, and equipage"; of the ancient "classics"—all of which constituted a conspicuous culture that helped confer legitimacy on the newly emergent groups. This helps explain the vogue during this period of manuals of etiquette, of private libraries and rare books, of European art and music displayed and performed in ornate—often neoclassical—museums and concert halls.

From Alicia Ostriker, "Loving Walt Whitman and the Problem of America," in Robert K. Martin, ed., *The Continuing Presence of Walt Whitman* (Iowa City: University of Iowa Press, 1992), pp. 217–32

Ostriker is one of a pioneering generation of feminist poets and literary critics who have found in Whitman a voice and vision that speaks meaningfully, if not always fully acceptably, to their sense of contemporary reality. Her recollection of how she, in her girlhood (rephrasing Wordsworth's well-known romantic aphorism in feminine terms, "the girl is mother of the woman"), discovered joy in "Song of Myself" was an act of female as well as male recognition that has been repeated many times over.

Her insistence, though, is on its particularity: how she, then and over an ensuing period of years, discovered herself as the poem's articulating "I" dis-covers itself. The process, she notes, is as much an act of seduction as of revelation. Although the point is not hers, one can construe her words and example as providing proof that Whitman's contemporaries were right in attacking his poetry, especially "Song of Myself," for its unhesitant play and display of eroticism. What his most vociferous early critics most objected to, even going so far as to try to ban its publication, is what Ostriker (and many other late-twentieth-century readers, female and male, gay and straight) most applaud: Whitman's unapologetic celebration of the body, its languages, and its processes.

The proof text for her reading is section 5 of "Song of Myself," arguably the most subversive set of verses in the entire poem, and quite possibly in all of his

---

6   Thorstein Veblen (1857–1929) was a social scientist best known for *The Theory of the Leisure Class* (1899), in which he developed a scathing critique of upper-class leisure and conspicuous consumption.

writing (see commentary in Key Passages and Full Text, **pp. 129–30**). Whereas some of her contemporaries have charged Whitman with being an inhibiting force as a poet who speaks *for* rather than *to* his readers, Ostriker finds Whitman's voice liberating and inviting and his message an inspiration for exploration of the depths of body and soul.

"There was a child went forth . . ."[1]

WHY HAVE I NEVER BEFORE written about Walt Whitman? I always identify myself to audiences as Whitmanic, and I have written about Blake[2] and Ginsberg,[3] who are important to me but surely not more important than Whitman. Perhaps it is because I read Whitman earliest and completely outside of school. We must of course have read "Oh Captain! My Captain!" in school, and I must have hated it. My parents' Untermeyer anthology[4] contained "Afoot and lighthearted I take to the open road" ("Song of the Open Road"), and I rather liked the swing of that. How "Song of Myself" fell into my hands I cannot say. What I remember is reading that poem straight through for the first time when I was thirteen, outdoors amid some uncut grass. That same year I decided Poe was mechanical, a puppet of a poet, all theatrical tricks, all indoors. This Whitman was a living creature, someone alive as I felt myself to be alive.

No, the location was not a meadow. I was a city girl. It was some grass and rocks in Manhattan's Central Park, where a scrim of forsythia announced April and the smell of dirt mingled with dog droppings. But the truth is that the girl is mother of the woman;[5] some portion of myself paused ecstatically at the moment when I (when it) encountered "Song of Myself" and elected thenceforth to celebrate itself and sing itself. Obviously those were the instructions conveyed by every line in the poem, for every atom belonging to the poet belonged to me.[6] To read Whitman was to experience self-recognition. Here were the self's not-yet-articulated perceptions of reality, its not-yet-formulated ideological biases, which plainly inhabited me already because I was an American. Or because I was a grandchild of Russian-Jewish immigrants? Or because I was young? The generosity of spirit meant that Whitman's energies could be mine if I chose. Like some improbably open-minded parent, he would permit everything.

He permitted love. That was the primary thing I noticed. The degree and quantity and variety of love in Whitman are simply astonishing. At thirteen I did not yet know the word *eroticism*, much less *auto-eroticism*, but I could tell when I encountered it, how much each manifestation was delicately, systematically

1 Her epigraph comes from the opening line of the tenth poem in the 1855 *Leaves of Grass*; the poem took its title from this line as of the 1871 edition.
2 William Blake (1757–1827), English poet and illustrator, was a major figure in the Romantic movement.
3 For Ginsberg, see p. 92.
4 Louis Untermeyer (1885–1977) was an indefatigable compiler of popular literary anthologies, including *Modern American Poetry*, which went through many editions and remained in print for decades, and *The Poetry and Prose of Walt Whitman* (1949).
5 Ostriker is re-gendering William Wordsworth's famous line "The Child is father of the Man" (from "My Heart Leaps Up When I Behold").
6 A personalized refiguring of l. 3 of "Song of Myself."

supporting all the others, like the network of filiations Whitman would later describe as spinning from the poet-spider's essence. Affection for one's own body, "that lot of me and all so luscious," "no sweeter fat than sticks to my own bones," underwrote the will to incorporate material phenomena—"All this I swallow, it tastes good, I like it well, it becomes mine" ("Song of Myself")[7]—the love of the world, the spectacle of other people, but also the love of what Whitman named the soul. Thus it was with ravishment that I read the amazing section 5:

Section 5 is cited in its entirety.

Though the temptation is simply to sigh, let me unravel something of what the green thirteen-year-old self must have apprehended in these lines, for the passage is a microcosm of Whitman's poetic method at its best. Outrageously elusive play is its essence. Describing (inventing) a scene (or fantasy) of masturbation, or of lovemaking with another person, or of mystical communion—if it is impossible to tell which, the point is that such scenes are equatable, just as "I" and "the other I am" and "you" stand in poised balance. The point is also that Whitman makes it humorously impossible to locate the relation of parts to whole, for each takes on the qualities normally assigned to another. "I" in this passage seems at first a kind of genial arbiter between "my soul" and "the other I am" (presumably the body), those famously rivalrous but insecure siblings. But the relationship immediately shifts. As soon as "I" invites an encounter with "you," "the other I am" disappears before it is even defined. If this term was to stand for "body," why was Whitman not more explicit? Was it to make body echo the cryptic self-identification of God to Moses in Midian, "I am that I am?"[8] In section 4 the mysterious entity "I am" was an observing ego. In section 5, if "you" is still "my soul," Whitman is clearly redefining the soul as separable from and equal to the self (instead of a portion of it), as nontranscendant, nonhierarchical, as in fact possessing its own body capable of relaxing and its own throat capable of humming. Whatever western philosophy from Plato through Protestant Christianity has made of the soul Whitman radically bypasses. Nor can one assimilate this image very easily to Emerson's Oversoul.[9] All that remains here of any notion of an immaterial essence is the sequence of cultural negatives which Whitman wishes away from the "stop" he wishes loosed. "Only the lull I like, the hum of your valvèd voice," with its seductive assonances, proposes a soul like the drone of Indian music, a vibrant fullness which is also void; "lull" would be a sound something like a lullaby, along with a cessation of movement.

Further melting takes place during and after the long four lines describing the lovemaking between self and soul. "I mind" seems a relaxed idiomatic equivalent of "I recall" or "I remember," while allowing "mind" to register almost as a

---

7   L. 831 of "Song of Myself."
8   Midian was the desert region east by southeast of the Jordan River to which Moses fled after killing an Egyptian and where God appeared to him in the form of a burning bush (the quote comes from Exodus 3:14).
9   Ralph Waldo Emerson's term for the divine presence and the title of one of his major meditative essays.

substantive noun. The "transparent" morning prepares us for perceptions and acts that will meet no obstacle. The future implied by the ego's invitation shifts to a recalled idyllic scene in which both self and soul are physically embodied, as if "the other I am" were diffused between them or distributed among them. The world of Eros, which is to join whatever is disconnected, required palpability; vision is not enough. The tacit action behind the described lovemaking resembles that in Donne's[10] "The Extasie," where the lovers mingle ("interinanimate") first their souls, then their bodies:

Ostriker quotes eight lines near the end of the poem.

Like Whitman, Donne wants to mediate the quarrel between the body's impurity and the soul's purity. The crucial difference is that soul and body remain logically distinguished and hierarchically conceived by Donne, whose theology requires the inferiority of bodies to souls, even while he boldly compares physical lovemaking to the incarnation. It is exactly that logical and hierarchical conception which Whitman opposes and rejects, in every inflection of his writing, as false.

The ego's penetrability in Whitman's poem provides one element of the passage's sweetness. There is something wonderful, always, in such moments of ecstatic male surrender. . . . Another element is its musicality, the assonance of "settled . . . head . . . gently" tied to the alliterated "head . . . hips," the p's and b's of "*p*arted my shirt from my *b*osom-*b*one, and *p*lunged your tongue to my *b*are-strip*t* heart," the off-rhyme of "shirt" and "heart," and above all the deep sound of "lull" and "hum" transformed to "plunged your tongue." Rhythmically the easy roll of mixed iambs and anapests, with the feminine endings of the first two lines, collects toward the successive stresses of "báre-strípt héart" and the tight, stretched, monosyllabic last line, with its long e's reinforcing the tension: "reach'd . . . beard . . . reach'd . . . feet."

Several particulars are important in Whitman's description of orgasm. "Swiftly arose and spread" marks the contrast after the sequence of iambs and anapests; the long line enacts the sensation of expansive ripples and "of the earth" suggests their extent, while "pass all the argument" conflates the sense of "surpass" with a suggestion that "argument" is static compared with the motion of peace and knowledge. Eros makes waves, but they are halcyon waves. The peace and knowledge that pass all the argument of the earth are what Eliot perhaps alludes to in the triple "Shantih" at the end of "The Waste Land,"[11] glossed as "the peace that passes understanding." Yet from Whitman's perspective, Eliot's fear and loathing of sexuality would make samadhi[12] unattainable. We might also contrast what happens in this passage with the climax of Dickinson's "Wild Nights! Wild Nights," another poem of autoerotic and androgynous fantasizing which uses the

---

10 John Donne (1572–1631) was one of the greatest religious and metaphysical poets of Elizabethan England.

11 *The Waste Land* (1922), written by the American poet and critic T. S. Eliot (1888–1965), quickly gained a reputation as one of the most visionary and influential poems of the twentieth century. It has often been compared to and contrasted with "Song of Myself."

12 The Hindu notion of a state of deep concentration leading to union with ultimate reality.

idea of a wide space of water but then brings it to closure in contraction instead of expansion:

> Rowing in Eden—
> Ah, the Sea!
> Might I but moor—Tonight—
> In Thee![13]

For Whitman the pull toward safety and enclosure never occurs. Instead, the rest of this passage dissolves the conventional division between sexual and mental gratification, returning us to a biblical sense of what it means to "know," without sin or grief or loss of self. Knowledge is cosmic and inclusive, then subsides, as the orgasmic sensation gently ebbs, back to perception of the physical environment. That environment is itself emblematic of sexuality, being "limitless" and including phallic leaves ("stiff or drooping") and vaginal earthy declivities ("wells") full of insect life, finally declining to weedy textural particularities.

During this process—as the reader may not notice—time past has returned to time present, and the "you" has disappeared from the description along with "the other I am." The soul as lover, as active partner, has been as it were reabsorbed into the self—did the reaching and plunging begin this reabsorption?—and has emitted waves of peace and knowledge, much as the fusion of two atoms produces radiation. By the close of the passage even the assertive repetitions of "I know" are gone, absorbed in their turn into the living minutiae of what is known.

Section 5 of "Song of Myself" either is or is not an objective correlative[14] for the reader's erotic experience. There I was, a palpitating adolescent, reading poetry to myself in the park as I so often did, with the noises of dogs, children, and a softball game in my circumference and airplanes periodically overhead—and it seemed to me he had it just right. He had me. He was me. Myself in the slippery moment when I was able to fall in love with anything, beautiful boys, hunched elderly women, frisky dogs, cerulean clouds above Fifth Avenue, mica in the sidewalk, softball teams. Writers commonly remain loyal to the enthusiastic creatures we are in adolescence. I hold dear the child who was simmering, simmering, simmering and was brought to a boil, given permission to exist by "Song of Myself."[15] For decades afterward, the activity of writing poetry seemed to me essentially erotic, as Whitman repeatedly insists it is. Poetry aroused me bodily, felt at once passive and active, derived from an unarguable consciousness of the vitality and beauty of the world, and rested on a conviction that what I could feel, see, know in states of excited joy was real. The erotic was not "sex." It had nothing to do with conquest. It was a means of knowledge.

---

13 Dickinson did not title her poems, which are typically referred to by number. This one is number 249, as assigned by editor Thomas Johnson in the text (*The Complete Poems of Emily Dickinson*) used by Ostriker.

14 Objective correlative, a term given critical currency by T. S. Eliot's 1919 essay "Hamlet and His Problem," refers to a situation, chain of events, or object that evokes a particular emotion in a reader.

15 This is Ostriker's play on Whitman's often quoted but variously interpreted remark: "I was simmering, simmering, simmering; Emerson brought me to a boil."

"Through me forbidden voices . . ."[16]

When a girl becomes a woman and discovers her disadvantaged cultural status, Whitman's presence may strengthen her incalculably. Both for my own poetry and for the poetry of many other American women, Whitman has been the exemplary precursor, killer of the censor and clearer of ground. Even his crudest statements on gender, the insistence in "Song of Myself" that "I am the poet of the woman the same as the man" or his equal-time advocacy of male and female bodies in "I Sing the Body Electric," are revolutionary compared to the sentimental conventions of his own time. I suspect they are still revolutionary compared to the psychoanalytic doctrines which pass for valid utterance about gender and sexuality today. The poet H.D.,[17] under analysis by Freud[18] in the thirties, struggled painfully uphill before she could write in "The Master" that "woman is perfect,"

> herself
> is that dart and pulse of the male,
> hands, feet, thighs,
> herself perfect.

But Whitman had already considered the topic of anatomy and concluded, "That of the male is perfect, and that of the female is perfect" ("I Sing the Body Electric"), adding of the female form that phallic "mad filaments, ungovernable shoots play out of it," much as he noticed at sunrise that "Something I cannot see puts upward libidinous prongs" ("Song of Myself"). He had already addressed "You workwomen and workmen of these States" in "A Song for Occupations." His Adam had already imagined his Eve "By my side or back of me . . . / Or in front, and I following her just the same" ("To the Garden the World").

But what moves me, and I suspect other American women poets, is less the agreeable programmatic utterances than the gestures whereby Whitman enacts the crossing of gender categories in his own person. It is not his claim to be "of the woman" that speeds us on our way but his capacity to be shamelessly receptive as well as active, to be expansive on an epic scale without a shred of nostalgia for narratives of conquest, to invent a rhetoric of power without authority, without hierarchy, and without violence. The omnivorous empathy of his imagination wants to incorporate All and therefore refuses to represent anything as unavailably Other. So long as femaleness in our culture signifies Otherness, Whitman's greed is our gain. In him we are freed to be what we actually are, in whatever portion of ourselves eludes society, system, and philosophy: not negative pole to positive pole, not adversarial half of some dichotomy, but figures in an energetic

---

16 L. 516 of "Song of Myself."
17 Hilda Doolittle (1886–1961), familiarly known as H. D., was an influential imagist poet. She clashed with Freud, her one-time psychoanalyst, over his view of the nature of women but helped to bring him to safety in England after the Nazi annexation of Austria.
18 A trained Viennese medical doctor and the founder of psychoanalysis, Sigmund Freud (1856–1939) was one of the most influential thinkers and writers of the late nineteenth and twentieth centuries.

dance. His sacralization of sexuality anticipates Audre Lorde's[19] widely read feminist manifesto, "The Erotic as Power." The phallic economy of which feminist theorists complain has no place in a diffuse polymorphous eroticism whereby the aggression supposedly proper to adult males yields to "that lot of me and all so luscious." Whitman's evocations of touch align him with female celebrants of tactile intimacy—from Anne Sexton,[20] who cries that "touch is all," to Luce Irigaray,[21] who argues that feminine pleasure depends upon touch as masculine pleasure depends upon the gaze. Above all, the woman in Whitman speaks to us through his impulse to question boundaries—to prefer fluidity to fixity, experiment to status quo. If women poets in America have written more boldly and experimentally in the last thirty years than our British equivalents, we have Whitman to thank.

I do not mean to say that Whitman is a man for all feminist purposes. He solves the problem of marginality by denying the existence of a center, transforming the figures of self, nation, cosmos into a vast floodplain of sensations, affections, filiations. For him there is no outsider position, hence no dilemma of powerlessness. High and low, rich and poor, the enslaved and the free are for him all actors in a pageant. Such a solution is beautiful but useless to one who is a slave. Whitman can write splendidly and deeply of death; he can write powerfully and glancingly of pain and doubt; he cannot write at all about chronic fear, anger, defeat, despair. Happily independent of institutions, including that of marriage, he has no sense of what it means to be crushed by them. If we want a nineteenth-century poet in whom the desire for power and the fact of powerlessness remain inescapably knotted, we turn to Emily Dickinson, whose poems are theaters of war, saturated in the language of politics. The poet who writes around 1864, "Peace is a fiction of our Faith."

I write this essay during the first weeks of a war, the Gulf War of the winter of 1991. My primary emotions since it began are gloom, fear, disgust with the stupidity of my species. William James[22] was quite right; people adore armed conflict while pretending not to. It would seem more appropriate to read Ecclesiastes or the Lamentations of Jeremiah than the cheerful Walt Whitman. I think of Virginia Woolf[23] in 1941 loading her pockets with stones and walking into the sea because she believed her sanity would not survive World War II. I think of Edna St. Vincent Millay[24] on the brink of the same war writing a poem entitled "Apostrophe to Man" which begins "Detestable race, continue to expunge yourself, die

---

19 Audre Lorde (1934–92), a New York poet of West Indian descent, wrote prolifically about womanhood, sexuality, and identity.
20 Anne Sexton (1928–74), like her one-time fellow student Sylvia Plath (1932–63), explored the innermost mental and physical depths of a woman's being in a poetry that was often painfully confessional.
21 Luce Irigaray is a contemporary French psycholinguist and philosopher with a continuing interest in gender formation and differentiation.
22 William James (1842–1910) was a pioneering figure in the formation of the fields of psychology and philosophy in the United States.
23 Virginia Woolf (1882–1941), English fiction writer and critic, ranks among the greatest novelists in the modernist canon. Subject to periods of intense depression, she committed suicide in 1941.
24 Edna St. Vincent Millay (1892–1950), a poet of great wit, challenged various social proprieties, most especially those that placed women in an inferior position to men. She was early to advocate US entrance into the Second World War.

out." Or Robinson Jeffers'[25] anguished monologue, "The Sword Will Decide."
When I read "Drum-Taps" I cannot forgive Whitman's representation of the Civil
War as spectacle, as pageantry, as tragic necessity. Six hundred thousand men
slaughtered one another because of intransigent male stupidity; I cannot think
otherwise. The bard's vision of a nation sealed in blood seems to me chillingly
close to a politician's vision. Dulce et decorum? Wilfred Owen[26] calls it an old lie.
The vampiric tenderness of "Vigil Strange," "A Sight in Camp," and "The
Wound-Dresser"[27] makes me shudder. I wish that agonies were not merely one of
Whitman's changes of garments. I wish, cruelly, that the soldiers dying in Whitman's arms could have driven him mad. I am sorry he said that there "will never
be any more perfection than there is now," because today that seems to me
intolerable, and I fear it is true.

Only one of Whitman's works seems to me adequate to the reality of America
at present. In *Democratic Vistas*,[28] the pessimist whom Whitman aimed always to
suppress is permitted sustained voice:

> I say we had best look at our times and lands searchingly in the face, like
> a physician diagnosing some deep disease. . . . The underlying principles
> of the States are not honestly believ'd in (for all this hectic glow, and
> these melodramatic screamings), nor is humanity itself believ'd in. . . .
> The depravity of the business classes of our country is not less than has
> been supposed, but infinitely greater. The official services of America,
> national, state and municipal, in all their branches and departments,
> except the judiciary, are saturated in corruption, bribery, falsehood,
> maladministration; and the judiciary is tainted. . . . The magician's ser-
> pent in the fable ate up all the other serpents; and moneymaking is our
> magician's serpent, remaining today sole master in the field. The best
> class we show, is but a mob of fashionable dress'd speculators and
> vulgarians.

And so on, windily, sadly, believably. As antidote for the "dry and flat Sahara"[29]
of American materialism, Whitman hopefully proposes a class of literatuses, "a
force-infusion" of the spirit, "or else our modern civilization, with all its
improvements, is in vain, and we are on the road to a destiny, a status, equivalent,
in the real world, to that of the fabled damned." The fabled damned. Only a man
who identified his immortality with his country's vitality could have written that.
Whitman's panoramic, spectacular, dynamic America exists. I too love it. I
experience surges of Whitmanian patriotism whenever I return from traveling
abroad to the welter of Kennedy Airport or walk a crowded city street. His

25 Robinson Jeffers (1887–1962) was a poet of nature much influenced by Whitman's prophetic tone
    and extended lines.
26 Wilfred Owen (1893–1918) was one of the outstanding young English poets killed on the battle-
    fields of the First World War.
27 These are three of Whitman's most highly regarded Civil War poems.
28 *Democratic Vistas* (1871) was a small prose volume Whitman composed in the years after the
    Civil War that expressed a savage critique of the current state of American life and culture. An
    appreciation of its acute analysis did not come until the twentieth century.
29 The term comes from *Democratic Vistas*; in Kaplan, *Whitman, Poetry and Prose*, p. 939.

shallow, corrupt, material America exists as well, and I too hate it passionately. Do we contradict ourselves? Very well then, we contradict ourselves.[30]

From Karen Sánchez-Eppler, *Touching Liberty: Abolition, Feminism, and the Politics of the Body* (Berkeley: University of California Press, 1993), pp. 74–82

This excerpt from Sánchez-Eppler's work serves as an outstanding example of the current critical practice of reading literary texts, even their aesthetics, for political meanings – a nearly complete reversal of the separation of form and style from context central to New Critical practice commonplace in the decades following the Second World War. Moreover, she follows the trend of recent literary criticism in reading the human body as a text analogous to printed texts. That interpretive strategy applies particularly well to Whitman, who not only vaunts the human physique as a central component of his poetics but produces exemplary contemporaneous instances of embodiment: sketches of the bodies of men, women, young, old, slaves, Native Americans, and workers – all categories that, for Sánchez-Eppler and her generation of literary historians, can be made to speak to current concerns with race, gender, sexuality, class, and literacy.

More specifically, she reads Whitman for relations between a poetics of embodiment and one of empowerment. She understands that it is one thing to say that Whitman opposed the degradation of African Americans (and their bodies) under the regulations of slavery but quite another to claim that his poetry effectively empowers them. Like D. H. Lawrence, she finds Whitman's form of literary sympathy for the downcast – or for the "other," however defined – problematic, though for different reasons.

Her analysis points up a fundamental paradox of "Song of Myself." The more its persona claims to transcend his own personhood, to enter into and merge with the bodies and souls of the myriad of people who inhabit its pages, the more strikingly the limitations not only of the act but of the writing are exposed. For her, the writer, the act of writing, and the text are themselves all subject to the conditions of their time no less than is the subject of the work.

In describing Whitman's vision of the mediating poet in terms of interacting lyric and narrative modes, I am suggesting that the choice and manipulation of poetic style can exert political force. Thus Whitman's conception of the poet as mediator itself establishes connections between literary and social practices. Such connections function not only to expand the notion of poetic efficacy but also to redefine what constitutes political action. What I have been calling Whitman's poetics of embodiment amounts to the aspect of his poetic style most deeply implicated in this process. For Whitman, the human body serves as the site where the issues of representation and the questions of political power intersect, and so

30 A paraphrase of ll. 1324–325 of "Song of Myself."

it is in his treatment of the human body that Whitman most explicitly establishes links between poetry and politics and most radically revises the assumptions and practices of both.

In "I Sing the Body Electric" Whitman presents the body of the slave as an exemplary instance of embodiment: the salable flesh of the slave attests to the role of the human body in designating identity.[1] It is not surprising, therefore, that Whitman's depictions of the slave serve to ground the poetics and politics of embodiment developed in "Song of Myself." Though other black bodies—most notably the negro driver and his team of horses[2]—appear in the 1855 version of this long poem, and more are added in the new catalogues of the 1856 edition, the figure of the fugitive, of the black body in transition between slavery and freedom, predominates. Just as the slave on the auction block, a piece of merchandise, appears to encapsulate the materiality of being, the transitional status of the fugitive seems to denote the fluidity of identity.

Yet as we have seen, Whitman's celebration of corporeality in "I Sing the Body Electric" strips away the flesh it claims to sing, while here the slave's attempt to change his condition, to disentangle blackness from slavery, is represented through brutal marks upon his body. Moreover, the two scenes in "Song of Myself" in which Whitman depicts an escape from slavery to freedom also involve a transformation of the relation between the poet and his subject, a grad-ual elimination of the initial distance between the "I" that speaks and the body of the fleeing slave. In short, the transition of the fugitive from slave to freeman manifests the structure and implications of Whitman's poetics of embodiment from a variety of perspectives: individual, aesthetic, and political. The relation between identity and the human body, the relation between the poet and his subject matter, and the relation between poetry and political practice all cohere in Whitman's representation of the fugitive.

The figure of the runaway slave first appears in a series of verse paragraphs[3] that pose varying personae for the poet: he is the solitary hunter, the ecstatic sailor on a Yankee Clipper, the playful companion of boatmen and clamdiggers, the witness of a marriage between a trapper and a squaw, and finally the host of a fugitive slave. As such a list makes clear, by the time the story of the slave is told, the flexibility of the poet's identity, the ease with which his "I" can be transferred from one subject to the next, has already been well established. Such meta-morphoses are so characteristic of Whitman's verse that readers generally take them for granted. In the depictions of the fugitive slave in "Song of Myself," however, Whitman carefully details this usually instantaneous transformation, laying bare some of the contradictions it entails. Anticipated by the fugitive "I" of Whitman's poem, the figure of the fugitive slave makes evident the predicament of that "I."

Section 10, ll. 189–98 are cited.

---

1   She is referring to sections 7–8 of "I Sing the Body Electric."
2   The reference is to the opening stanza of section 13.
3   In section 10.

While the fugitive remains outside of the house, the speaker retains the fixed integrity of an observing "I" clearly distinct from what it observes: "I heard his motions," "I saw him"; but once the speaker begins to tend the slave, he relinquishes this self-defining pronoun. In washing and clothing and giving and remembering, the unique identity of the server is gradually absorbed by the body being served as each "and" further separates the act that follows from the "I" that designates the actor. Only after the fugitive leaves for the north, becoming, for the first time since entering the house, an actor rather than a body being acted upon, does the speaker again assert his "I." Whitman's deployment of pronouns presents physical contact as capable of holding the differentiations of identity in abeyance.

Whitman claims in this passage that the slave's body not only represents but is the locus of social divisions, so that healing the galls caused by the physical iron fetters of slavery actually sutures the divisions between the enslaved and the free, black and white. The healing of the slave's body enables him to claim a free identity and become a grammatical subject. In this passage physical contact merges the identities of host and slave, but the successful outcome of this merger, the slave's transformation into a freeman, requires that the barrier of pronominal difference be rejected. If the assertion of a separate "he" and "I" is necessary for the achievement of freedom, it nevertheless reinscribes the divisions emancipation hoped to remove. The "firelock leaned in the corner" offers a sad reminder of the violence those divisions produced within antebellum society. Indeed the question of the host's relation to the fugitive gains urgency from the presence of the gun: how secure is their merger, how wary is their difference? A pious abolitionist sentiment would simply interpret the firelock as a promise of protection against external enemies, but within the house, self and other, enemy and friend, merger and difference are not so easily and perfectly identified. The waiting gun could equally well indicate the host's trust in the stranger beside him or his vigilant lack of trust. In the previous scene a gun has already suggested the precariousness and explosiveness of interracial contact. Whitman describes the trapper bridegroom: "One hand rested on his rifle . . . the other hand held firmly the wrist of the red girl."[4]

Over six hundred lines later, the figure of the fugitive reappears, and this time Whitman attempts a more radical union, as if to demonstrate the limitations of his earlier strategy.

Section 33, ll. 830–39 are cited.

The transference of the poet's "I" to the figure of the hounded slave, and the consequent merger of these two identities, is marked by the drib and ooze of wounded flesh. Here Whitman employs a manifestly corporeal vocabulary to articulate the union of poet and fugitive, demonstrating how his poetics of merger depends upon the notion of embodiment. There is a Doubting Thomas quality to

---

4   Her citation comes from l. 189 of the 1855 edition; mention of the rifle was dropped by the time of the 1881 edition.

this passage, as if probing the fugitive's wounds would assure the veracity of Whitman's poetic miracle: he would become the other, and so otherness would be eliminated. The fugitive's attempt to change his status and the poet's attempt to write this poem share, for Whitman, the same assumptions about the corporeality of identity: for the slave, escaping to freedom or returning to captivity entails a harrowing of his flesh; for the poet, telling this story involves representing that flesh as his own. Whitman's equation of poetry with bodily experience strives to defy any distinction between the written and the physical world.

Whitman's poetics of embodiment always, however, remains a poetics. Indeed what is so searing about his exorbitant claims to inhabit another's body is that the more fervently he asserts them, the more extravagant and impossible they appear. The pathos of this inevitably failed poetic ideal is inscribed within the poem itself. Indeed Whitman's most adamant assertions of his poetics of embodiment consistently work to undermine their own authority. So Whitman's insistence that he does not describe the slave's experience, but rather embodies that experience, contains its own caveat: "All these I feel or am,"[5] he writes, suggesting that the tangible claims of embodiment may amount to nothing more than an imaginative projection of feeling. Moreover, the alternatives of feeling or being relate to the scene described with a remarkable lack of specificity. It is not just that the triumph of embodiment (I feel the bullets, I am the hounded slave) so easily collapses into the far lesser claim of sympathetic feeling, but that the assertion of embodiment expands to permeate the entire scene so that Whitman's "I" belongs to it "all," not only to the fugitive but to the fence that supports him and the buckshot and bullets that wound him. Normal distinctions between the animate and the inanimate are denied. The bullets gain a murderous intentionality; twinges of pain become the agents that inflict pain. Thus the embodiment claimed in these lines relies on a sense of identity that remains distinct from any specific corporeal manifestation and instead moves between them. Identity appears infinitely flexible and transferable at the very moment when Whitman attempts to locate it in the human body.

In asserting his poetics of embodiment Whitman thus raises questions about the validity of this ideal from two seemingly opposite perspectives: either poetic embodiment is impossible, bodies are discrete objects, and no amount of will or desire can eradicate their otherness, so that a poetics of embodiment can offer only the representations of a sympathetic but nevertheless alien imagination; or embodiment is possible, and the body is not a barrier to identification (since identity appears fluid, transferable, and only incidentally associated with any individual corporeal form), so that a poetics of embodiment can offer only the disintegration of all links between the body and identity. If the body defines identity, then a poetics of embodiment remains a potent fantasy; if, on the other hand, identity can be transferred from one body to another, then a poetics of embodiment might be achievable, but it would also be meaningless. As a defense against these undesirable positions Whitman redefines his poetics of embodiment so that it simultaneously insists that identity inheres in the flesh and that it is a matter of representation, infinitely mobile and ultimately indeterminate.

5   L. 837 of "Song of Myself."

Agonies are one of my changes of garments;
I do not ask the wounded person how he feels. . . . I myself become the
   wounded person,
My hurt turns livid upon me as I lean on a cane and observe.[6]

These lines provide a frequently quoted synopsis of Whitman's poetics of
embodiment. What is finally most significant about them, however, is not the
exorbitant claim to become the other, to put on another's body with the ease of
changing clothes, but the odd doubleness with which Whitman retains the distance and difference of the observer. As he leans on a cane and observes, Whitman
simultaneously presents himself as object and as subject, embodied and
disembodied, the wounded person and the voice which describes that livid flesh.

   The case of the fugitive slave provides Whitman with an extreme and definitive
instance of the problematics of embodiment characteristic of his poetry as a
whole. Whitman's focus on the body has a political as well as a poetic meaning.
He proposes in *Leaves of Grass* that the divisions in the social fabric, the nature of
identity, and the relation of the poet's word to the external world are not simply
analogous, but finally identical questions. For in trying to reconcile an embodied
and a disembodied conception of identity, Whitman makes clear that the divisions between self and other (white and black, master and slave) that inform the
political delineations of personhood can be located with equal force within each
person and within every act of utterance. I have suggested as much already in
arguing that Whitman's first notebook poetry presents the relation between slave
and master as an alternative means of articulating the relation between body and
soul and in showing that Whitman's most powerful image for the comingling of
body and soul reiterates the scene of miscegenation. The import of bodily difference manifested by American slavery challenges not only national unity but also
any unitive conception of identity. By literalizing this challenge Whitman dis-
mantles traditional distinctions between what is a personal and what a political
issue: each stands equally well as an emblem for the other. Moreover, Whitman
finds that poetry is constituted out of the same divide between the disembodied
and the embodied, the intangible words that demand to be felt as a palpable
world. What the miscegenating embrace of body and soul produces in "Song of
Myself" is poetry:[7]

Section 5, ll. 84–90 are cited.

Not only does the pair of body and soul indicate the divided nature of identity,
but viewed separately body and soul each display the same split between the
embodied and the disembodied. The soul has a corporeal form (a throat, a head),
while the body lacks the impermeability, the strict boundaries, normally associated with flesh, so that a bosom-bone may be parted as easily as a shirt. This

6   Ll. 844–46 of "Song of Myself."
7   Sánchez-Eppler follows the pattern of Alicia Ostriker (see pp. 100–2) and others of reading the
    body–soul interchange of section 5 as crucial to the poem, although she injects into her reading of
    that passage a novel, racially based interpretation.

passage establishes not one mode for poetic production, but two: the regulated but undifferentiated lull that the body requests from the soul, and the fleshy communication of a plunging tongue. The dual conception of identity as simultaneously corporeal and incorporeal with which Whitman responds to the challenge of bodily difference results in a similarly dualistic notion of poetry.

In reading the relation Whitman traces between body and soul, or between hum and tongue, as reinscribing the problematics of a corporeal identity charac-teristic of American slavery, I am, therefore, also examining the erasure of such historical markers: Whitman's consistent decontextualizing of his imagery. "Song of Myself," for example, forges a conception of self and of song that is notorious for its claims of expansive universality. If I have presented miscegenation as an historically grounded model of Whitman's poetic practice, it nevertheless remains clear that Whitman's depiction of the sexual union of radically different kinds as the embrace of body and soul entails a dramatic relocation of social divisions, and hence the absorption of the political realm into the person of the poet. Whitman concluded his preface to the 1855 edition by setting up a criterion by which to judge the poems that follow: "The proof of a poet is that his country absorbs him as affectionately as he has absorbed it." The claim of affection acknowledges the erotic nature of this standard. Whitman's ideal of absorption is fulfilled. For if Whitman's poetry does absorb the social divisions of antebellum America, and particularly the crisis over slavery, it is also absorbed by it. Thus the poet, the person whom Whitman imagined as capable of mediating between the social divisions exemplified by American slavery, finally comes to incarnate those divisions.

From Susan S. Williams, *Confounding Images: Photography and Portraiture in Antebellum American Fiction* (Philadelphia: University of Pennsylvania Press, 1997), pp. 42–45

Williams' analysis of the circulation of images and texts in the recently indus-trialized, capitalized economy of antebellum America represents another major topic in recent literary studies: the material and cultural production of works of art. It is not hard to see why Whitman has served as a prime figure as much for scholars such as Williams studying the creation and circulation of cultural arti-facts as for those examining the construction of race, gender, sexuality, and class. What makes her approach all the more interesting is its multimedia exam-ination of photographic images in combination with printed texts, an approach well matched to Whitman's own fascination with images, whether produced photographically, verbally, or both, as in the case of the daguerreotype illustra-tion printed in the 1855 *Leaves of Grass* and its counterparts in later editions.

Williams' discussion of the divorce of the cultural artifact from its unique original as a result of the industrialized processes of reproduction has distinct implications for *Leaves of Grass* as both an aesthetic and a material form of expression. In one of his poetry's most famous figurative statements, Whit-man's speaker declares: "Camerado, this is no book, Who touches this book touches a man" ("So Long!," the closing poem of *Leaves of Grass* from 1860 on).

Two separate but related questions need to be asked. How can one touch a person by touching his/her verbal or pictorial likeness? And how does the nature of that contact get altered when the likeness is not handcrafted in single units but machine made in units of hundreds and thousands? When Whitman asks rhetorically in one of the closing lines of "Song of Myself," "If you want me again look for me under your boot-soles," one is left to ponder the uniqueness or even particularity of the "I," "you," even boot soles in a circulating system of interconnected units numbering in the millions.

But Williams also raises questions relating to the embedded issues of authorship and readership. How does an author create his/her image ("self-posturing" is the term that she assigns to Whitman)? And how, in turn, does the reader respond? The answers to these questions, which capture a central dynamic of literary and cultural communication, will also depend on the context in which they are located. In a poem such as "Song of Myself" that seems preoccupied with formations and valuations of selfhood, the very nature of self agency becomes complicated by the technological consequences of mass reproduction, as Williams argues.

The most famous case of a writer using a daguerreotype for publicity purposes is that of Walt Whitman. When he first published *Leaves of Grass* in 1855, he included an engraving of himself based on a daguerreotype by Gabriel Harrison.[1] Whitman had long admired daguerreotypes for "their *naturalness*, and the *life-look* of the eye—that soul of the face!"[2] In the 1855 *Leaves of Grass*, the portrait functioned as his "natural" signature, since the book contained no other identifying material about the author.

For Whitman, the portrait signaled his ownership of his text; to insert a portrait in a book was to connect author and text. Such an idea was not entirely new. A few decades earlier, Washington Irving[3] had explored the connection between portraits and literary property in "The Art of Book Making" (1819), a sketch in which portraits hanging on the walls of the British Museum become animated and spring from their frames in order to stop literary thieves from pilfering their works. Yet what makes Whitman's case especially interesting is the position of studied ease he adopts in the portrait: he slouches slightly, chewing a blade of grass and looking straight at the camera (and reader). Whitman fully understood that his seemingly "natural" portraits were constructed identities. He continued such experiments in self-posturing throughout his life. There are at least 130 known photographs of Whitman, including the so-called "Butterfly Portrait" of 1889, which was taken with a wooden butterfly wired to his finger. In this way he

---

1   See Figure 2, p. 16.
2   The reference comes from an article Whitman wrote during the period in which he edited the *Brooklyn Daily Eagle*, "Visit to Plumbe's Gallery," in *The Gathering of the Forces,* ed. Cleveland Rodgers and John Black, 2 vols. (New York: G. P. Putnam's Sons, 1920), 2: 117.
3   Washington Irving (1783–1859) was an American prose writer highly regarded in his own time, less so in ours. The most popular of his works then and now is *The Sketch-Book* (1820), in which "The Art of Book Making" was published.

challenged the idea of the "reality" behind the imitation of the photograph, knowing that such a reality was made by the sitter and the photographer.

The 1855 edition of *Leaves of Grass* had only a small circulation, but Whitman's use of the image signals a larger cultural interest in the circulation of images in the public sphere that the daguerreotype helped inaugurate. The growth of illustrated books and magazines combined with the proliferation of daguerreotypes on center tables and in public galleries meant that portraits were constantly on display, subject to the inspection of a wide variety of readers and viewers. Many daguerreotypes were themselves sixth-plate miniatures that could be held in the palm of the hand, usually protected by an elaborate case. In this sense, they were not conducive to display but rather were objects to be intimately examined and possessed. At the same time, this miniature size also made daguerreotypes readily portable: they could be sent through the mail, carried in breast pockets, and traded like calling cards. Later, with the advent of paper prints made from negatives, images became even more transportable. "*Form is henceforth divorced from matter*," Oliver Wendell Holmes[4] declared in 1859. Given "a few negatives of a thing worth seeing," the thing itself becomes redundant and necessary. "Matter in large masses must always be fixed and dear; form is cheap and transportable."

Holmes is commenting on the way in which the photographic portrait would come to function as a double that could circulate in place of the real thing. Friends and lovers exchanged photographs as a sign of their bond; fans purchased portraits of celebrities without ever having seen them in person; armchair travelers toured the world without leaving their homes. Such possibilities of vicarious experience, which we now take for granted, represented a profound shift not only in perception but also in the social order. Activities that had previously been possible only in public shifted to the home, while certain private documents— such as the portrait of a beloved—could be carried and exchanged within the public sphere. As photographers displayed and sold portraits of their customers, images became negotiable within a market economy that detached them from their original referent. As a result, the self became an exchangeable form of social currency. Photography and money became "homologous forms of social power," in Jonathan Crary's terms, since they were "equally totalizing systems for binding and unifying all subjects within a single global network of valuation and desire."[5] Both systems engaged in a process of reification whereby an abstract sign became "real."

This process detached the images from what Walter Benjamin[6] terms their "aura," as they were removed from their original historical context and made into portable, everyday objects. Benjamin defines the aura as the quality of

4   Oliver Wendell Holmes (1809–94) was a renowned physician and professor of anatomy at Harvard but is today chiefly known for his humorous poems and essays.
5   [Williams' note.] Jonathan Crary, *Techniques of the Observer* (Cambridge, Mass.: MIT Press, 1990), p. 13.
6   A German-Jewish philosopher and social critic associated with the Frankfurt School of the 1930s and 1940s, Walter Benjamin (1892–1940) is today recognized as one of the most perceptive, formative thinkers and commentators on modern life and culture. The reference here is to his widely influential essay "The Work of Art in the Age of Mechanical Reproduction," in *Illuminations*, ed. Hannah Arendt (New York: Schocken, 1969), pp. 217–51.

unapproachability and authenticity inherent to original—as opposed to mechanically reproduced—works of art. Since the daguerreotype was reproducible only through engravings that were not exact copies, it maintained its aura. "For the last time the aura emanates from the early photographs in the fleeting expression of a human face," he writes: a face that remains hauntingly present and authentic despite the absence of the sitter it depicts. Yet antebellum writers frequently represented the portability of daguerreotypes as threatening this aura, since the images could be examined through magnifiers, used as advertisements, and viewed—and even possessed—by strangers. "I cannot consent to submit you too frequently to the gaze of strangers," a soldier fighting in the Mexican War wrote to his wife; although her daguerreotype was a comforting presence for him, he resisted showing it to the prying eyes of strangers.[7] This portability thus created an ease of circulation that, when combined with their ready availability in daguerrian galleries and in reproductions, made these images an important component of an increasingly commercialized public sphere.

---

7 [Williams' note.] Quoted in Martha A. Sandweiss, "Daguerreotypes of the Mexican War," in *Eyewitness to War: Prints and Daguerreotypes of the Mexican War, 1846–1848*, ed. Martha A. Sandweiss, Rick Stewart, and Ben W. Huseman (Forth Worth, Tex.: Amon Carter Museum and Washington, D.C.: Smithsonian Institution Press, 1989), 58–60.

3

Key Passages and Full Text

Approaching the Text

Textual History

Writing, revising, and republishing *Leaves of Grass* was Whitman's life work. He fell into the habit in later years of using the phrase "My Book and I," and in so doing he succinctly labeled the most significant relationship in his life. The idea of *Leaves of Grass* as his life work has an appropriateness that transcends even the intensely autobiographical character of its contents. In a more basic sense yet, it was the essential, continuing fact of his existence. Whitman lived the second half of his life in the closest possible contact with his book, composing and recomposing, publishing and promoting it. He was still working on it at the time of his death at the age of 72.

The life of the text (or, to use Robert Darnton's useful term, the biography of the text[1]) was as protean as that of its author. Whitman produced six editions of *Leaves of Grass* in the United States over the second half of his life: 1855, 1856, 1860, 1867, 1871–72, and 1881–82. There were, in addition, numerous reprintings, several piratings, one authorized British edition (1868), and a small number of translations into other European languages during his later years.

The life of "Song of Myself" was similarly dynamic. It was the opening and keynote poem in the first *Leaves of Grass*, running forty-four large octavo-sized pages, longer than all the other eleven poems collectively and the poem that best corresponded verbally to the frontispiece daguerreotype of Whitman as workingman poet. The poem appeared in that first printing without a specific title (all the poems had the generic title "Leaves of Grass"), section division, or line numbers. Its punctuation was as unconventional (ellipses outnumbering all other forms of internal punctuation) as its long lines and colloquial verbiage. The end rhyme, regular prosody, and formal diction that had characterized his periodical poems of the 1840s was entirely gone, replaced by free verse, a loose, ambling rhythmic gait, and a streetwise vocabulary that included such "unpoetic" terms as "Cuff," "blab," "foo foos," "sponger," "poke-easy," "heave'e'yo,"

---

1 Robert Darnton, "What is the History of Books?" in Cathy N. Davidson, ed., *Reading in America: Literature and Social History* (Baltimore: Johns Hopkins University Press, 1989), p. 30.

"life-lumps," "father-stuff," "venerealee," and, perhaps most famously, "barbaric yawp."

It remained the opening poem in the 1856 edition as well, though now given the title "Poem of Walt Whitman, an American." Its second-edition printing looked significantly different to the eye, with the long lines of verse frequently wrapping around one or more additional lines as a result of the much smaller sized paper. The text itself, however, was only marginally altered, with ellipses giving way to commas and double dashes and spelling very slightly regularized. Although there were now thirty-two poems in the edition, all formally titled "Poem of . . .," the primacy of "Song of Myself" in the volume remained clear.

Whitman hoped to bring out yet a new edition of *Leaves of Grass* in 1857, but harsh economic conditions forestalled that plan. By the time he was able to publish a third edition, in 1860, the contents of the volume had grown to 178 poems and the format had changed considerably. Whitman's most significant organizational move was the grouping of many of the new poems and some of the old ones into seven "clusters," the two most important being the fifteen heterosexual "Enfans d'Adam" and the forty-five homosexual "Calamus" poems, whose individual poems he numbered sequentially. The volume opened with a long new opening poem, "Proto-Leaf" (later retitled "Starting from Paumanok"), which formed a book-end with the new closing poem, "So long!," in an attempt to impose greater structure on the whole volume. The original opening poem was now renamed "Walt Whitman," its title until 1881, and was positioned after "Proto-Leaf," though not included in any of the clusters. Complementing his attempt to organize the contents into an overarching pattern, Whitman now numbered the older poem's stanzas, as he did those of all the long poems, as a means of regularizing their internal structure. In this vastly enlarged, segmented edition, "Walt Whitman" necessarily lost some of its prominence as the volume lost some of its original unity.

Whitman continued to work on his volume assiduously during and after the Civil War to produce a new edition (1867) suited to dramatically changing times. As in years past, that process meant standardizing certain aspects of the text (as by indicating past tenses by the contraction "'d"), revising old poems, composing new ones, and reorganizing the positioning of both in the expanding volume. The most important change to the text of "Walt Whitman" in its immediate post-Civil War incarnation was its segmentation into fifty-two sections, a feature that it retained in all subsequent printings. He also updated the poem's contents to reflect the fact and incorporate events of the recent war. The poem was now repositioned near the front of the volume, directly after the short, new programmatic poem "Inscription" (eventually revised and renamed "One's-Self I Sing"), which remained the opening poem in all subsequent editions. Meanwhile, this fourth edition of *Leaves of Grass* incorporated relatively few new poems (only six), although it did feature as annexes two important new clusters of Civil War poems, 'Drum-Taps' and 'Sequel to Drum-Taps'.

With the two *Drum-Taps* annexes trailing after its main contents, the 1867 edition of *Leaves of Grass* had the look and feel of a work-in-progress, even judged by the volatile standards of the evolving volume. Unsatisfied as always with the state of the text, Whitman resumed work on it in the summer of 1869 in a burst of renewed activity that eventuated in a fifth edition (1871–72), although the outcome was hardly less a work-in-progress. The new edition integrated the *Drum-Taps* annex into the main text, incorporating some of the poems in a new cluster called "Drum Taps" but dispersing others into two other new Civil War clusters. It also included two large new annexes, named after his ambitious new poems "Passage to India" and "After All, Not to Create Only." The text of "Walt Whitman" in this fifth edition was little changed, with sections and stanza numbers retained. As always, however, Whitman tinkered with the text, adding and deleting lines and changing phraseology.

Whitman would continue to revise the text of the poem and the volume during the last twenty years of his life, but the only new American edition of *Leaves of Grass* to appear during those two decades was the sixth (1881–82). (For an account of the tangled publication history of this edition, which was threatened with censorship shortly after publication, see **p. 4**.) The sixth edition, however, was a heavily revised one to which Whitman dedicated a great deal of concentrated energy and force. He had good reason to do so, since he brought out the new edition in cooperation with the most respected, established publisher he had ever worked with, James Osgood of Boston, and had high hopes for it. He not only attended carefully to the text of the volume but also came up to Boston to help to oversee production, as he had with the third edition in 1860. For this "definitive" new edition he significantly reorganized the contents of the volume, introducing new clusters, eliminating thirty-nine old poems and adding seventeen new ones, and lightly editing the texts of earlier poems. He now gave his originating poem of 1855 the enduring title "Song of Myself" but reprinted its text with only slight changes. Ever since, that 1881–82 text has been the most nearly authoritative and frequently reprinted text of "Song of Myself."

Chronology of "Song of Myself" and *Leaves of Grass*

Date	"Song of Myself"	Leaves of Grass
c. 1848–54	Composition of trial lines and stanzas in home-made notebooks and loose leaves	
1855	First publication of poem, untitled and unsectioned	Publication of first edition, consisting of a prose manifesto and twelve untitled poems (the first of which is "Song of Myself")
1856	New printing of poem, now titled "Poem of Walt Whitman, an American" but still unsectioned	Publication of second edition, consisting of thirty-two poems and containing the text of Emerson's letter, Whitman's open letter in response, and a small compilation of reviews of the first edition

Date	"Song of Myself"	Leaves of Grass
1860	New printing of poem, now titled "Walt Whitman" (its name in all subsequent editions until 1881) and fitted with stanza numbers; positioned as the second poem of the volume	Publication of third edition, in Boston, by firm of Thayer and Eldridge, best known for their antislavery list; contents are much expanded and rearranged as "clusters"
1867	New printing of poem, with numerous minor changes of wording and spelling, added references to the Civil War, and segmentation of the text into fifty-two sections	Publication of fourth edition, in New York, with contents reorganized and much expanded by the appending of *Drum-Taps*, Whitman's Civil War poems, to most copies
1871	New printing of poem, still titled "Walt Whitman," with previous edition's text largely intact	Publication of fifth edition, in New York, expanded by inclusion of *Passage to India* as an annex and by formal incorporation of *Drum-Taps* into the text
1876	Reprinting of poem	Publication of second issue, fifth edition, now in two volumes, the second (*Two Rivulets*) containing his prose works
1881–82	New printing of poem, now titled "Song of Myself" and set in its final text	Publication of sixth and final American edition, in Boston, by James Osgood; when Osgood succumbed to pressure to suppress the volume, Whitman transferred it first to Rees, Welsh, then to David McKay, both commercial publishers in Philadelphia

"Song of Myself" Manuscripts

The stunningly innovative poetics and bold ideology of "Song of Myself" invite discussion of origins. In fact, the text teases the reader to read it as a drama of origination: "Stop this day and night with me and you shall possess the origin of all poems" (l. 33). Not surprisingly, readers have done just that since the 1850s and interpreted it as Whitman's most fundamental poem. Ever since the study of American literature became formalized and its primary materials collected in archives by the mid twentieth century, critics have been able to substantiate their readings by tracing trial lines and passages eventually incorporated into "Song of Myself" back to Whitman's earliest known notebooks, many of which have

Figure 7 Title page of *Leaves of Grass*, 1855 (Courtesy of University of
South Carolina Library)

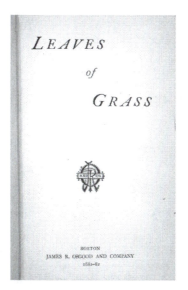

Figure 8 Title page of *Leaves of Grass*, 1881 (Courtesy of University of
South Carolina Library)

survived and are now preserved in a variety of US libraries (with the greatest concentrations at the Library of Congress, Washington, DC; Perkins Library, Duke University; and Alderman Library, University of Virginia). Those note-books, which number among the most intriguing and consequential literary manuscripts in American culture, contain not only lines and stanzas that made their way into *Leaves of Grass* but experiments with poetic techniques, such as catalogs, first-person "speaking," and direct addresses to the reader, that would characterize Whitman's boldest and most original poetry.

Figure 9 reproduces passages from a pre-1855 manuscript notebook into which Whitman wrote down, among other jottings, trial lines and stanzas for the future "Song of Myself." The lines in this manuscript, which at this stage were clearly still being formulated in both their wording and their placement, can readily be identified as lines that emerge with different phrasing and in separate places in the printed poem: "I celebrate myself to celebrate [you] every man and woman" anticipates the opening line of the poem; "I loosen the tongue that was tied in [you] them" anticipates "I act as the tongue of you,/ Tied in your mouth, in mine it begins to be loosen'd" (section 47, ll. 1248–249); and the last two lines antici-pate both the opening lines of section 5 and even more directly the related, open-ing lines of section 48, "I have said that the soul is not more than the body,/ And I have said that the body is not more than the soul."

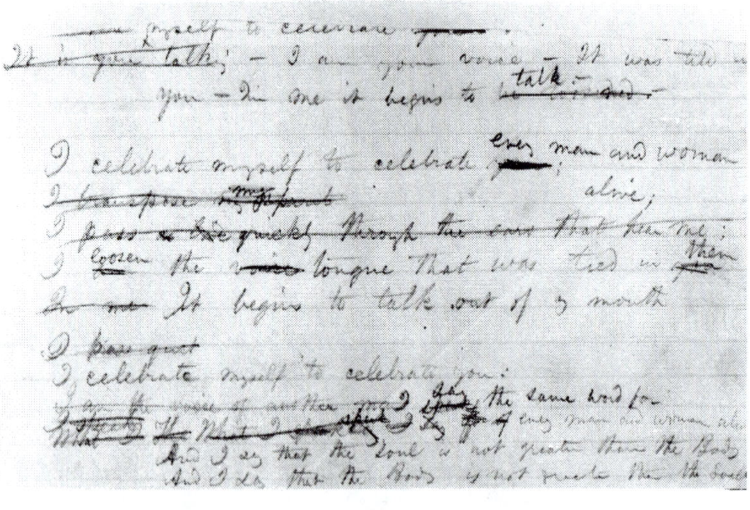

Figure 9 **Pre-1855 manuscript scrap showing trial lines eventually incorporated, with changes, into different parts of "Song of Myself" (Trent Collection, Duke University Library)**

Figure 10 indicates how Whitman tinkered with these lines, as was his habitual practice with all of his poems. The changes were made on printed sheets of the previous edition of "Song of Myself" that he used as copy-text in preparation for the "final" 1881 edition. Some of the changes are major: the addition of the new title, the elaboration of the opening line to include a second predicate, the revision

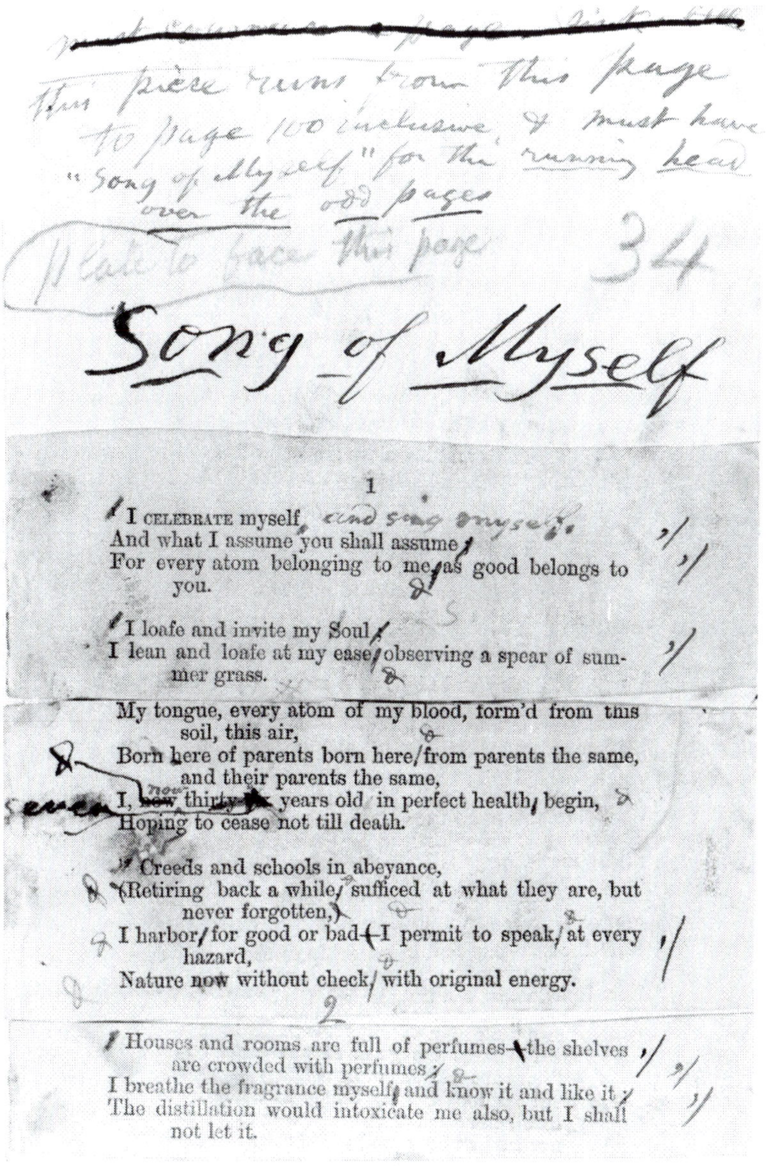

*This piece runs from this page
to page 100 inclusive, & must have
"Song of Myself" for the running head
over the odd pages*

Plate to face this page

34

Song of Myself

1

I CELEBRATE myself, *and sing myself,*
And what I assume you shall assume,
For every atom belonging to me as good belongs to
   you.

I loafe and invite my Soul,
I lean and loafe at my ease observing a spear of summer grass.

My tongue, every atom of my blood, form'd from this
   soil, this air,
Born here of parents born here from parents the same,
   and their parents the same,
I, now thirty years old in perfect health begin,
Hoping to cease not till death.

Creeds and schools in abeyance,
(Retiring back a while sufficed at what they are, but
   never forgotten,)
I harbor for good or bad, I permit to speak at every
   hazard,
Nature now without check with original energy.

2

Houses and rooms are full of perfumes, the shelves
   are crowded with perfumes,
I breathe the fragrance myself and know it and like it,
The distillation would intoxicate me also, but I shall
   not let it.

Figure 10 Whitman customarily prepared a new edition of *Leaves of Grass* from the printed sheets of a previous one. This typescript reveals the verbal and grammatical emendations he introduced in arriving at the final (1881) text of "Song of Myself," as well as the instructions he left the printer for its setting (Trent Collection, Duke University Library)

of his persona's age by a year. What one can readily learn from viewing *Leaves of Grass* manuscripts such as this one is how dynamic the process of composition was. Words, lines, and stanzas got shaped and reshaped as Whitman worked from draft to "finished" poem, then from one edition of his poems to the next.

The illustration also reveals Whitman's habitual manner, the result of his training as a printer, of leaving instructions about layout and other technical matters for the printer, whether engaged by him directly or indirectly through his publisher. Among the instructions here was advice about the placement of his 1855 engraved likeness, which he had printed only sparingly since the second (1856) edition of *Leaves of Grass*. Although little the worse for wear, the engraving represented the once virile poet, by 1881 afflicted with various ailments and slowed by partial paralysis, in a posture as far removed from his earlier self as did the rewritten poems.

Documents like these, which are surprisingly numerous because of the fact that Whitman was compulsive about both his own reputation and retention of scraps of paper and documents, allow fascinating ingress to his habitual method of composition. Still, for all the evidence they supply about Whitman's compositional habits and history, it remains as difficult to explain the origins of "Song of Myself" as those of any great work of art.

Reading "Song of Myself"

One of the overriding tendencies of readers over the years, especially those trained in formalist poetics and reading practices, has been to conceive of this long, complicated poem as a coherent narrative, with an identifiable beginning, middle, and end. Consequently, for more than a hundred years readers have attempted to break the poem down into its component parts by assigning it a partitive structure. A recent discovery by the literary historian and critic Ed Folsom reveals that Whitman himself thought along similar lines. The evidence Folsom adduces is a manuscript page (now at the Humanities Research Center, University of Texas) on which, he observes, Whitman jotted down notes in the Rome brothers' printing office as his poems went to press in 1855. Among them were markings that indicate that at that decisive moment Whitman considered "Song of Myself" to consist of five parts, which corresponded roughly to the 1881 poem's sections 1–15, 16–27, 28–34, 35–42, 43–52.[2]

For lack of any additional manuscript evidence, that document may be called the first and originating attempt to divide this poem interpretively into parts. Since then, readers have responded in like fashion; dozens of schematic interpretations have been published in the twentieth century (not to mention many more unpublished), all assuming that a skein of narrative structure or thematic continuity can be read into or out of the poem. They vary widely and pursue remarkably

---

2   Folsom's website, "The 'Song of Myself' Manuscripts," can be accessed at either of two internet locations: alone, at <http://bailiwick.lib.uiowa.edu/whitman/index.html>, or in concert with many other valuable web-based analyses of Whitman and Emily Dickinson mounted jointly as "The Classroom Electric: Dickinson, Whitman, and American Culture," at <http://jefferson.village.virginia.edu/fdw/>.

divergent lines of thought, ranging from Christian to post-Christian, Buddhist to pantheist, spiritualist to self-reforming.

On the other hand, readers in recent years have increasingly pursued radically anti-narrative modes of interpretation that focus on the process rather than the story of the poem. A useful starting point for this mode of inquiry is contemporary literary critic Joseph Frank's idea of the work of modernist literature as having a "spatial" rather than a temporal form.[3] With its circling movements, nonsequential connections, and preoccupation with rendering the physical territory of the United States, "Song of Myself" seems to inhabit the dimension of space more than of time. Not surprisingly, "Song of Myself" has struck many twentieth-century readers as familiarly modernist or even postmodernist, an uncanny anticipation of twentieth-century aesthetic practices in its challenge to conventional linear, narrative-centered practices of writing and reading. Indeed, the spatially based practices of reading and rereading to which twentieth-century critics have subjected the poem are precisely the kinds of reading strategies increasingly taught in colleges and universities since the 1990s.

During the past two decades, there has emerged a third pattern of reading "Song of Myself," which mirrors the self-conscious politicization of the academy and the formation of area-studies programs. As traditional disciplines, such as literature, art, and history, have been refashioned along gender, racial, ethnic, and class lines, works such as "Song of Myself" have been re-evaluated accordingly and re-assessed for the kind of "cultural work" they do.[4] Because of its rich and complicated representation of a broad swath of Americans and Americana, "Song of Myself" has had a special status and generated intense interest among readers pursuing these lines of analysis.

---

3 Joseph Frank, *The Widening Gyre: Crisis and Mastery in Modern Literature* (Bloomington: Indiana University Press, 1968), pp. 3–14.
4 I borrow the term from the influential book by Jane Tompkins, *Sensational Designs: The Cultural Work of American Fiction, 1790–1860* (New York: Oxford University Press, 1985).

Key Passages

Selection of Key Passages

Isolating key passages in a poem such as "Song of Myself" is problematic; the 1855 text not only lacked section divisions but also possessed a loose fluidity that seemingly complicated removal of parts of the poem from the whole. But once the poem was reorganized into fifty-two sections in the 1867 edition and all subsequent printings, identification of sections – no less, key sections – became a simplified task.

Just the same, the first readers were quick to draw attention to particular lines and passages of the poem. There was an obvious reason for this; nineteenth-century reviewing typically consisted of more citation than commentary, and "Song of Myself," with its flamboyantly unconventional poetics, undoubtedly invited excerpting more than did most poems. For some reviewers, no doubt, the poem had to be seen and sampled for their remarks to be appreciated.

The seven key passages (that is, numbered sections of the poem) reproduced below are selected on the basis of their centrality to the critical commentary on "Song of Myself." These passages have all received extensive attention over the years from critics and general readers, have proven in most cases to be among the poem's most controversial, and have lent themselves to vigorous, many-sided debate over the most pressing questions raised in the past and today about the poem, ranging from form and style to ideological issues pertaining to sexuality, gender, race, class, nationalism, and globalism.

The text for the key passages is that of the 1855 edition, the earliest and aesthetically and ideologically most radical version of the poem, whereas the full text of the poem printed on **pp. 142–95** is that of the 1881 edition. The reader is thereby provided the basis for a comparative look at Whitman's shifting text and an understanding of the text as a living, evolving phenomenon.

Several editorial practices need to be pointed out. First, each passage and its headnote is preceded by an indicative "heading" in square brackets, provided as a point of reference for those looking for a particular passage that they have previously encountered. The headings draw upon frequently quoted lines in each passage and should not be seen as an attempt to impose titles on the parts of Whitman's poems. Second, section numbers are given in brackets above each of the key passages; no such divisions existed in the 1855 edition. Finally, headnotes to the key passages give general background and critical information, as well as guidelines to interpretation. To avoid duplication, however, annotation of unfamiliar words and concepts is reserved to the footnotes attached to the full text of the poem.

Key Passages (from 1855 edition)

Section I ["I celebrate myself"]

One may fairly claim that the opening lines of a poem (or, for that matter, of any literary text) are the most crucial of the work. Their composition requires an author to make a wide range of decisions that determine fundamental aspects of the entire work, including subject, voice, tone, setting, direction, and duration. For this reason alone, the opening lines of "Song of Myself" would invite attention. But they have received extraordinary attention ever since their publication on their particular merits as well.

The poem begins with the most famous opening line in American poetry. Lauded for its liberating energy and affirmation of selfhood, derided for its egotism and bombast, this line gained fame (and notoriety) immediately following publication. In more recent decades it has been interpreted by numerous critics and writers as one of the boldest assertions in all modern literature of individuality – by some even as a signature opening of American and/or modern verse. One way that critics have made this point is to compare and contrast the opening of "Song of Myself" with that of Virgil's *Aeneid* and Milton's *Paradise Lost*, finding it a modern alternative to the formal invocations to the muses or gods customary in epic poems. Whitman's, they point out, is a path-breaking modern variation on the classical epic, one that sings the song of selfhood and therefore has no external authority other than its own self to invoke at its outset.

Critics in the Cold War generation tended to focus on what they perceived to be the untrammeled freedom of the self in this poem and in nineteenth-century American literature generally. Reacting consciously in opposition, the post-Vietnam War generation has tended to see both author and subject as more strictly bound by the discursive and ideological practices of their time. Thus, they argue that Whitman's attempts to celebrate modern freedom are compromised and complicated by the immersion of author, subject, and text in the social, political, economic, and print-making structures of the day.

Alternatively, critics have understood these lines more simply as introducing the central figure of the poem, the "I." Readers may make sense of the poem by following up on this point and noting that the omnipresence of that character as much as any other aspect of the poem gives it continuity and unity. That is, the "I" will be present at all phases, acts, and settings of the poem's long, looping journey as it travels through time and space, intruding itself into even the most unlikely scenes, as in the twenty-eight bathers interlude in section 11 and the roll call of heroic victims in section 33. Similarly, it will be always and exclusively the "I" that will speak and sometimes perform the words of the poem. In this sense, "Song of Myself" may be read as a poem of, about, and – in the most immediate sense – by the self.

The last two lines of the opening stanza have also been widely discussed, especially in the past two decades, as literary criticism has reoriented its focus from the author to the reader, as well as to the complicated pathways joining the two. As a result, recent commentators have repeatedly focused on the poem's direct address to the reader, which begins in these lines but continues intermittently throughout the poem. (See, for instance, the analysis of audience address in Ezra Greenspan, *Walt Whitman and the American Reader*, New York: Cambridge University Press, 1990, chapter 6.) They have pointed out that the persona seeks to involve the reader as an active partner in the journey/ enterprise of the poem, not just as a passive listener and recipient. But even on this point opinions have differed significantly. Does the voice of the persona subsume that of the reader, as though via dictation? Or does it empower the reader to think and speak for himself/herself?

The brief second stanza has also proven a popular and controversial subject of discussion. It speedily caught the eyes of Whitman's supporters and detractors, who alike adopted the nineteenth-century reading practice of deducing evidence of "character" from first-person writing and consequently interpreted these lines as signs, alternatively, of independence or of laziness. The earliest response of this sort was that of journalist Charles Dana, who referred just a few weeks after publication to the author of *Leaves of Grass* as a "loafer" (see **p. 40**). A century later, a generation marching to the rhythm of the Beatniks and their followers found in this figure of speech a term of praise.

A different approach to the second stanza has been taken by aesthetic-minded critics, who, like Randall Jarrell (see **pp. 87–91**), have broadly refuted the charges dating from 1855 (as of Rufus Griswold, see **pp. 55–56**) and continuing well into the twentieth century against Whitman of being a literary barbarian. Critics reading this stanza, for example, have discerned a carefully calculated repetitive use of long-drawn vowel sounds ("loafe," "invite," "soul," "lean and loafe," "ease") to reinforce the leisured sense of the stanza. A third motif of commentary has been to direct close attention to the recurring figure of the spear of grass, which has been interpreted throughout the twentieth century as the central symbol of the poem. There is good reason to believe that Whitman intended it as such in 1855. He not only named the volume *Leaves of Grass* but also printed each of the poems under that heading and repeatedly featured grass in crucial parts of "Song of Myself" (corresponding, in later editions, to sections 5, 6, 17, 31, 33, 34, and 52). Indeed, the framing of the poem by grass in the opening and closing sections seems quite likely to be intentional.

Whitman composed two additional stanzas for this section in 1881 to make it a more expansive, four-stanza opening. But, as early as 1867, when he first imposed section divisions on the poem, he set this one off as a four-stanza section that included the two stanzas that in 1881 he would reset at the beginning of section 2.

[1]

I celebrate myself,
And what I assume you shall assume,
For every atom belonging to me as good belongs to you.

I loafe and invite my soul,
I lean and loafe at my ease . . . . observing a spear of summer grass.

Section 5 ["I believe in you my soul"]

Although these stanzas have evoked an extraordinarily divergent array of interpretations ranging from devotional and pastoral to orgiastic, readers have read
them perhaps most often in a religious context. One persistent tendency has
been to see them as pantheistic, with comparisons made with the thought and
expression of Ralph Waldo Emerson and/or the Transcendentalists. By contrast,
more conservative readers, especially in Whitman's own time, tended to casti-
gate them as sacrilegious. In the past generation, however, critics and scholars
have more frequently interpreted these stanzas in sexual than in religious
terms.

The opening stanza invokes the traditional Christian dichotomy of the soul
and the body ("the other I am"), only to subvert it by declaring belief in both –
and not just belief but equal belief, stated in rhythmically balanced verbal units.
Furthermore, the poet deliberately puts these two traditional antagonists into
relation by neutralizing the judgmental term "abase," in effect declaring that the
body is no baser than the soul. That iconoclastic declaration comes, by this
point in the poem, well prepared for, especially after the stunningly bold portrayal in section 2 of the human body stripped naked, its parts detailed, and its
biological processes vaunted.

The second stanza repeats the emphatic term/action "loafe" and its association with the unspecified location of "on the grass" introduced in section 1,
though here for the first time stated in the imperative voice. As in the opening
section, the action associated with it is lyrical, the production – or, more accurately, the process – of vocalizing sounds. Once again, Whitman associates this
process lyrically via alliteration, this time with word pairs ("loafe" and "loose,"
"lull" and "like," "valved" and "voice").

The emphasis on voice and vocalization deserves elaboration. The poem
begins, as mentioned, with the vocalized act of "celebrat[tion]," an act that in
1881 got strengthened when Whitman added the significant parallel predicate
"and sing" (see Figure 10, **p. 123**). Likewise, in the third stanza that he also
added in 1881 to the opening section, he introduced the first use of "tongue"
(1.6) and, in the new fourth stanza, a further act of "speak[ing]." From this point
on, voice, tongue, speech, utterance, song, and sounds will fill the poem as both
terms and acts. The entirety of section 26, for instance, consists of a prolonged
act of listening to surrounding sounds. Furthermore, the underlying mode of

the poem, at each and every moment, is one of incessant speech: the persona expressing his mind to the reader, I to you, and repeatedly making the reader aware that an act of verbal exchange is taking place.

The third stanza may be and has often been read as devotional. Or it may be – and increasingly in our generation is – read as frankly erotic: an act of oral and/ or oral-genital coupling. Either reading permits an interpretation of the fourth stanza as the resultant euphoric release, whether as religious vision or orgasmic peace in which the parts of nature, human and animal, cohere in a seamless whole.

[5]

I believe in you my soul . . . . the other I am must not abase itself to you,
And you must not be abased to the other.

Loafe with me on the grass . . . . loose the stop from your throat,
Not words, not music or rhyme I want . . . . not custom or lecture, not
    even the best,
Only the lull I like, the hum of your valved voice.

I mind how we lay in June, such a transparent summer morning;
You settled your head athwart my hips and gently turned over upon me,
And parted the shirt from my bosom-bone, and plunged your tongue to
    my barestript heart,
And reached till you felt my beard, and reached till you held my feet.

Swiftly arose and spread around me the peace and joy and knowledge
    that pass all the art and argument of the earth;
And I know that the hand of God is the elderhand of my own,
And I know that the spirit of God is the eldest brother of my own,
And that all the men ever born are also my brothers . . . . and the women
    my sisters and lovers,
And that a kelson of the creation is love;
And limitless are leaves stiff or drooping in the fields,
And brown ants in the little wells beneath them,
And mossy scabs of the wormfence, and heaped stones, and elder and
    mullen and pokeweed.

Section 6 ["A child said"]

George Eliot excerpted the first stanza of this section in her notice of the 1855 *Leaves of Grass* (*Westminster and Foreign Quarterly Review* 9 [1 April 1856]). Various other contemporary readers were also quick to fasten upon it, perhaps because of its portrayal of the child, which could be seen as exemplifying the era's romantic association of childhood with innocence, intuition, and nature.

The sudden appearance (then disappearance) of "the child" is striking. How can one explain it, and why does it occur at this moment in the poem? Perhaps the child is "the produced babe" (the phrase used in the third stanza) of the act of sexual union that took place in the previous section. Or perhaps the child simply appears transcendently, supernally to time and place, in a way that challenges linear notions of narrativity (precisely as the speaker's presence can be read as doing). Whatever the explanation, the effect is not simply charming but profound. The child holds up the central symbol of the poem and raises the fundamental question: What is the grass? The remainder of the section – one might even say, the remainder of the poem – attempts to fashion a response to that question.

The speaker's answer, introduced by the colloquial sequence of "guess[es]," is presented as provisional. Contemplating out loud, he retorts with a variety of interpretations that test the symbol's richness: grass as representing self, God, childhood, life's common denominator, and, finally, death. As he ponders these ideas more rigorously, he discerns connections between them: life and death, young and old, humanity and God – and, underlying them all, the essential continuity of existence.

Whitman put the child's question "What is the grass?" (and also the third question in this section, in stanza three) into italics beginning in 1860. The effect, intensified by the addition of a section-division number right before the introduction of the child, was to set the child and its question off somewhat from the flow of the poem.

[6]

A child said, What is the grass? fetching it to me with full hands;
How could I answer the child? . . . . I do not know what it is any more
    than he.

I guess it must be the flag of my disposition, out of hopeful green stuff
    woven.

Or I guess it is the handkerchief of the Lord,
A scented gift and remembrancer designedly dropped,
Bearing the owner's name someway in the corners, that we may see and
    remark, and say Whose?

Or I guess the grass is itself a child . . . . the produced babe of the
    vegetation.

Or I guess it is a uniform hieroglyphic,
And it means, Sprouting alike in broad zones and narrow zones,
Growing among black folks as among white,
Kanuck, Tuckahoe, Congressman, Cuff, I give them the same, I receive
    them the same.

And now it seems to me the beautiful uncut hair of graves.

Tenderly will I use you curling grass,
It may be you transpire from the breasts of young men,
It may be if I had known them I would have loved them;
It may be you are from old people and from women, and from offspring
    taken soon out of their mothers' laps,
And here you are the mothers' laps.

This grass is very dark to be from the white heads of old mothers,
Darker than the colorless beards of old men,
Dark to come from under the faint red roofs of mouths.

O I perceive after all so many uttering tongues!
And I perceive they do not come from the roofs of mouths for nothing.

I wish I could translate the hints about the dead young men and women,
And the hints about old men and mothers, and the offspring taken soon
    out of their laps.

What do you think has become of the young and old men?
And what do you think has become of the women and children?

They are alive and well somewhere;
The smallest sprout shows there is really no death,
And if ever there was it led forward life, and does not wait at the end to
    arrest it,
And ceased the moment life appeared.

All goes onward and outward . . . . and nothing collapses,
And to die is different from what any one supposed, and luckier.

Section 10 ["The runaway slave came to my house"]

Whitman had stated forcefully in the 1855 Preface his programmatic goal for
poetry to document and represent a wide array of people, places, and activities
from all parts of the United States. This section, like sections 15–16 and 33,
epitomizes that goal. This sequence of stanzas projects the poem's omnipresent
persona to a series of remote locations around the United States. Some scenes,
such as those of the clam diggers and possibly the clipper ship, must have drawn
on personal memories on and off Long Island; others, such as the hunting,
trapping, and fugitive slave scenes, were more purely invented (Whitman did not
keep a gun, did not hunt, had not yet traveled to the western plains or mountains, and did not engage in abolitionist activities). As occurs throughout the
poem, the thread of continuity attaches to and unravels from the person of the
speaker. Thus, the indicative actions of the passage relate to or derive from him:

"I hunt," "My eyes settle the land," "stopped for me," "I tucked," "I saw," and "I heard." What happens here, as throughout the poem, happens because of the presence and mediation of the "I."

Whereas most contemporary readers derided the catalog technique he employed in the poem as banal or antipoetic, readers in our own generation have applauded the inclusiveness of Whitman's treatment of his fellow Americans. More than half a century ago, F. O. Matthiessen famously pointed out correspondences between Whitman's verbal paintings of common people and settings, prominent in this section and elsewhere, and those of contemporary genre artists, especially the Long Island-based William Sidney Mount with whose work Whitman was familiar.[1] But in more recent years, critics have asked a different set of questions probing Whitman's representation of his diverse subjects. They have made clear that these are not simply genre paintings of local color settings and provincial activities but controversial renderings of taboo subjects: sexuality, miscegenation, and slavery.

Two of the genre portraits that have received the most attention in this regard in all of *Leaves of Grass* come from this section: the trapper and his Native American bride, and the runaway slave. Signs of Whitman's meditation over the latter passage can be found in a sequence of two trial stanzas that he composed in a pre-1855 manuscript notebook (Notebook 80, Library of Congress):

> I am the poet of slaves and of the masters of slaves
> I am the poet of the body
> And I am
>
> I am the poet of the body
> And I am the poet of the soul
> I go with the slaves of the earth equally with the masters
> And I will stand between the masters and the slaves,
> Entering into both so that both will understand me alike.

These lines were part of Whitman's puzzling out of a central proposition in his self-conception as a poet, as he struggled to determine to his own satisfaction what kind of a poet he was. In the pre-1855 manuscript notebooks he repeatedly responded to the implied rhetorical question, What am I the poet of?, with the deceptively simple declarative sentence: "I am the poet of . . . ." In this fascinating trial passage, he was answering, in effect, in terms of two of the most powerful pairs of antitheses present in antebellum culture: body and soul, and slave and master. Those pairs, he understood furthermore, were related; to

<hr />

1   F. O. Matthiessen, *American Renaissance: Art and Expression in the Age of Emerson and Whitman* (New York: Oxford University Press, 1941), pp. 596–601. Matthiessen also shrewdly observed correspondences between a different aspect of Whitman's poetry, its fascination with the male body, and the painting of Whitman's friend, the major American artist Thomas Eakins (1844–1916). Matthiessen singled out for comparison Eakins' *The Swimming Hole* and section 11 of "Song of Myself" (p. 610).

speak of slavery and freedom was necessarily to speak not only of body and soul but of them in terms of possession.

The fundamental issue in these trial passages is mediation between these antitheses by the "I." The mediation in the last line is so strong, in fact, that the point of attention is deflected from master and slave to the "I." A related issue occurs in the fugitive-slave stanza of section 10, where the relative standing between speaker and fugitive is in question. For a far-reaching analysis of this complicated act of verbal mediation and representation, see Karen Sánchez-Eppler's essay in the Interpretations section (**pp. 106–11**). For a very different poetic approach to and rendering of the treatment of fugitive slaves, see Whitman's seethingly sarcastic poem about the arrest of Anthony Burns, "A Boston Ballad," which was another of the original twelve poems of the 1855 *Leaves of Grass*.

[10]

Alone far in the wilds and mountains I hunt,
Wandering amazed at my own lightness and glee,
In the late afternoon choosing a safe spot to pass the night,
Kindling a fire and broiling the freshkilled game,
Soundly falling asleep on the gathered leaves, my dog and gun by my
    side.

The Yankee clipper is under her three skysails . . . . she cuts the sparkle
    and scud,
My eyes settle the land . . . . I bend at her prow or shout joyously from
    the deck.

The boatmen and clamdiggers arose early and stopped for me,
I tucked my trowser-ends in my boots and went and had a good time,
You should have been with us that day round the chowder-kettle.

I saw the marriage of the trapper in the open air in the far-west . . . . the
    bride was a red girl,
Her father and his friends sat near by crosslegged and dumbly smoking
    . . . . they had moccasins to their feet and large thick blankets
    hanging from their shoulders;
On a bank lounged the trapper . . . . he was dressed mostly in skins . . . .
    his luxuriant beard and curls protected his neck,
One hand rested on his rifle . . . . the other hand held firmly the wrist of
    the red girl,
She had long eyelashes . . . . her head was bare . . . . her coarse straight
    locks descended upon her voluptuous limbs and reached to her feet.

The runaway slave came to my house and stopped outside,
I heard his motions crackling the twigs of the woodpile,

Through the swung half-door of the kitchen I saw him limpsey and
   weak,
And went where he sat on a log, and led him in and assured him,
And brought water and filled a tub for his sweated body and bruised
   feet,
And gave him a room that entered from my own, and gave him some
   coarse clean clothes,
And remember perfectly well his revolving eyes and his awkwardness,
And remember putting plasters on the galls of his neck and ankles;
He staid with me a week before he was recuperated and passed north,
I had him sit next me at table . . . . my firelock leaned in the corner.

Section 11 ["along the beach came the twenty-ninth bather"]

"Well, did the lady fall in love with the twenty-ninth bather, or *vice versa?*" asked
the anonymous critic writing in the *Brooklyn Daily Eagle* in September 1855 (see
p. 47). An era accustomed to think according to the psychoanalytical theories
of Freud and his successors may smile at this ingenuousness, but not of all this
reviewer's contemporaries missed the erotic exhibitionism of this passage, or
that of other parts of the poem. Few who did approved of it, although Whitman
was not without occasional defenders, such as Fanny Fern, in his own day even
on these delicate grounds (see **pp. 57–61**).

This passage exemplifies a host of issues related to what Vivian Pollak has
recently labeled "the erotic Whitman."[1] It demonstratively indicates Whitman's
own commitment, despite strict Victorian taboos, to the treatment of eroticism
in poetry. Most of the eroticism in Whitman is male centered, as in his now
famous "Calamus" poems first published in the 1860 edition, and certainly
Whitman is today widely regarded as the premier gay poet of his culture. What
is distinctive about this passage, however, is the fact that the eroticism is lodged
primarily in the woman – if anything, an even more powerful transgression
against poetic and social propriety. In fact, it is she, the missing twenty-ninth
bather whose hand and body are powerfully projected onto the scene of male
camaraderie, who figures along with the voyeuristic narrator as the active agent
of secret eroticism in this passage.

Despite Whitman's growing conservatism as he entered old age, he left this
provocative section largely untouched internally during the years 1855–81,
making only minor changes of punctuation and wording. On the other hand, the
most serious change over that period was a direct result of his decision to
segment the entire poem into numbered sections. In 1855, the poem flowed
unbrokenly from the treatment of the fugitive slave to that of the twenty-eight
bathers and one, with nothing but a normal stanza line break to separate them.
The result is a much greater continuity between the two scenes.

---

1   *The Erotic Whitman* (Berkeley: University of California Press, 2000).

[11]

Twenty-eight young men bathe by the shore,
Twenty-eight young men, and all so friendly,
Twenty-eight years of womanly life, and all so lonesome.

She owns the fine house by the rise of the bank,
She hides handsome and richly drest aft the blinds of the window.

Which of the young men does she like the best?
Ah the homeliest of them is beautiful to her.

Where are you off to, lady? for I see you,
You splash in the water there, yet stay stock still in your room.

Dancing and laughing along the beach came the twenty-ninth bather,
The rest did not see her, but she saw them and loved them.

The beards of the young men glistened with wet, it ran from their long
     hair,
Little streams passed all over their bodies.

An unseen hand also passed over their bodies,
It descended tremblingly from their temples and ribs.

The young men float on their backs, their white bellies swell to the sun
     . . . . they do not ask who seizes fast to them,
They do not know who puffs and declines with pendant and bending
     arch,
They do not think whom they souse with spray.

Section 33 (excerpted) ["I am the hounded slave"]

The pervasive identification by the speaker with the world around him, which
D. H. Lawrence famously deplored (see **pp. 79–81**), is fully on display in this
sequence of passages. Lawrence was so exercised that he sometimes overlooked Whitman's deliberately comic overstatement, but his criticism is a serious one. At some point, the identification of the speaker with the people most
distant from him (the wife, the skipper, the hounded slave) in a socially and
racially torn society becomes not just trite but objectionable. Furthermore, the
speaker's assertion that he not only feels with but actually becomes the "other"
raises more issues than it resolves.

A window on the impassioned verse of these stanzas is provided by one of
Whitman's earliest manuscript notebooks (Notebook 85, Library of Congress),
into which he drafted parts of individual poems. One set of verses clearly
anticipates the collage of first-person scenarios of section 33:

All this I swallow in my soul, and it becomes mine, and I likes it well,
I am the man; I suffered, I was there:
All the beautiful disdain and calmness of martyrs
The old woman that was chained and burnt with dry wood, and her
    children looking on,
The great queens that walked serenely to the block,
The hunted slave who flags in the race at last, and leans up by the fence,
    blowing and covered with sweat,
And the twinges that sting like needles his breast and neck
The murderous buck-shot and the bullets.
All this I not only feel and see but am.
I am the hunted slave
Damnation and despair are close upon me
I clutch the rail of the fence.
My gore presently trickles thinned with ooze of my skin as I
    fall on the reddened grass and stones,
And the hunters haul up close with their unwilling horses,
Till taunt and oath swim away from my dim dizzy ears
What the rebel, felt gaily adjusting his neck to the rope noose,
What the savage, lashed to the stump, spirting yells and laughter at every
    foe
What rage of hell urged the lips and hands of the victors.
How fared the young captain pale and flat on his own bloody deck
The pangs of defeat sharper then the green edged wounds of his side
What choked the throat of the general when he surrendered his army
What heightless dread falls in the click of a moment

This particular manuscript entry contains one of the keys to Whitman's experimentation. At a number of places in the manuscript, Whitman originally inscribed "he," which he erased and rewrote as "I." For example, the important line "I am the man; I suffered, I was there," which passed virtually unchanged into the published version of "Song of Myself," was originally drafted "He is the man; he suffered, he was there." Similarly, the first-person identification of the persona with the "hunted slave" was originally written in the third person, to clearly different effect. It is no exaggeration to say that the future "Song of Myself" would have been an entirely different poem had Whitman not decided to write it consistently and exhaustively in the first person.

The stanza beginning "I am the hounded slave" demonstrates that sometimes the sense of a verse, stanza, or poem is as dependent on what the reader brings to as what the author inscribes in the act of literary communication. The main change introduced by Whitman over the years was the substitution of commas for ellipses, but by 1885, twenty-two years after the Emancipation Proclamation, twenty years after the end of the Civil War, and nearly a decade after the end of Reconstruction, the scene no longer had the immediacy it once had to readers and the issues may well have had a different resonance.

This is by far the longest section in the poem; the selection below begins about two-thirds of the way though the section.

[33]

I am a free companion . . . . I bivouac by invading watchfires.

I turn the bridegroom out of bed and stay with the bride myself,
And tighten her all night to my thighs and lips.

My voice is the wife's voice, the screech by the rail of the stairs,
They fetch my man's body up dripping and drowned.

I understand the large hearts of heroes,
The courage of present times and all times;
How the skipper saw the crowded and rudderless wreck of the
    steamship, and death chasing it up and down the storm,
How he knuckled tight and gave not back one inch, and was faithful of
    days and faithful of nights,
And chalked in large letters on a board, Be of good cheer, We will not
    desert you;
How he saved the drifting company at last,
How the lank loose-gowned women looked when boated from the side
    of their prepared graves,
How the silent old-faced infants, and the lifted sick, and the sharp-
    lipped unshaved men;
All this I swallow and it tastes good . . . . I like it well, and it becomes
    mine,
I am the man . . . . I suffered . . . . I was there.

The disdain and calmness of martyrs,
The mother condemned for a witch and burnt with dry wood, and her
    children gazing on;
The hounded slave that flags in the race and leans by the fence, blowing
    and covered with sweat,
The twinges that sting like needles his legs and neck,
The murderous buckshot and the bullets,
All these I feel or am.

I am the hounded slave . . . . I wince at the bite of the dogs,
Hell and despair are upon me . . . . crack and again crack the marksmen,
I clutch the rails of the fence . . . . my gore dribs thinned with the ooze of
    my skin,
I fall on the weeds and stones,
The riders spur their unwilling horses and haul close,

They taunt my dizzy ears . . . . they beat me violently over the head with
     their whip-stocks.

Agonies are one of my changes of garments;
I do not ask the wounded person how he feels . . . . I myself become the
     wounded person,
My hurt turns livid upon me as I lean on a cane and observe.

Section 52 ["I sound my barbaric yawp"]

Contemporaries were quick to fasten on to the phrase "barbaric yawp"
to characterize the outré quality of Whitman's verse. The parodist of the
1860 "Counter-Jumps," for instance, rephrased it "feeble yelp" (see **p. 29**).
But there is as surely a "kangaroo among the beauty" quality in these richly
articulated stanzas – and, for that matter, in the entire poem – as in Emily
Dickinson's arch self-description, and little reason to doubt that Whitman was
self-confidently flaunting it.
   The poem circles back in its closing lines to its point of origination. It
reinscribes elements established in its early moments: grass, the paradoxical
merging of life and death, the exchange between "I" and "you." Remarkably, the
poem ends without a closing period. Might Whitman, an experienced printer,
editor, and proofreader, have overlooked so conspicuous an omission? More
likely, he was incorporating an open-ended conclusion to relations between
speaker and reader consistent with the logic of the entire poem, a poem that
celebrates the unceasing process of life.

[52]

The spotted hawk swoops by and accuses me . . . . he complains of my
     gab and my loitering.

I too am not a bit tamed . . . . I too am untranslatable,
I sound my barbaric yawp over the roofs of the world.

The last scud of day holds back for me,
It flings my likeness after the rest and true as any on the shadowed wilds,
It coaxes me to the vapor and the dusk.

I depart as air . . . . I shake my white locks at the runaway sun,
I effuse my flesh in eddies and drift it in lacy jags.

I bequeath myself to the dirt to grow from the grass I love,
If you want me again look for me under your bootsoles.

You will hardly know who I am or what I mean,
But I shall be good health to you nevertheless,
And filter and fibre your blood.

Failing to fetch me at first keep encouraged,
Missing me one place search another,
I stop some where waiting for you[1]

---

1   In all subsequent editions, Whitman inserted a period at the end of this line.

Full 1881–82 Text

Selection of Full Text Edition

The text of "Song of Myself" printed below is that of the 1881–82 edition of *Leaves of Grass*, the last edition published in Whitman's lifetime. It remained without challenge the standard text for the poem until the publication of Malcolm Cowley's 1959 "facsimile" edition of the 1855 *Leaves of Grass*. Cowley's edition brought renewed attention to the first edition for the first time in a century, although few critics or textual editors followed up on his editorial decision for yet another generation. Only in the past generation have an increasing number of scholars expressed a preference for Whitman's poetry in its earliest, freshest state. One of the best arguments made for privileging the 1855 edition is that given by the editors of the *Heath Anthology of American Literature* in adopting the first edition for their text: "in later editions of the poems, Whitman toned down some of the more radical stylistic, linguistic, and thematic features of the original edition of *Leaves of Grass*."[1] To add further weight to their rationale, one may note that he also retreated in his later years (and editions) from some of his edgier ideological positions. But most other anthologies of American writing, including the popular *Norton Anthology of American Literature*, still print the 1881–82 text, as do most recent collections of Whitman's poetry.

Choosing between the 1855 and 1881–82 texts raises in intriguing fashion the classic textual editorial dilemma: how does one choose between two masterfully crafted editions that were both produced with the consent, authority, and oversight of the author? Indeed, given Whitman's all-purpose involvement in the production of both editions, we know with unusual certainty that both of these texts were largely uncorrupted by the intrusion of outside hands. When the censor (or the publisher acting at the command of the censor) tried to interfere with the text of individual poems in 1881–82, Whitman ultimately refused to cooperate and took control over the edition himself.

That question, in turn, raises a second classic textual editorial question: whose priorities should take precedence, those of the author or those of the

---

1   Paul Lauter *et al.*, *Heath Anthology of American Literature*, 2 vols., 4th ed. (Boston: Houghton Mifflin, 2002), 1: 2863, n1.

contemporary reader? In an era such as ours in which the theoretical and oper-
ational centrality of individualized authorship has been challenged by a new,
mounting awareness of and respect for the role of readers in the creation of texts,
that question takes on heightened urgency and complexity.

We know where Whitman's preference lay. The 1881–82 text of "Song of
Myself" was not only the final text chronologically but also the one that alone
carried Whitman's ultimate authorization, a point he made unequivocally. Even
though he continued to write poems during the remaining ten years of his life and
to assemble around them new annexes to *Leaves of Grass*, he left the volume
proper, including "Song of Myself," completely intact. Those facts notwithstand-
ing, a twenty-first-century reader is hardly obligated to respect the wish of a
nineteenth-century author.

Ultimately, an editor has to choose. This editor has chosen the 1881–82 text
because that text best allows readers to see the cumulative outcome of the long,
twisting evolution of this volatile text. Readers who wish a comparative understanding of the two texts may refer back in this sourcebook to Key Passages for
the 1855 text of those seven sections, or to the various print or online versions
listed in Further Reading for the entire 1855 text.

"Song of Myself" (1881–82 Edition)

1

I celebrate myself, and sing myself,[1]
And what I assume you shall assume,
For every atom belonging to me as good belongs to you.

I loafe and invite my soul,
I lean and loafe at my ease observing a spear of summer grass.   5

My tongue, every atom of my blood, form'd[2] from this soil,
    this air,
Born here of parents born here from parents the same, and
    their parents the same,
I, now thirty-seven years old in perfect health begin,
Hoping to cease not till death.

Creeds and schools in abeyance,   10
Retiring back a while sufficed at what they are, but never
    forgotten,

---

1   Whitman turned the simple predicate of 1855 and subsequent editions into this compound predi-
    cate only in 1881. What, if anything, is gained by the repetition of "celebrate myself" and "sing
    myself" has been a matter of debate among critics.
2   Whitman began the stylized practice of replacing the final "e" in past participles with an apos-
    trophe in 1867. One can view this systematic practice of revision in the facsimile edition of his
    "blue book," his personal copy of the third edition of *Leaves of Grass* that he used as copy-text in
    preparing a new text for the fourth edition of 1867. For a modern reprint of this copy-text, see the
    Arthur Golden entry in Further Reading.

I harbor for good or bad, I permit to speak at every hazard,
Nature without check with original energy.[3]

2

Houses and rooms are full of perfumes, the shelves are
  crowded with perfumes,
I breathe the fragrance myself and know it and like it,   15
The distillation would intoxicate me also, but I shall not
  let it.

The atmosphere is not a perfume, it has no taste of the
  distillation, it is odorless,
It is for my mouth forever, I am in love with it,
I will go to the bank by the wood and become undisguised
  and naked,
I am mad for it to be in contact with me.[4]   20

The smoke of my own breath,
Echoes, ripples, buzz'd whispers, love-root, silk-thread,
  crotch and vine,
My respiration and inspiration, the beating of my heart, the
  passing of blood and air through my lungs,
The sniff of green leaves and dry leaves, and of the shore
  and dark-color'd sea-rocks, and of hay in the barn,
The sound of the belch'd words of my voice loos'd to the
  eddies of the wind,   25
A few light kisses, a few embraces, a reaching around of arms,
The play of shine and shade on the trees as the supple
  boughs wag,
The delight alone or in the rush of the streets, or along the
  fields and hill-sides,
The feeling of health, the full-noon trill, the song of me
  rising from bed and meeting the sun.[5]

Have you reckon'd a thousand acres much? have you
  reckon'd the earth much?   30
Have you practis'd so long to learn to read?
Have you felt so proud to get at the meaning of poems?

---

3   One of the most important textual changes in the compositional history of "Song of Myself" was
    the addition of the last two stanzas of this section in 1881, which have the effect of linking the
    poem more directly to Whitman himself in time and place (although Whitman was 37 years old in
    1856, not 1855).
4   The identification between intoxication and creativity and the juxtaposition between artificiality
    and nature in the first two stanzas of this section are standard fare in nineteenth-century romanti-
    cism, but the quick turn toward nakedness, a major motif of the poem, is a distinctly Whitmanian
    variation.
5   This stunning display of the biological processes of the human anatomy and sense impressions
    corresponds to the remarkable catalog of the body that Whitman added to the 1856 text of what
    came eventually to be called "I Sing the Body Electric." In his own day, however, such bold,
    explicit, and often erotic representations of the body were considered offensive.

Stop this day and night with me and you shall possess the
    origin of all poems,
You shall possess the good of the earth and sun, (there are
    millions of suns left,)
You shall no longer take things at second or third hand, nor
    look through the eyes of the dead, nor feed on the
    spectres in books,   35
You shall not look through my eyes either, nor take things
    from me,
You shall listen to all sides and filter them from your self.

                    3
I have heard what the talkers were talking, the talk of the
    beginning and the end,
But I do not talk of the beginning or the end.

There was never any more inception than there is now,   40
Nor any more youth or age than there is now,
And will never be any more perfection than there is now,
Nor any more heaven or hell than there is now.

Urge and urge and urge,
Always the procreant urge of the world.   45

Out of the dimness opposite equals advance, always
    substance and increase, always sex,
Always a knit of identity, always distinction, always a breed
    of life.

To elaborate is no avail, learn'd and unlearn'd feel that it is so.

Sure as the most certain sure, plumb in the uprights, well
    entretied,[6] braced in the beams,
Stout as a horse, affectionate, haughty, electrical,   50
I and this mystery here we stand.

Clear and sweet is my soul, and clear and sweet is all that is
    not my soul.

Lack one lacks both, and the unseen is proved by the seen,
Till that becomes unseen and receives proof in its turn.

Showing the best and dividing it from the worst age vexes age,   55
Knowing the perfect fitness and equanimity of things, while
    they discuss I am silent, and go bathe and admire myself.

---

6   A carpenter's term for "cross-braced." Whitman was drawing on his experience as a house builder
     in Brooklyn during the years immediately preceding the publication of the 1855 *Leaves of Grass*.
     This is one of many instances in which the poem draws for its metaphors and content on popular
     and professional discourses then in circulation.

Welcome is every organ and attribute of me, and of any man
  hearty and clean,
Not an inch nor a particle of an inch is vile, and none shall
  be less familiar than the rest.

I am satisfied—I see, dance, laugh, sing;
As the hugging and loving bed-fellow sleeps at my side
  through the night, and withdraws at the peep of the
  day with stealthy tread,   60
Leaving me baskets cover'd with white towels swelling the
  house with their plenty,
Shall I postpone my acceptation and realization and scream
  at my eyes,
That they turn from gazing after and down the road,
And forthwith cipher and show me to a cent,
Exactly the value of one and exactly the value of two, and
  which is ahead?   65

          4
Trippers and askers surround me,
People I meet, the effect upon me of my early life or the
  ward and city I live in, or the nation,
The latest dates, discoveries, inventions, societies, authors
  old and new,
My dinner, dress, associates, looks, compliments, dues,
The real or fancied indifference of some man or woman I
  love,   70
The sickness of one of my folks or of myself, or ill-doing or
  loss or lack of money, or depressions or exaltations,
Battles, the horrors of fratricidal war, the fever of doubtful
  news, the fitful events;
These come to me days and nights and go from me again,
But they are not the Me myself.

Apart from the pulling and hauling stands what I am,   75
Stands amused, complacent, compassionating, idle, unitary,
Looks down, is erect, or bends an arm on an impalpable
  certain rest,
Looking with side-curved head curious what will come next,
Both in and out of the game and watching and wondering
  at it.

Backward I see in my own days where I sweated through fog with
  linguists and contenders,   80
I have no mockings or arguments, I witness and wait.

5[7]

I believe in you my soul, the other I am must not abase
    itself to you,
And you must not be abased to the other.

Loafe with me on the grass, loose the stop from your throat,
Not words, not music or rhyme I want, not custom or
    lecture, not even the best,   85
Only the lull I like, the hum of your valvèd voice.

I mind how once we lay such a transparent summer morning,
How you settled your head athwart my hips and gently
    turn'd over upon me,
And parted the shirt from my bosom-bone, and plunged
    your tongue to my bare-stript heart,
And reach'd till you felt my beard, and reach'd till you held
    my feet.   90

Swiftly arose and spread around me the peace and knowledge
    that pass all the argument of the earth,
And I know that the hand of God is the promise of my own,
And I know that the spirit of God is the brother of my own,
And that all the men ever born are also my brothers, and the
    women my sisters and lovers,
And that a kelson[8] of the creation is love,   95
And limitless are leaves stiff or drooping in the fields,
And brown ants in the little wells beneath them,
And mossy scabs of the worm fence, heap'd stones, elder,
    mullein and poke-weed.

6

A child said *What is the grass?* fetching it to me
    with full hands;
How could I answer the child? I do not know what it is any
    more than he.   100

I guess it must be the flag of my disposition, out of hopeful
    green stuff woven.

Or I guess it is the handkerchief of the Lord,
A scented gift and remembrancer designedly dropt,
Bearing the owner's name someway in the corners, that we
    may see and remark, and say *Whose?*

7   See the excerpt from Alicia Ostriker in Interpretations (pp. 100–2) for a commentary on this
    section.
8   Term drawn from shipbuilding to describe a longitudinal structure of timbers (in wooden ships) or
    of plates (in metal ones) designed to provide strength and firmness to a vessel's keel.

Or I guess the grass is itself a child, the produced babe of
    the vegetation.   105

Or I guess it is a uniform hieroglyphic,
And it means, Sprouting alike in broad zones and narrow
    zones,
Growing among black folks as among white,
Kanuck, Tuckahoe, Congressman, Cuff,[9] I give them the
    same, I receive them the same.

And now it seems to me the beautiful uncut hair of graves.   110

Tenderly will I use you curling grass,
It may be you transpire from the breasts of young men,
It may be if I had known them I would have loved them,
It may be you are from old people, or from offspring taken
    soon out of their mothers' laps,
And here you are the mothers' laps.   115

This grass is very dark to be from the white heads of old
    mothers,
Darker than the colorless beards of old men,
Dark to come from under the faint red roofs of mouths.

O I perceive after all so many uttering tongues,
And I perceive they do not come from the roofs of mouths
    for nothing.   120

I wish I could translate the hints about the dead young men
    and women,
And the hints about old men and mothers, and the offspring
    taken soon out of their laps.

What do you think has become of the young and old men?
And what do you think has become of the women and
    children?

They are alive and well somewhere,   125
The smallest sprout shows there is really no death,
And if ever there was it led forward life, and does not wait
    at the end to arrest it,
And ceas'd the moment life appear'd.

All goes onward and outward, nothing collapses,
And to die is different from what any one supposed, and
    luckier.   130

---

9   "Kanuck," slang for French Canadian; "Tuckahoe," slang for Virginian; "Cuff," slang for African
American. Whitman is provocatively linking these slang terms and their conventionally disreput-
able designees to the more respectable term and designee of "Congressman."

7

Has any one supposed it lucky to be born?
I hasten to inform him or her it is just as lucky to die, and I
    know it.

I pass death with the dying and birth with the new-wash'd
    babe, and am not contain'd between my hat and boots,
And peruse manifold objects, no two alike and every one good,
The earth good and the stars good, and their adjuncts all
    good.   135

I am not an earth nor an adjunct of an earth,
I am the mate and companion of people, all just as immortal
    and fathomless as myself,
(They do not know how immortal, but I know.)

Every kind for itself and its own, for me mine male and
    female,
For me those that have been boys and that love women,   140
For me the man that is proud and feels how it stings to be
    slighted,
For me the sweet-heart and the old maid, for me mothers
    and the mothers of mothers,
For me lips that have smiled, eyes that have shed tears,
For me children and the begetters of children.

Undrape! you are not guilty to me, nor stale nor discarded,   145
I see through the broadcloth and gingham whether or no,
And am around, tenacious, acquisitive, tireless, and cannot
    be shaken away.

8

The little one sleeps in its cradle,
I lift the gauze and look a long time, and silently brush away
    flies with my hand.

The youngster and the red-faced girl turn aside up the bushy
    hill,   150
I peeringly view them from the top.

The suicide sprawls on the bloody floor of the bedroom,
I witness the corpse with its dabbled hair, I note where the
    pistol has fallen.

The blab of the pave, tires of carts, sluff of boot-soles, talk
    of the promenaders,[10]

---

10 The phraseology here ("blab," "sluff," "talk") is typical of Whitman's attempt throughout the
   poem to replicate the sound and appearance of a newly urbanizing society.

The heavy omnibus, the driver with his interrogating thumb,
   the clank of the shod horses on the granite floor,   155
The snow-sleighs, clinking, shouted jokes, pelts of snow-balls,
The hurrahs for popular favorites, the fury of rous'd mobs,
The flap of the curtain'd litter, a sick man inside borne to
   the hospital,
The meeting of enemies, the sudden oath, the blows and fall,
The excited crowd, the policeman with his star quickly
   working his passage to the centre of the crowd,   160
The impassive stones that receive and return so many echoes,
What groans of over-fed or half-starv'd who fall sunstruck or
   in fits,
What exclamations of women taken suddenly who hurry
   home and give birth to babes,
What living and buried speech is always vibrating here, what
   howls restrain'd by decorum,
Arrests of criminals, slights, adulterous offers made,
   acceptances, rejections with convex lips,   165
I mind them or the show or resonance of them – I come
   and I depart.

9

The big doors of the country barn stand open and ready,
The dried grass of the harvest-time loads the slow-drawn
   wagon,
The clear light plays on the brown gray and green intertinged,
The armfuls are pack'd to the sagging mow.   170

I am there, I help, I came stretch'd atop of the load,
I felt its soft jolts, one leg reclined on the other,
I jump from the cross-beams and seize the clover and timothy,[11]
And roll head over heels and tangle my hair full of wisps.

10

Alone far in the wilds and mountains I hunt,   175
Wandering amazed at my own lightness and glee,
In the late afternoon choosing a safe spot to pass the night,
Kindling a fire and broiling the fresh-kill'd game,
Falling asleep on the gather'd leaves with my dog and gun
   by my side.

The Yankee clipper is under her sky-sails, she cuts the
   sparkle and scud,   180
My eyes settle the land, I bend at her prow or shout
   joyously from the deck.

---

11 A common meadow grass in the United States.

The boatmen and clam-diggers arose early and stopt for me,
I tuck'd my trowser-ends in my boots and went and had a
    good time;
You should have been with us that day round the
    chowder-kettle.

I saw the marriage of the trapper in the open air in the far
    west, the bride was a red girl,   185
Her father and his friends sat near cross-legged and dumbly
    smoking, they had moccasins to their feet and large
    thick blankets hanging from their shoulders,
On a bank lounged the trapper, he was drest mostly in skins,
    his luxuriant beard and curls protected his neck, he held
    his bride by the hand,
She had long eyelashes, her head was bare, her coarse straight
    locks descended upon her voluptuous limbs and reach'd
    to her feet.[12]

The runaway slave[13] came to my house and stopt outside,
I heard his motions crackling the twigs of the woodpile,   190
Through the swung half-door of the kitchen I saw him
    limpsy and weak,
And went where he sat on a log and led him in and assured
    him,
And brought water and fill'd a tub for his sweated body and
    bruis'd feet,
And gave him a room that enter'd from my own, and gave
    him some coarse clean clothes,
And remember perfectly well his revolving eyes and his
    awkwardness,   195
And remember putting plasters on the galls of his neck and
    ankles;
He staid with me a week before he was recuperated and
    pass'd north,
I had him sit next me at table, my fire-lock lean'd in the
    corner.

---

12 Both the erotic portrayal of the "red" woman's body and the suggestion of miscegenation – a vexed
   subject in a society uncomfortable with its multiethnic, multiracial population – were distinctly
   unconventional in mid-century American poetry.
13 This stanza recreates a scenario of fugitive slaves escaping north to freedom via the underground
   railroad. Scenarios of this sort would have been familiar to antebellum American readers from
   popular ex-slave narratives, such as those of Frederick Douglass, Henry Bibb, and Josiah Henson
   (all influences on Harriet Beecher Stowe's *Uncle Tom's Cabin*), as well as from antislavery journalism, literature, and lectures. The scenario recurs, with significant variations, in section 33, ll. 838–
   43. Both scenes are fictitious; Whitman was neither a participant nor even a fellow traveler in the
   abolitionist movement.

11

Twenty-eight[14] young men bathe by the shore,
Twenty-eight young men and all so friendly;   200
Twenty-eight years of womanly life and all so lonesome.

She owns the fine house by the rise of the bank,
She hides handsome and richly drest aft the blinds of the
    window.

Which of the young men does she like the best?
Ah the homeliest of them is beautiful to her.   205

Where are you off to, lady? for I see you,
You splash in the water there, yet stay stock still in your room.

Dancing and laughing along the beach came the twenty-ninth
    bather,
The rest did not see her, but she saw them and loved them.

The beards of the young men glisten'd with wet, it ran from
    their long hair,   210
Little streams pass'd all over their bodies.

An unseen hand also pass'd over their bodies,
It descended tremblingly from their temples and ribs.

The young men float on their backs, their white bellies bulge
    to the sun, they do not ask who seizes fast to them,
They do not know who puffs and declines with pendant and
    bending arch,   215
They do not think whom they souse with spray.

12

The butcher-boy puts off his killing-clothes, or sharpens his
    knife at the stall in the market,
I loiter enjoying his repartee and his shuffle and break-down.

Blacksmiths with grimed and hairy chests environ the anvil,
Each has his main-sledge, they are all out, there is a great
    heat in the fire.   220

From the cinder-strew'd threshold I follow their movements,
The lithe sheer of their waists plays even with their massive
    arms,

---

14 Critics have offered a myriad of interpretations of the number twenty-eight. Perhaps the most
common has been the association of the number with the number of days in the lunar calendar and
a woman's reproductive cycle.

Overhand the hammers swing, overhand so slow, overhand
 so sure,
They do not hasten, each man hits in his place.

13

The negro holds firmly the reins of his four horses, the block
 swags underneath on its tied-over chain,   225
The negro that drives the long dray of the stone-yard, steady
 and tall he stands pois'd on one leg on the string-piece,[15]
His blue shirt exposes his ample neck and breast and loosens
 over his hip-band,
His glance is calm and commanding, he tosses the slouch of
 his hat away from his forehead,
The sun falls on his crispy hair and mustache, falls on the
 black of his polish'd and perfect limbs.

I behold the picturesque giant and love him, and I do not
 stop there,   230
I go with the team also.

In me the caresser of life wherever moving, backward as well
 as forward sluing,
To niches aside and junior bending, not a person or object
 missing,
Absorbing all to myself and for this song.

Oxen that rattle the yoke and chain or halt in the leafy
 shade, what is that you express in your eyes?   235
It seems to me more than all the print I have read in my life.

My tread scares the wood-drake and wood-duck on my
 distant and day-long ramble,
They rise together, they slowly circle around.

I believe in those wing'd purposes,
And acknowledge red, yellow, white, playing within me,   240
And consider green and violet and the tufted crown
 intentional,
And do not call the tortoise unworthy because she is not
 something else,
And the jay in the woods never studied the gamut, yet trills
 pretty well to me,
And the look of the bay mare shames silliness out of me.

14

The wild gander leads his flock through the cool night,   245

---

15 A large piece of lumber, generally laid horizontally in construction.

Ya-honk he says, and sounds it down to me like an
    invitation,
The pert may suppose it meaningless, but I listening close,
Find its purpose and place up there toward the wintry sky.

The sharp-hoof'd moose of the north, the cat on the house-sill,
    the chickadee, the prairie-dog,
The litter of the grunting sow as they tug at her teats,   250
The brood of the turkey-hen and she with her half-spread
    wings,
I see in them and myself the same old law.

The press of my foot to the earth springs a hundred affections,
They scorn the best I can do to relate them.

I am enamour'd of growing out-doors,   255
Of men that live among cattle or taste of the ocean or woods,
Of the builders and steerers of ships and the wielders of axes
    and mauls, and the drivers of horses,
I can eat and sleep with them week in and week out.

What is commonest, cheapest, nearest, easiest, is Me,
Me going in for my chances, spending for vast returns,   260
Adorning myself to bestow myself on the first that will take me,
Not asking the sky to come down to my good will,
Scattering it freely forever.

            15[16]
The pure contralto sings in the organ loft,
The carpenter dresses his plank, the tongue of his foreplane
    whistles its wild ascending lisp,   265
The married and unmarried children ride home to their
    Thanksgiving dinner,
The pilot seizes the king-pin, he heaves down with a strong arm,
The mate stands braced in the whale-boat, lance and harpoon
    are ready,
The duck-shooter walks by silent and cautious stretches,
The deacons are ordain'd with cross'd hands at the altar,   270
The spinning-girl retreats and advances to the hum of the
    big wheel,
The farmer stops by the bars as he walks on a First-day[17] loafe
    and looks at the oats and rye,

16 This section's long list of people, professions, and activities chronicling the daily life of mid-nine-
    teenth-century America was generally derided as banal and unpoetic in its own time, but it has been
    lauded as inclusive and democratic in our own.
17 Quaker term for "Sunday," the latter being the term used in the 1855 edition. Whitman, who had
    fond memories of the Society of Friends from his Long Island childhood, changed the vocabulary of
    days and dates for the third edition (1860) in order to incorporate the descriptive power of Quaker
    terminology into his poetry.

The lunatic is carried at last to the asylum a confirm'd case,
(He will never sleep any more as he did in the cot in his
    mother's bed-room;)
The jour printer[18] with gray head and gaunt jaws works at his case,   275
He turns his quid of tobacco while his eyes blurr with the
    manuscript;
The malform'd limbs are tied to the surgeon's table,
What is removed drops horribly in a pail;
The quadroon[19] girl is sold at the auction-stand, the drunkard
    nods by the bar-room stove,
The machinist rolls up his sleeves, the policeman travels his
    beat, the gate-keeper marks who pass,   280
The young fellow drives the express-wagon, (I love him,
    though I do not know him;)
The half-breed straps on his light boots to compete in the race,
The western turkey-shooting draws old and young, some
    lean on their rifles, some sit on logs,
Out from the crowd steps the marksman, takes his position,
    levels his piece;
The groups of newly-come immigrants cover the wharf or levee,   285
As the woolly-pates hoe in the sugar-field, the overseer views
    them from his saddle,
The bugle calls in the ball-room, the gentlemen run for their
    partners, the dancers bow to each other,
The youth lies awake in the cedar-roof'd garret and harks to
    the musical rain,
The Wolverine sets traps on the creek that helps fill the Huron,
The squaw wrapt in her yellow-hemm'd cloth is offering
    moccasins and bead-bags for sale,   290
The connoisseur peers along the exhibition-gallery with half-shut
    eyes bent sideways,
As the deck-hands make fast the steamboat the plank is
    thrown for the shore-going passengers,
The young sister holds out the skein while the elder sister
    winds it off in a ball, and stops now and then for the knots,
The one-year wife is recovering and happy having a week
    ago borne her first child,
The clean-hair'd Yankee girl works with her sewing-machine
    or in the factory or mill,   295
The paving-man leans on his two-handed rammer, the
    reporter's lead flies swiftly over the note-book, the
    sign-painter is lettering with blue and gold,

18 That is, journeyman printer, a role known to Whitman personally from his training and occupation
    as a printer in his teens and twenties.
19 A quadroon was a person of one-fourth Negro blood. During Whitman's time, the term "visible
    admixture of Negro [or African] blood" was the commonly invoked legal term determining a
    person's race. In many Southern states, the category of Negro encompassed not only quadroons
    but also octoroons, relegating them potentially to the classification of slaves.

The canal boy trots on the tow-path, the book-keeper counts
    at his desk, the shoemaker waxes his thread,
The conductor beats time for the band and all the performers
    follow him,
The child is baptized, the convert is making his first professions,
The regatta is spread on the bay, the race is begun, (how the
    white sails sparkle!)   300
The drover watching his drove sings out to them that would
    stray,
The pedler sweats with his pack on his back, (the purchaser
    higgling about the odd cent;)
The bride unrumples her white dress, the minute-hand of
    the clock moves slowly,
The opium-eater reclines with rigid head and just-open'd lips,
The prostitute draggles her shawl, her bonnet bobs on her
    tipsy and pimpled neck,   305
The crowd laugh at her blackguard oaths, the men jeer and
    wink to each other,
(Miserable! I do not laugh at your oaths nor jeer you;)
The President holding a cabinet council is surrounded by the
    great Secretaries,
On the piazza walk three matrons stately and friendly with
    twined arms,
The crew of the fish-smack pack repeated layers of halibut in
    the hold,[20]   310
The Missourian crosses the plains toting his wares and his
    cattle,
As the fare-collector goes through the train he gives notice
    by the jingling of loose change,
The floor-men are laying the floor, the tinners are tinning
    the roof, the masons are calling for mortar,
In single file each shouldering his hod pass onward the
    laborers;
Seasons pursuing each other the indescribable crowd is
    gather'd, it is the fourth of Seventh-month,[21] (what
    salutes of cannon and small arms!)   315
Seasons pursuing each other the plougher ploughs, the
    mower mows, and the winter-grain falls in the ground;
Off on the lakes the pike-fisher watches and waits by the
    hole in the frozen surface,
The stumps stand thick round the clearing, the squatter
    strikes deep with his axe,
Flatboatmen make fast towards dusk near the cotton-wood
    or pecan-trees,

20 The juxtaposition of the President with the prostitute, and matrons with fishermen, is indicative of
    Whitman's disrespect for normative class decorum.
21 Quaker term for "Fourth of July," the phrasing used in the 1855 edition. See note 17.

Coon-seekers go through the regions of the Red river or
    through those drain'd by the Tennessee, or through
    those of the Arkansas,   320
Torches shine in the dark that hangs on the Chattahooche[22] or
    Altamahaw,[23]
Patriarchs sit at supper with sons and grandsons and great-grandsons
    around them,
In walls of adobie, in canvas tents, rest hunters and trappers
    after their day's sport,
The city sleeps and the country sleeps,
The living sleep for their time, the dead sleep for their time,   325
The old husband sleeps by his wife and the young husband
    sleeps by his wife;
And these tend inward to me, and I tend outward to them,
And such as it is to be of these more or less I am,
And of these one and all I weave the song of myself.

16

I am of old and young, of the foolish as much as the wise,   330
Regardless of others, ever regardful of others,
Maternal as well as paternal, a child as well as a man,
Stuff'd with the stuff that is coarse and stuff'd with the stuff
    that is fine,
One of the Nation of many nations, the smallest the same
    and the largest the same,
A Southerner soon as a Northerner, a planter nonchalant
    and hospitable down by the Oconee[24] I live,   335
A Yankee bound my own way ready for trade, my joints the
    limberest joints on earth and the sternest joints on earth,
A Kentuckian walking the vale of the Elkhorn[25] in my deer-skin
    leggings, a Louisianian or Georgian,
A boatman over lakes or bays or along coasts, a Hoosier,
    Badger, Buckeye;[26]
At home on Kanadian[27] snow-shoes or up in the bush, or
    with fishermen off Newfoundland,
At home in the fleet of ice-boats, sailing with the rest and tacking,   340
At home on the hills of Vermont or in the woods of Maine,
    or the Texan ranch,
Comrade of Californians, comrade of free North-Westerners,
    (loving their big proportions,)

---

22 Normally spelled "Chattahoochie," a river that flows primarily through the upcountry of Georgia.
23 A river that flows through the high country of western North Carolina.
24 A river that flows through Georgia and South Carolina.
25 A creek that flows through the Bluegrass region of Kentucky.
26 Nicknames of denizens, respectively, of Indiana, Wisconsin, and Ohio.
27 The sometimes irregular spelling of geographical names in the poem derives from both the unfixed
    spellings for name places still novel or exotic in Whitman's time and his own willfully idiosyncratic
    practice.

Comrade of raftsmen and coalmen, comrade of all who
    shake hands and welcome to drink and meat,
A learner with the simplest, a teacher of the thoughtfullest,
A novice beginning yet experient of myriads of seasons,   345
Of every hue and caste am I, of every rank and religion,
A farmer, mechanic, artist, gentleman, sailor, quaker,
Prisoner, fancy-man, rowdy, lawyer, physician, priest.

I resist any thing better than my own diversity,
Breathe the air but leave plenty after me,   350
And am not stuck up, and am in my place.

(The moth and the fish-eggs are in their place,
The bright suns I see and the dark suns I cannot see are in
    their place,
The palpable is in its place and the impalpable is in its place.)

            17
These are really the thoughts of all men in all ages and lands,
    they are not original with me,   355
If they are not yours as much as mine they are nothing, or
    next to nothing,
If they are not the riddle and the untying of the riddle they
    are nothing,
If they are not just as close as they are distant they are nothing.

This is the grass that grows wherever the land is and the water is,
This the common air that bathes the globe.   360

            18
With music strong I come, with my cornets and my drums,
I play not marches for accepted victors only, I play marches
    for conquer'd and slain persons.

Have you heard that it was good to gain the day?
I also say it is good to fall, battles are lost in the same spirit
    in which they are won.

I beat and pound for the dead,   365
I blow through my embouchures[28] my loudest and gayest for
    them.

Vivas to those who have fail'd!
And to those whose war-vessels sank in the sea!

---

28 The mouthpiece of wind instruments, though here more likely the shape of the mouth in the act of
    blowing. Whitman favored the term for its metaphorical capacity to express the musicality of the
    mouth and body. His most striking use of the term occurs in the 1855 Preface, where he refers to
    the interflow between the ideal poet and natural geography in saying of the great North American
    rivers and seas that they "do not embouchure where they spend themselves more than they
    embouchure into him"; Kaplan, *Whitman: Poetry and Prose*, p. 7.

And to those themselves who sank in the sea!
And to all generals that lost engagements, and all overcome
    heroes!   370
And the numberless unknown heroes equal to the greatest
    heroes known!

19

This is the meal equally set, this the meat for natural hunger,
It is for the wicked just the same as the righteous, I make
    appointments with all,
I will not have a single person slighted or left away,
The kept-woman, sponger, thief, are hereby invited,   375
The heavy-lipp'd slave is invited, the venerealee[29] is invited;
There shall be no difference between them and the rest.

This is the press of a bashful hand, this the float and odor of
    hair,
This the touch of my lips to yours, this the murmur of
    yearning,
This the far-off depth and height reflecting my own face,   380
This the thoughtful merge of myself, and the outlet again.

Do you guess I have some intricate purpose?
Well I have, for the Fourth-month[30] showers have, and the
    mica on the side of a rock has.

Do you take it I would astonish?
Does the daylight astonish? does the early redstart twittering
    through the woods?   385
Do I astonish more than they?

This hour I tell things in confidence,
I might not tell everybody, but I will tell you.

20

Who goes there? hankering, gross, mystical, nude;
How is it I extract strength from the beef I eat?   390

What is a man anyhow? what am I? what are you?

All I mark as my own you shall offset it with your own,
Else it were time lost listening to me.

I do not snivel that snivel the world over,

---

29 Apparently, a Whitman neologism (the term appears in neither the *Oxford English Dictionary* nor
    Webster's) for a person suffering from venereal disease.
30 Quaker term for "April." See note 17.

That months are vacuums and the ground but wallow and
    filth.   395

Whimpering and truckling fold with powders for invalids,
    conformity goes to the fourth-remov'd,
I wear my hat as I please indoors or out.

Why should I pray? why should I venerate and be
    ceremonious?

Having pried through the strata, analyzed to a hair,
    counsel'd with doctors and calculated close,
I find no sweeter fat than sticks to my own bones.   400

In all people I see myself, none more and not one a barley-corn
    less,
And the good or bad I say of myself I say of them.

I know I am solid and sound,
To me the converging objects of the universe perpetually flow,
All are written to me, and I must get what the writing means.   405

I know I am deathless,
I know this orbit of mine cannot be swept by a carpenter's
    compass,
I know I shall not pass like a child's carlacue[31] cut with a
    burnt stick at night.

I know I am august,
I do not trouble my spirit to vindicate itself or be understood,   410
I see that the elementary laws never apologize,
(I reckon I behave no prouder than the level I plant my
    house by, after all.)

I exist as I am, that is enough,
If no other in the world be aware I sit content,
And if each and all be aware I sit content.   415

One world is aware and by far the largest to me, and that is
    myself,
And whether I come to my own to-day or in ten thousand
    or ten million years,
I can cheerfully take it now, or with equal cheerfulness I
    can wait.

My foothold is tenon'd and mortis'd in granite,

---

31 Variant of the more common "curlicue," a curled flourish, as in writing or decoration.

I laugh at what you call dissolution,   420
And I know the amplitude of time.

            21
I am the poet of the Body and I am the poet of the Soul,
The pleasures of heaven are with me and the pains of hell
     are with me,
The first I graft and increase upon myself, the latter I
     translate into a new tongue.

I am the poet of the woman the same as the man,   425
And I say it is as great to be a woman as to be a man,
And I say there is nothing greater than the mother of men.

I chant the chant of dilation or pride,
We have had ducking and deprecating about enough,
I show that size is only development.   430

Have you outstript the rest? are you the President?
It is a trifle, they will more than arrive there every one, and
     still pass on.

I am he that walks with the tender and growing night,
I call to the earth and sea half-held by the night.

Press close bare-bosom'd night—press close magnetic
     nourishing night!   435
Night of south winds—night of the large few stars!
Still nodding night—mad naked summer night.

Smile O voluptuous cool-breath'd earth!
Earth of the slumbering and liquid trees!
Earth of departed sunset—earth of the mountains misty-topt!   440
Earth of the vitreous pour of the full moon just tinged with
     blue!
Earth of shine and dark mottling the tide of the river!
Earth of the limpid gray of clouds brighter and clearer for
     my sake!
Far-swooping elbow'd earth—rich apple-blossom'd earth!
Smile, for your lover comes.   445

Prodigal, you have given me love—therefore I to you give
     love!
O unspeakable passionate love.

            22
You sea! I resign myself to you also—I guess what you mean,
I behold from the beach your crooked inviting fingers,

I believe you refuse to go back without feeling of me,   450
We must have a turn together, I undress, hurry me out of
    sight of the land,
Cushion me soft, rock me in billowy drowse,
Dash me with amorous wet, I can repay you.

Sea of stretch'd ground-swells,
Sea breathing broad and convulsive breaths,   455
Sea of the brine of life and of unshovell'd yet always-ready
    graves,
Howler and scooper of storms, capricious and dainty sea,
I am integral with you, I too am of one phase and of all phases.

Partaker of influx and efflux I, extoller of hate and conciliation,
Extoller of amies[32] and those that sleep in each others' arms.   460

I am he attesting sympathy,
(Shall I make my list of things in the house and skip the
    house that supports them?)

I am not the poet of goodness only, I do not decline to be
    the poet of wickedness also.

What blurt is this about virtue and about vice?
Evil propels me and reform of evil propels me, I stand
    indifferent,   465
My gait is no fault-finder's or rejecter's gait,
I moisten the roots of all that has grown.

Did you fear some scrofula out of the unflagging pregnancy?
Did you guess the celestial laws are yet to be work'd over
    and rectified?

I find one side a balance and the antipodal side a balance,   470
Soft doctrine as steady help as stable doctrine,
Thoughts and deeds of the present our rouse and early start.

This minute that comes to me over the past decillions,[33]
There is no better than it and now.

What behaved well in the past or behaves well to-day is not
    such a wonder,   475

---

32 French for "friends" – a classic instance of the banal use of foreign borrowings that Randall Jarrell
    bemoans in Whitman (see **p. 89**).
33 A million to the tenth power. Whitman is pressing language to its quantitative limits to express his
    exuberant sense of the individual's place in the universe. In l. 799 he reduces the geometric scale a
    bit to quintillions.

The wonder is always and always how there can be a mean
    man or an infidel.

23

Endless unfolding of words of ages!
And mine a word of the modern, the word En-Masse.[34]

A word of the faith that never balks,
Here or henceforward it is all the same to me, I accept Time
    absolutely.   480

It alone is without flaw, it alone rounds and completes all,
That mystic baffling wonder alone completes all.

I accept Reality and dare not question it,
Materialism first and last imbuing.

Hurrah for positive science![35] long live exact demonstration!   485
Fetch stonecrop mixt with cedar and branches of lilac,
This is the lexicographer, this the chemist, this made a
    grammar of the old cartouches,
These mariners put the ship through dangerous unknown seas,
This is the geologist, this works with the scalpel, and this is
    a mathematician.

Gentlemen, to you the first honors always!   490
Your facts are useful, and yet they are not my dwelling,
I but enter by them to an area of my dwelling.

Less the reminders of properties told my words,
And more the reminders they of life untold, and of freedom
    and extrication,
And make short account of neuters and geldings, and favor
    men and women fully equipt,   495
And beat the gong of revolt, and stop with fugitives and
    them that plot and conspire.

24

Walt Whitman, a kosmos, of Manhattan the son,[36]
Turbulent, fleshy, sensual, eating, drinking and breeding,

---

34 The term, borrowed from the French, was of recent origin (first English usage, according to the
   Oxford English Dicitonary, 1802), although Whitman more likely is referring to it as a recent
   sociological rather than etymological phenomenon. He favored the word, using it most famously in
   his signature poem "One's-Self I Sing" to denote not just a social totality but democracy.
35 This exclamatory approval of science may surprise those who expect a lyric poet such as Whitman
   to take the hostile view of the English Romantic poet William Wordsworth (1770–1850): "We
   murder to dissect." Whitman read broadly in the 1840s and 1850s in the popularized literature of
   science and incorporated strands of the discourses of astronomy, cosmology, geology, and arche-
   ology in "Song of Myself."
36 An adopted son, of course, since he was born on Long Island and grew up and lived most of his pre-
   Leaves of Grass life in Brooklyn.

No sentimentalist, no stander above men and women or
    apart from them,
No more modest than immodest.   500

Unscrew the locks from the doors!
Unscrew the doors themselves from their jambs!

Whoever degrades another degrades me,
And whatever is done or said returns at last to me.

Through me the afflatus[37] surging and surging, through me
    the current and index.   505

I speak the pass-word primeval, I give the sign of democracy,
By God! I will accept nothing which all cannot have their
    counterpart of on the same terms.

Through me many long dumb voices,
Voices of the interminable generations of prisoners and slaves,
Voices of the diseas'd and despairing and of thieves and
    dwarfs,   510
Voices of cycles of preparation and accretion,
And of the threads that connect the stars, and of wombs and
    of the father-stuff,
And of the rights of them the others are down upon,
Of the deform'd, trivial, flat, foolish, despised,
Fog in the air, beetles rolling balls of dung.   515

Through me forbidden voices,
Voices of sexes and lusts, voices veil'd and I remove the veil,
Voices indecent by me clarified and transfigur'd.

I do not press my fingers across my mouth,
I keep as delicate around the bowels as around the head and
    heart,   520
Copulation is no more rank to me than death is.

I believe in the flesh and the appetites,
Seeing, hearing, feeling, are miracles, and each part and tag
    of me is a miracle.

Divine am I inside and out, and I make holy whatever I
    touch or am touch'd from,
The scent of these arm-pits aroma finer than prayer,   525
This head more than churches, bibles, and all the creeds.

---

37 From the Latin *afflatus* for "blown or breathed on," here used to suggest an act of supernal
inflation, as in inspiration.

If I worship one thing more than another it shall be the
    spread of my own body, or any part of it,
Translucent mould of me it shall be you!
Shaded ledges and rests it shall be you!
Firm masculine colter[38] it shall be you!   530
Whatever goes to the tilth of me it shall be you!
You my rich blood! your milky stream pale strippings of
    my life!
Breast that presses against other breasts it shall be you!
My brain it shall be your occult convolutions!
Root of wash'd sweet-flag![39] timorous pond-snipe! nest of
    guarded duplicate eggs! it shall be you!   535
Mix'd tussled hay of head, beard, brawn, it shall be you!
Trickling sap of maple, fibre of manly wheat, it shall be you!
Sun so generous it shall be you!
Vapors lighting and shading my face it shall be you!
You sweaty brooks and dews it shall be you!   540
Winds whose soft-tickling genitals rub against me it shall be you!
Broad muscular fields, branches of live oak, loving lounger
    in my winding paths, it shall be you!
Hands I have taken, face I have kiss'd, mortal I have ever
    touch'd, it shall be you.

I dote on myself, there is that lot of me and all so luscious,
Each moment and whatever happens thrills me with joy,   545
I cannot tell how my ankles bend, nor whence the cause of
    my faintest wish,
Nor the cause of the friendship I emit, nor the cause of the
    friendship I take again.

That I walk up my stoop, I pause to consider if it really be,
A morning-glory[40] at my window satisfies me more than the
    metaphysics of books.

To behold the day-break!   550
The little light fades the immense and diaphanous shadows,
The air tastes good to my palate.

Hefts of the moving world at innocent gambols silently
    rising freshly exuding,
Scooting obliquely high and low.

Something I cannot see puts upward libidinous prongs,   555
Seas of bright juice suffuse heaven.

---

38 A cutting tool, such as a knife, attached to the beam of a plow; here used phallically.
39 A synonym for "calamus," a swamp plant Whitman also favors for its phallic shape.
40 A climbing plant whose flowers open early in the morning.

The earth by the sky staid with, the daily close of their
    junction,
The heav'd challenge from the east that moment over my head,
The mocking taunt, See then whether you shall be master!

25

Dazzling and tremendous how quick the sun-rise would kill
    me,   560
If I could not now and always send sun-rise out of me.

We also ascend dazzling and tremendous as the sun,
We found our own O my soul in the calm and cool of the
    day-break.

My voice goes after what my eyes cannot reach,
With the twirl of my tongue I encompass worlds and
    volumes of worlds.   565

Speech is the twin of my vision, it is unequal to measure itself,
It provokes me forever, it says sarcastically,
Walt you contain enough, why don't you let it out then?

Come now I will not be tantalized, you conceive too much
    of articulation,
Do you not know O speech how the buds beneath you are
    folded?   570
Waiting in gloom, protected by frost,
The dirt receding before my prophetical screams,
I underlying causes to balance them at last,
My knowledge my live parts, it keeping tally with the
    meaning of all things,
Happiness, (which whoever hears me let him or her set out
    in search of this day.)   575

My final merit I refuse you, I refuse putting from me what I
    really am,
Encompass worlds, but never try to encompass me,
I crowd your sleekest and best by simply looking toward you.

Writing and talk do not prove me,
I carry the plenum of proof and every thing else in my face,   580
With the hush of my lips I wholly confound the skeptic.

26

Now I will do nothing but listen,
To accrue what I hear into this song, to let sounds contribute
    toward it.

I hear bravuras of birds, bustle of growing wheat, gossip of
    flames, clack of sticks cooking my meals,
I hear the sound I love, the sound of the human voice,   585
I hear all sounds running together, combined, fused or
    following,
Sounds of the city and sounds out of the city, sounds of the
    day and night,
Talkative young ones to those that like them, the loud laugh
    of work-people at their meals,
The angry base of disjointed friendship, the faint tones of
    the sick,
The judge with hands tight to the desk, his pallid lips
    pronouncing a death-sentence,   590
The heave'e'yo of stevedores unlading ships by the wharves,
    the refrain of the anchor-lifters,
The ring of alarm-bells, the cry of fire, the whirr of swift-streaking
    engines and hose-carts with premonitory
    tinkles and color'd lights,
The steam-whistle, the solid roll of the train of approaching
    cars,
The slow march play'd at the head of the association
    marching two and two,
(They go to guard some corpse, the flag-tops are draped
    with black muslin.)   595

I hear the violoncello, ('tis the young man's heart's complaint,)
I hear the key'd cornet, it glides quickly in through my ears,
It shakes mad-sweet pangs through my belly and breast.

I hear the chorus, it is a grand opera,
Ah this indeed is music – this suits me.   600

A tenor large and fresh as the creation fills me,
The orbic flex of his mouth is pouring and filling me full.

I hear the train'd soprano (what work with hers is this?)
The orchestra whirls me wider than Uranus flies,
It wrenches such ardors from me I did not know I possess'd
    them,   605
It sails me, I dab with bare feet, they are lick'd by the
    indolent waves,
I am cut by bitter and angry hail, I lose my breath,
Steep'd amid honey'd morphine, my windpipe throttled in
    fakes[41] of death,
At length let up again to feel the puzzle of puzzles,
And that we call Being.   610

---

41 Coils, as of rope.

27

To be in any form, what is that?
(Round and round we go, all of us, and ever come back thither,)
If nothing lay more develop'd the quahaug in its callous
    shell were enough.

Mine is no callous shell,
I have instant conductors all over me whether I pass or stop,   615
They seize every object and lead it harmlessly through me.

I merely stir, press, feel with my fingers, and am happy,
To touch my person to some one else's is about as much as I
    can stand.

28

Is this then a touch? quivering me to a new identity,
Flames and ether making a rush for my veins,   620
Treacherous tip of me reaching and crowding to help them,
My flesh and blood playing out lightning to strike what is
    hardly different from myself,
On all sides prurient provokers stiffening my limbs,
Straining the udder of my heart for its withheld drip,
Behaving licentious toward me, taking no denial,   625
Depriving me of my best as for a purpose,
Unbuttoning my clothes, holding me by the bare waist,
Deluding my confusion with the calm of the sunlight and
    pasture-fields,
Immodestly sliding the fellow-senses away,
They bribed to swap off with touch and go and graze at the
    edges of me,   630
No consideration, no regard for my draining strength or my
    anger,
Fetching the rest of the herd around to enjoy them a while,
Then all uniting to stand on a headland and worry me.

The sentries desert every other part of me,
They have left me helpless to a red marauder,   635
They all come to the headland to witness and assist against me.

I am given up by traitors,
I talk wildly, I have lost my wits, I and nobody else am the
    greatest traitor,
I went myself first to the headland, my own hands carried
    me there.

You villain touch! what are you doing? my breath is tight in
    its throat,   640
Unclench your floodgates, you are too much for me.

29

Blind loving wrestling touch, sheath'd hooded sharp-tooth'd
    touch!
Did it make you ache so, leaving me?

Parting track'd by arriving, perpetual payment of perpetual
    loan,
Rich showering rain, and recompense richer afterward.   645

Sprouts take and accumulate, stand by the curb prolific and
    vital,
Landscapes projected masculine, full-sized and golden.

30

All truths wait in all things,
They neither hasten their own delivery nor resist it,
They do not need the obstetric forceps of the surgeon,   650
The insignificant is as big to me as any,
(What is less or more than a touch?)

Logic and sermons never convince,
The damp of the night drives deeper into my soul.

(Only what proves itself to every man and woman is so,   655
Only what nobody denies is so.)

A minute and a drop of me settle my brain,
I believe the soggy clods shall become lovers and lamps,
And a compend of compends is the meat of a man or woman,
And a summit and flower there is the feeling they have for
    each other,   660
And they are to branch boundlessly out of that lesson until
    it becomes omnific,[42]
And until one and all shall delight us, and we them.

31

I believe a leaf of grass is no less than the journey-work of
    the stars,
And the pismire[43] is equally perfect, and a grain of sand, and
    the egg of the wren,
And the tree-toad is a chef-d'œuvre for the highest,   665
And the running blackberry would adorn the parlors of
    heaven,

---

42 In this stanza, as in other parts of the poem, Whitman is reaching for a vocabulary to express his
    exuberant sense of life based on a romantic faith in the powers of "positive science" (l. 485). A
    "compend of compends" (or, more conventionally, "compendium of compendiums") denotes an
    ultimate distillation or condensation; "omnific" denotes an all-creating capacity.
43 Antiquated term for "ant."

And the narrowest hinge in my hand puts to scorn all
    machinery,
And the cow crunching with depress'd head surpasses any
    statue,
And a mouse is miracle enough to stagger sextillions of
    infidels.

I find I incorporate gneiss, coal, long-threaded moss, fruits,
    grains, esculent roots,   670
And am stucco'd with quadrupeds and birds all over,
And have distanced what is behind me for good reasons,
But call any thing back again when I desire it.

In vain the speeding or shyness,
In vain the plutonic rocks send their old heat against my
    approach,   675
In vain the mastodon retreats beneath its own powder'd
    bones,
In vain objects stand leagues off and assume manifold shapes,
In vain the ocean settling in hollows and the great monsters
    lying low,
In vain the buzzard houses herself with the sky,
In vain the snake slides through the creepers and logs,   680
In vain the elk takes to the inner passes of the woods,
In vain the razor-bill'd auk sails far north to Labrador,
I follow quickly, I ascend to the nest in the fissure of the cliff.

        32
I think I could turn and live with animals, they are so placid
    and self-contain'd,
I stand and look at them long and long.   685

They do not sweat and whine about their condition,
They do not lie awake in the dark and weep for their sins,
They do not make me sick discussing their duty to God,
Not one is dissatisfied, not one is demented with the mania
    of owning things,
Not one kneels to another, nor to his kind that lived
    thousands of years ago,   690
Not one is respectable or unhappy over the whole earth.

So they show their relations to me and I accept them,
They bring me tokens of myself, they evince them plainly in
    their possession.

I wonder where they get those tokens,
Did I pass that way huge times ago and negligently drop
    them?   695

Myself moving forward then and now and forever,
Gathering and showing more always and with velocity,
Infinite and omnigenous,[44] and the like of these among them,
Not too exclusive toward the reachers of my remembrancers,
Picking out here one that I love, and now go with him on
        brotherly terms.   700

A gigantic beauty of a stallion, fresh and responsive to my
        caresses,
Head high in the forehead, wide between the ears,
Limbs glossy and supple, tail dusting the ground,
Eyes full of sparkling wickedness, ears finely cut, flexibly moving.

His nostrils dilate as my heels embrace him,   705
His well-built limbs tremble with pleasure as we race around
        and return.

I but use you a minute, then I resign you, stallion,
Why do I need your paces when I myself out-gallop them?
Even as I stand or sit passing faster than you.

        33[45]
Space and Time! now I see it is true, what I guess'd at,   710
What I guess'd when I loaf'd on the grass,
What I guess'd while I lay alone in my bed,
And again as I walk'd the beach under the paling stars of the
        morning.

My ties and ballasts leave me, my elbows rest in sea-gaps,
I skirt sierras, my palms cover continents,   715
I am afoot with my vision.

By the city's quadrangular houses—in log huts, camping
        with lumbermen,
Along the ruts of the turnpike, along the dry gulch and
        rivulet bed,
Weeding my onion-patch or hoeing rows of carrots and
        parsnips, crossing savannas, trailing in forests,
Prospecting, gold-digging, girdling the trees of a new
        purchase,   720
Scorch'd ankle-deep by the hot sand, hauling my boat down
        the shallow river,
Where the panther walks to and fro on a limb overhead,
        where the buck turns furiously at the hunter,

---

44 Of all kinds.
45 This section begins the poem's longest, broadest cataloging of America, expanding on that of
   section 15.

Where the rattlesnake suns his flabby length on a rock,
    where the otter is feeding on fish,
Where the alligator in his tough pimples sleeps by the bayou,
Where the black bear is searching for roots or honey, where
    the beaver pats the mud with his paddle-shaped tail;   725
Over the growing sugar, over the yellow-flower'd cotton
    plant, over the rice in its low moist field,
Over the sharp-peak'd farm house, with its scallop'd scum
    and slender shoots from the gutters,
Over the western persimmon,[46] over the long-leav'd corn, over
    the delicate blue-flower flax,
Over the white and brown buckwheat, a hummer and
    buzzer there with the rest,
Over the dusky green of the rye as it ripples and shades in
    the breeze;   730
Scaling mountains, pulling myself cautiously up, holding on
    by low scragged limbs,
Walking the path worn in the grass and beat through the
    leaves of the brush,
Where the quail is whistling betwixt the woods and the
    wheat-lot,
Where the bat flies in the Seventh-month eve, where the
    great goldbug drops through the dark,
Where the brook puts out of the roots of the old tree and
    flows to the meadow,   735
Where cattle stand and shake away flies with the tremulous
    shuddering of their hides,
Where the cheese-cloth hangs in the kitchen, where andirons
    straddle the hearth-slab, where cobwebs fall in festoons
    from the rafters;
Where trip-hammers crash, where the press is whirling its
    cylinders,
Wherever the human heart beats with terrible throes under
    its ribs,
Where the pear-shaped balloon is floating aloft, (floating in
    it myself and looking composedly down,)   740
Where the life-car[47] is drawn on the slip-noose, where the heat
    hatches pale-green eggs in the dented sand,
Where the she-whale swims with her calf and never forsakes it,
Where the steam-ship trails hind-ways its long pennant of
    smoke,
Where the fin of the shark cuts like a black chip out of the
    water,

---

46 A fruit tree native to North America whose name is of Algonquian origin. Captain John Smith took
    note of the astringent fruit during his residence in Virginia.
47 A watertight boat or chamber used in rescues to haul people through surf too unsettled for open
    boats.

Where the half-burn'd brig is riding on unknown currents,   745
Where shells grow to her slimy deck, where the dead are
    corrupting below;
Where the dense-starr'd flag[48] is borne at the head of the
    regiments,
Approaching Manhattan up by the long-stretching island,[49]
Under Niagara, the cataract falling like a veil over my
    countenance,
Upon a door-step, upon the horse-block[50] of hard wood
    outside,   750
Upon the race-course, or enjoying picnics or jigs or a good
    game of baseball,
At he-festivals, with blackguard gibes, ironical license, bull-dances,
    drinking, laughter,
At the cider-mill tasting the sweets of the brown mash,
    sucking the juice through a straw,
At apple-peelings wanting kisses for all the red fruit I find,
At musters, beach-parties, friendly bees, huskings,
    house-raisings;[51]   755
Where the mocking-bird sounds his delicious gurgles,
    cackles, screams, weeps,
Where the hay-rick stands in the barn-yard, where the dry-stalks
    are scatter'd, where the brood-cow waits in the hovel,
Where the bull advances to do his masculine work, where
    the stud to the mare, where the cock is treading the hen,
Where the heifers browse, where geese nip their food with
    short jerks,
Where sun-down shadows lengthen over the limitless and
    lonesome prairie,   760
Where herds of buffalo make a crawling spread of the square
    miles far and near,
Where the humming-bird shimmers, where the neck of the
    long-lived swan is curving and winding,
Where the laughing-gull scoots by the shore, where she
    laughs her near-human laugh,
Where bee-hives range on a gray bench in the garden half
    hid by the high weeds,
Where band-neck'd partridges roost in a ring on the ground
    with their heads out,   765
Where burial coaches enter the arch'd gates of a cemetery,
Where winter wolves bark amid wastes of snow and icicled trees,

---

48 The flag is presumably the Stars and Stripes, which had thirty-one stars when Whitman first
    published the poem in 1855, thirty-eight at the time of this final edition of the text in 1881, and
    forty-four at the time of his death in 1892.
49 Whitman presumably has in mind the approach to Manhattan Island from his native Long Island,
    appropriately named, which lies immediately to the east.
50 A platform, often of wood, used in mounting or dismounting from horse or vehicle.
51 All five of the nouns in this line denote gatherings of people, typically of a rural or pioneer nature.

Where the yellow-crown'd heron comes to the edge of the
    marsh at night and feeds upon small crabs,
Where the splash of swimmers and divers cools the warm
    noon,
Where the katy-did[52] works her chromatic reed on the walnut-tree
    over the well,   770
Through patches of citrons and cucumbers with silver-wired
    leaves,
Through the salt-lick or orange glade, or under conical firs,[53]
Through the gymnasium, through the curtain'd saloon,
    through the office or public hall;
Pleas'd with the native and pleas'd with the foreign, pleas'd
    with the new and old,
Pleas'd with the homely woman as well as the handsome,   775
Pleas'd with the quakeress as she puts off her bonnet and
    talks melodiously,
Pleas'd with the tune of the choir of the whitewash'd
    church,
Pleas'd with the earnest words of the sweating Methodist
    preacher, impress'd seriously at the camp-meeting;
Looking in at the shop-windows of Broadway the whole
    forenoon, flatting the flesh of my nose on the thick
    plate glass,
Wandering the same afternoon with my face turn'd up to
    the clouds, or down a lane or along the beach,   780
My right and left arms round the sides of two friends, and I
    in the middle;
Coming home with the silent and dark-cheek'd bush-boy,
    (behind me he rides at the drape of the day,)
Far from the settlements studying the print of animals' feet,
    or the moccasin print,
By the cot in the hospital reaching lemonade to a feverish
    patient,
Nigh the coffin'd corpse when all is still, examining with a
    candle;   785
Voyaging to every port to dicker[54] and adventure,
Hurrying with the modern crowd as eager and fickle as any,
Hot toward one I hate, ready in my madness to knife him,
Solitary at midnight in my back yard, my thoughts gone
    from me a long while,
Walking the old hills of Judæa with the beautiful gentle God
    by my side,   790
Speeding through space, speeding through heaven and the stars,

---

52 Alternative spelling of "katydid," a common, green, long-horned grasshopper.
53 Three remarkably different ecological zones, designed to convey the breadth and diversity of the
   American landscape.
54 A colloquial term meaning "to trade" or "to bargain."

Speeding amid the seven satellites and the broad ring, and
    the diameter of eighty thousand miles,
Speeding with tail'd meteors, throwing fire-balls like the rest,
Carrying the crescent child that carries its own full mother
    in its belly,
Storming, enjoying, planning, loving, cautioning,   795
Backing and filling, appearing and disappearing,
I tread day and night such roads.

I visit the orchards of spheres and look at the product,
And look at quintillions[55] ripen'd and look at quintillions green.

I fly those flights of a fluid and swallowing soul,   800
My course runs below the soundings of plummets.

I help myself to material and immaterial,
No guard can shut me off, no law prevent me.

I anchor my ship for a little while only,
My messengers continually cruise away or bring their returns
    to me.   805

I go hunting polar furs and the seal, leaping chasms with a
    pike-pointed staff, clinging to topples of brittle and blue.

I ascend to the foretruck,
I take my place late at night in the crow's-nest,
We sail the arctic sea, it is plenty light enough,
Through the clear atmosphere I stretch around on the
    wonderful beauty,   810
The enormous masses of ice pass me and I pass them, the
    scenery is plain in all directions,
The white-topt mountains show in the distance, I fling out
    my fancies toward them,
We are approaching some great battle-field in which we are
    soon to be engaged,
We pass the colossal outposts of the encampment, we pass
    with still feet and caution,
Or we are entering by the suburbs some vast and ruin'd city,   815
The blocks and fallen architecture more than all the living
    cities of the globe.

I am a free companion, I bivouac by invading watchfires,
I turn the bridegroom out of bed and stay with the bride
    myself,

---

55 A million to the third power. See note 33.

I tighten her all night to my thighs and lips.

My voice is the wife's voice, the screech by the rail of the
    stairs,   820
They fetch my man's body up dripping and drown'd.

I understand the large hearts of heroes,
The courage of present times and all times,
How the skipper saw the crowded and rudderless wreck of
    the steam-ship,[56] and Death chasing it up and down the
    storm,
How he knuckled tight and gave not back an inch, and was
    faithful of days and faithful of nights,   825
And chalk'd in large letters on a board, *Be of good
    cheer, we will not desert you;*
How he follow'd with them and tack'd with them three
    days and would not give it up,
How he saved the drifting company at last,
How the lank loose-gown'd women look'd when boated
    from the side of their prepared graves,
How the silent old-faced infants and the lifted sick, and the
    sharp-lipp'd unshaved men   830
All this I swallow, it tastes good, I like it well, it becomes
    mine,
I am the man, I suffer'd, I was there.

The disdain and calmness of martyrs,
The mother of old, condemn'd for a witch, burnt with dry
    wood, her children gazing on,
The hounded slave that flags in the race, leans by the fence,
    blowing, cover'd with sweat,   835
The twinges that sting like needles his legs and neck, the
    murderous buckshot and the bullets,
All these I feel or am.

I am the hounded slave, I wince at the bite of the dogs,
Hell and despair are upon me, crack and again crack the
    marksmen,
I clutch the rails of the fence, my gore dribs, thinn'd with
    the ooze of my skin,   840
I fall on the weeds and stones,
The riders spur their unwilling horses, haul close,
Taunt my dizzy ears and beat me violently over the head
    with whip-stocks.

---

56 Wrecks of steamships were common in the nineteenth century and received press coverage comparable to media coverage today of airplane crashes. This episode is based on the January 1854
sinking of the *San Francisco*, caught in a storm shortly after embarking for South America from
New York City, with all hands lost.

Agonies are one of my changes of garments,
I do not ask the wounded person how he feels, I myself
  become the wounded person,   845
My hurts turn livid upon me as I lean on a cane and observe.

I am the mash'd fireman with breast-bone broken,
Tumbling walls buried me in their debris,
Heat and smoke I inspired, I heard the yelling shouts of my
  comrades,
I heard the distant click of their picks and shovels,   850
They have clear'd the beams away, they tenderly lift me forth.

I lie in the night air in my red shirt, the pervading hush is
  for my sake,
Painless after all I lie exhausted but not so unhappy,
White and beautiful are the faces around me, the heads are
  bared of their fire-caps,
The kneeling crowd fades with the light of the torches.   855

Distant and dead resuscitate,
They show as the dial or move as the hands of me, I am the
  clock myself.

I am an old artillerist, I tell of my fort's bombardment,
I am there again.

Again the long roll of the drummers,   860
Again the attacking cannon, mortars,
Again to my listening ears the cannon responsive.

I take part, I see and hear the whole,
The cries, curses, roar, the plaudits for well-aim'd shots,
The ambulanza[57] slowly passing trailing its red drip,   865
Workmen searching after damages, making indispensable
  repairs,
The fall of grenades through the rent roof, the fan-shaped
  explosion,
The whizz of limbs, heads, stone, wood, iron, high in the air.

Again gurgles the mouth of my dying general, he furiously
  waves with his hand,
He gasps through the clot *Mind not me—mind—the*
  entrenchments.   870

        34
Now I tell what I knew in Texas in my early youth,

---

57 Whitman's mistaken Spanish for "ambulance." On his bombastic use of foreign languages, again
  see the comment by Randall Jarrell (p. 89).

(I tell not the fall of Alamo,[58]
Not one escaped to tell the fall of Alamo,
The hundred and fifty are dumb yet at Alamo,)
'Tis the tale of the murder in cold blood of four hundred
    and twelve young men.   875

Retreating they had form'd in a hollow square with their
    baggage for breastworks,
Nine hundred lives out of the surrounding enemy's, nine
    times their number, was the price they took in advance,
Their colonel was wounded and their ammunition gone,
They treated for an honorable capitulation, receiv'd writing
    and seal, gave up their arms and march'd back prisoners
    of war.

They were the glory of the race of rangers,   880
Matchless with horse, rifle, song, supper, courtship,
Large, turbulent, generous, handsome, proud, and
    affectionate,
Bearded, sunburnt, drest in the free costume of hunters,
Not a single one over thirty years of age.

The second First-day[59] morning they were brought out in
    squads and massacred, it was beautiful early summer,   885
The work commenced about five o'clock and was over by
    eight.

None obey'd the command to kneel,
Some made a mad and helpless rush, some stood stark and
    straight,
A few fell at once, shot in the temple or heart, the living and
    dead lay together,
The maim'd and mangled dug in the dirt, the new-comers
    saw them there,   890
Some half-kill'd attempted to crawl away,
These were despatch'd with bayonets or batter'd with the
    blunts of muskets,
A youth not seventeen years old seiz'd his assassin till two
    more came to release him,
The three were all torn and cover'd with the boy's blood.

At eleven o'clock began the burning of the bodies;   895
That is the tale of the murder of the four hundred and
    twelve young men.

---

58 The battle is that of Goliad (27 March 1836), which took place three weeks after the Alamo and
    which likewise ended in the massacre of American troops by Mexican, though in this instance after
    an arranged truce.
59 Quaker term for "Sunday." See note 17.

35⁶⁰

Would you hear of an old-time sea-fight?
Would you learn who won by the light of the moon and stars?
List to the yarn, as my grandmother's father the sailor told
   it to me.

Our foe was no skulk in his ship I tell you, (said he,⁶¹)   900
His was the surly English pluck, and there is no tougher or
   truer, and never was, and never will be;
Along the lower'd eve he came horribly raking us.

We closed with him, the yards entangled, the cannon touch'd,
My captain lash'd fast with his own hands.

We had receiv'd some eighteen pound shots under the water,   905
On our lower-gun-deck two large pieces had burst at the
   first fire, killing all around and blowing up overhead.

Fighting at sun-down, fighting at dark,
Ten o'clock at night, the full moon well up, our leaks on the
   gain, and five feet of water reported,
The master-at-arms loosing the prisoners confined in the
   after-hold to give them a chance for themselves.

The transit to and from the magazine is now stopt by the
   sentinels,   910
They see so many strange faces they do not know whom to
   trust.

Our frigate takes fire,
The other asks if we demand quarter?
If our colors are struck and the fighting done?

Now I laugh content, for I hear the voice of my little captain,   915
We have not struck, he composedly cries, *we have just begun our
   part of the fighting.*

Only three guns are in use,
One is directed by the captain himself against the enemy's
   mainmast,
Two well serv'd with grape and canister silence his musketry
   and clear his decks.

---

60 This section and the next recount the legendary 23 September 1779 naval battle in the American
    War of Independence off the coast of Yorkshire between John Paul Jones's *Bonhomme Richard* and
    the British *Serapis*.
61 The narration switches here from the voice of the unnamed "I" to that of his great-grandfather.
    That switch, signaled by the parenthetical "said he," was added to the poem only from the 1867
    edition on.

The tops alone second the fire of this little battery, especially
    the main-top,   920
They hold out bravely during the whole of the action.

Not a moment's cease,
The leaks gain fast on the pumps, the fire eats toward the
    powder-magazine.

One of the pumps has been shot away, it is generally thought
    we are sinking.

Serene stands the little captain,   925
He is not hurried, his voice is neither high nor low,
His eyes give more light to us than our battle-lanterns.

Toward twelve there in the beams of the moon they
    surrender to us.

36

Stretch'd and still lies the midnight,
Two great hulls motionless on the breast of the darkness,   930
Our vessel riddled and slowly sinking, preparations to pass
    to the one we have conquer'd,
The captain on the quarter-deck coldly giving his orders
    through a countenance white as a sheet,
Near by the corpse of the child that serv'd in the cabin,
The dead face of an old salt with long white hair and
    carefully curl'd whiskers,
The flames spite of all that can be done flickering aloft and
    below,   935
The husky voices of the two or three officers yet fit for duty,
Formless stacks of bodies and bodies by themselves, dabs of
    flesh upon the masts and spars,
Cut of cordage, dangle of rigging, slight shock of the soothe
    of waves,
Black and impassive guns, litter of powder-parcels, strong
    scent,
A few large stars overhead, silent and mournful shining,   940
Delicate sniffs of sea-breeze, smells of sedgy grass and fields
    by the shore, death-messages given in charge to survivors,
The hiss of the surgeon's knife, the gnawing teeth of his saw,
Wheeze, cluck, swash of falling blood, short wild scream,
    and long, dull, tapering groan,
These so, these irretrievable.

37

You laggards there on guard! look to your arms!   945
In at the conquer'd doors they crowd! I am possess'd!

Embody all presences outlaw'd or suffering,
See myself in prison shaped like another man,
And feel the dull unintermitted pain.

For me the keepers of convicts shoulder their carbines and
    keep watch,   950
It is I let out in the morning and barr'd at night.

Not a mutineer walks handcuff'd to jail but I am handcuff'd
    to him and walk by his side,
(I am less the jolly one there, and more the silent one with
    sweat on my twitching lips.)

Not a youngster is taken for larceny but I go up too, and
    am tried and sentenced.

Not a cholera patient lies at the last gasp but I also lie at the
    last gasp,   955
My face is ash-color'd, my sinews gnarl, away from me
    people retreat.

Askers embody themselves in me and I am embodied in them,
I project my hat, sit shame-faced, and beg.

      38
Enough! enough! enough!
Somehow I have been stunn'd. Stand back!   960
Give me a little time beyond my cuff'd head, slumbers,
    dreams, gaping,
I discover myself on the verge of a usual mistake.

That I could forget the mockers and insults!
That I could forget the trickling tears and the blows of the
    bludgeons and hammers!
That I could look with a separate look on my own crucifixion
    and bloody crowning.   965

I remember now,
I resume the overstaid fraction,
The grave of rock multiplies what has been confided to it, or
    to any graves,
Corpses rise, gashes heal, fastenings roll from me.

I troop forth replenish'd with supreme power, one of an
    average unending procession,   970
Inland and sea-coast we go, and pass all boundary lines,
Our swift ordinances on their way over the whole earth,
The blossoms we wear in our hats the growth of thousands
    of years.

Eleves,[62] I salute you! come forward!
Continue your annotations, continue your questionings.   975

39

The friendly and flowing savage, who is he?
Is he waiting for civilization, or past it and mastering it?

Is he some Southwesterner rais'd out-doors? is he Kanadian?
Is he from the Mississippi country? Iowa, Oregon, California?
The mountains? prairie-life, bush-life? or sailor from the sea?   980

Wherever he goes men and women accept and desire him,
They desire he should like them, touch them, speak to them,
    stay with them.

Behavior lawless as snow-flakes, words simple as grass,
    uncomb'd head, laughter, and naivetè,
Slow-stepping feet, common features, common modes and
    emanations,
They descend in new forms from the tips of his fingers,   985
They are wafted with the odor of his body or breath, they
    fly out of the glance of his eyes.

40

Flaunt of the sunshine I need not your bask—lie over!
You light surfaces only, I force surfaces and depths also.

Earth! you seem to look for something at my hands,
Say, old top-knot,[63] what do you want?   990

Man or woman, I might tell how I like you, but cannot,
And might tell what it is in me and what it is in you, but
    cannot,
And might tell that pining I have, that pulse of my nights
    and days.

Behold, I do not give lectures or a little charity,
When I give I give myself.   995

You there, impotent, loose in the knees,
Open your scarf'd chops till I blow grit within you,
Spread your palms and lift the flaps of your pockets,
I am not to be denied, I compel, I have stores plenty and
    to spare,
And any thing I have I bestow.   1000

---

62 Another of Whitman's borrowings, the French word for "students," although he may mean it in a
    more elevated sense.
63 Crest or tuft of hair, as on top of the skull, or of feathers, as on a bird.

I do not ask who you are, that is not important to me,
You can do nothing and be nothing but what I will
    infold you.

To cotton-field drudge or cleaner of privies I lean,
On his right cheek I put the family kiss,
And in my soul I swear I never will deny him.   1005

On women fit for conception I start bigger and nimbler babes,
(This day I am jetting[64] the stuff of far more arrogant republics.)

To any one dying, thither I speed and twist the knob of the
    door,
Turn the bed-clothes toward the foot of the bed,
Let the physician and the priest go home.   1010

I seize the descending man and raise him with resistless will,
O despairer, here is my neck,
By God, you shall not go down! hang your whole weight
    upon me.

I dilate you with tremendous breath, I buoy you up,
Every room of the house do I fill with an arm'd force,   1015
Lovers of me, bafflers of graves.

Sleep—I and they keep guard all night,
Not doubt, not decease shall dare to lay finger upon you,
I have embraced you, and henceforth possess you to myself,
And when you rise in the morning you will find what I tell
    you is so.   1020

                    41
I am he bringing help for the sick as they pant on their backs,
And for strong upright men I bring yet more needed help.

I heard what was said of the universe,
Heard it and heard it of several thousand years;
It is middling well as far as it goes—but is that all?   1025

Magnifying and applying come I,
Outbidding at the start the old cautious hucksters,
Taking myself the exact dimensions of Jehovah,[65]

---

64 That is, ejaculating – not a term or activity likely to endear this poem to its Victorian audience.
65 Beginning with Jehovah (a transliteration from the Hebrew for the four-letter name of the Biblical
    deity), Whitman lists a litany of the world's gods, monotheistic and pagan: Kronos, the greatest of
    the mythological Titans; Zeus, his son and successor; Hercules, a lesser, more anthropomorphic
    deity fabled for his strength; Osiris, Egyptian god of the underworld; Isis, Egyptian goddess of
    fertility; Belus, fabled king of Assyria; Brahma, the Hindu supreme soul; Buddha, the supreme
    philosopher of the Asian religion he founded; Manito, Algonquian god of nature; Allah, deity of
    Islam; Odin, god of war in Norse mythology; Mexitli, Aztec god of war.

Lithographing Kronos, Zeus his son, and Hercules his grandson,
Buying drafts of Osiris, Isis, Belus, Brahma, Buddha,   1030
In my portfolio placing Manito loose, Allah on a leaf, the
    crucifix engraved,
With Odin and the hideous-faced Mexitli and every idol
    and image,
Taking them all for what they are worth and not a cent more,
Admitting they were alive and did the work of their days,
(They bore mites as for unfledg'd birds who have now to
    rise and fly and sing for themselves,)   1035
Accepting the rough deific sketches to fill out better in myself,
    bestowing them freely on each man and woman I see,
Discovering as much or more in a framer framing a house,
Putting higher claims for him there with his roll'd-up sleeves
    driving the mallet and chisel,
Not objecting to special revelations, considering a curl of
    smoke or a hair on the back of my hand just as curious as any
    revelation,
Lads ahold of fire-engines and hook-and-ladder ropes no less
    to me than the gods of the antique wars,   1040
Minding their voices peal through the crash of destruction,
Their brawny limbs passing safe over charr'd laths, their
    white foreheads whole and unhurt out of the flames;
By the mechanic's wife with her babe at her nipple interceding
    for every person born,
Three scythes at harvest whizzing in a row from three lusty
    angels with shirts bagg'd out at their waists,
The snag-tooth'd hostler[66] with red hair redeeming sins past
    and to come,   1045
Selling all he possesses, traveling on foot to fee lawyers for
    his brother and sit by him while he is tried for forgery;
What was strewn in the amplest strewing the square rod
    about me, and not filling the square rod then,
The bull and the bug never worshipp'd half enough,
Dung and dirt more admirable than was dream'd,
The supernatural of no account, myself waiting my time to
    be one of the supremes,   1050
The day getting ready for me when I shall do as much good
    as the best, and be as prodigious;
By my life-lumps![67] becoming already a creator,
Putting myself here and now to the ambush'd womb of the
    shadows.

---

66 A keeper of horses at an inn, often a person of low socioeconomic standing.
67 A term borrowed from the popular mid-century pseudo-science of phrenology, whose practitioners
   mapped the terrain of the skull, lumps and all, which they deciphered as markers of human
   psychology and personality. A true believer, Whitman had sat in 1849 for such an examination at
   the offices of Fowlers and Wells, who published in this field and served Whitman in 1855 as
   distributors of the first edition of *Leaves of Grass*.

42

A call in the midst of the crowd,
My own voice, orotund sweeping and final.   1055

Come my children,
Come my boys and girls, my women, household and
    intimates,
Now the performer launches his nerve, he has pass'd his
    prelude on the reeds within.

Easily written loose-finger'd chords—I feel the thrum of
    your climax and close.

My head slues round on my neck,   1060
Music rolls, but not from the organ,
Folks are around me, but they are no household of mine.

Ever the hard unsunk ground,
Ever the eaters and drinkers, ever the upward and downward
    sun, ever the air and the ceaseless tides,
Ever myself and my neighbors, refreshing, wicked, real,   1065
Ever the old inexplicable query, ever that thorn'd thumb,
    that breath of itches and thirsts,
Ever the vexer's *hoot! hoot!* till we find where the sly one
    hides and bring him forth,
Ever love, ever the sobbing liquid of life,
Ever the bandage under the chin, ever the trestles of death.

Here and there with dimes on the eyes walking,   1070
To feed the greed of the belly the brains liberally spooning,
Tickets buying, taking, selling, but in to the feast never once
    going,
Many sweating, ploughing, thrashing, and then the chaff for
    payment receiving,
A few idly owning, and they the wheat continually claiming.

This is the city and I am one of the citizens,   1075
Whatever interests the rest interests me, politics, wars,
    markets, newspapers, schools,
The mayor and councils, banks, tariffs, steamships, factories,
    stocks, stores, real estate and personal estate.

The little plentiful manikins skipping around in collars and
    tail'd coats,
I am aware who they are, (they are positively not worms or
    fleas,)
I acknowledge the duplicates of myself, the weakest and
    shallowest is deathless with me,   1080
What I do and say the same waits for them,
Every thought that flounders in me the same flounders in
    them.

I know perfectly well my own egotism,
Know my omnivorous lines and must not write any less,
And would fetch you whoever you are flush with myself.   1085

Not words of routine this song of mine,
But abruptly to question, to leap beyond yet nearer bring;
This printed and bound book—but the printer and the
    printing-office boy?
The well-taken photographs—but your wife or friend close
    and solid in your arms?
The black ship mail'd with iron, her mighty guns in her
    turrets—but the pluck of the captain and engineers?   1090
In the houses the dishes and fare and furniture—but the
    host and hostess, and the look out of their eyes?
The sky up there—yet here or next door, or across the way?
The saints and sages in history—but you yourself?
Sermons, creeds, theology—but the fathomless human brain,
And what is reason? and what is love? and what is life?   1095

43

I do not despise you priests, all time, the world over,
My faith is the greatest of faiths and the least of faiths,
Enclosing worship ancient and modern and all between
    ancient and modern,
Believing I shall come again upon the earth after five
    thousand years,
Waiting responses from oracles, honoring the gods, saluting
    the sun,   1100
Making a fetich of the first rock or stump, powowing with
    sticks in the circle of obis,
Helping the llama or brahmin as he trims the lamps of the idols,
Dancing yet through the streets in a phallic procession, rapt
    and austere in the woods a gymnosophist,[68]
Drinking mead from the skull-cup, to Shastas and Vedas[69]
    admirant, minding the Koran,
Walking the teokallis,[70] spotted with gore from the stone and
    knife, beating the serpent-skin drum,   1105
Accepting the Gospels, accepting him that was crucified,
    knowing assuredly that he is divine,
To the mass kneeling or the puritan's prayer rising, or sitting
    patiently in a pew,
Ranting and frothing in my insane crisis, or waiting dead-like
    till my spirit arouses me,

---

68 Member of an ancient Hindu ascetic order, who often went naked.
69 Shastas (more correctly, "shastras" or "sastras") and Vedas are sacred scriptures of Hinduism.
70 Ancient temples of Mexico or Central America, usually built on the summit of a truncated
    pyramidal mound.

Looking forth on pavement and land, or outside of pavement
and land,
Belonging to the winders of the circuit of circuits.   1110

One of that centripetal and centrifugal gang I turn and talk
like a man leaving charges before a journey.

Down-hearted doubters dull and excluded,
Frivolous, sullen, moping, angry, affected, dishearten'd,
atheistical,
I know every one of you, I know the sea of torment, doubt,
despair and unbelief.

How the flukes splash!   1115
How they contort rapid as lightning, with spasms and spouts
of blood!

Be at peace bloody flukes of doubters and sullen mopers,
I take my place among you as much as among any,
The past is the push of you, me, all, precisely the same,
And what is yet untried and afterward is for you, me, all,
precisely the same.   1120

I do not know what is untried and afterward,
But I know it will in its turn prove sufficient, and cannot fail.

Each who passes is consider'd, each who stops is consider'd,
not a single one can it fail.

It cannot fail the young man who died and was buried,
Nor the young woman who died and was put by his side,   1125
Nor the little child that peep'd in at the door, and then drew
back and was never seen again,
Nor the old man who has lived without purpose, and feels it
with bitterness worse than gall,
Nor him in the poor house tubercled by rum and the bad
disorder,
Nor the numberless slaughter'd and wreck'd, nor the brutish
koboo[71] call'd the ordure of humanity,
Nor the sacs merely floating with open mouths for food to
slip in,   1130
Nor any thing in the earth, or down in the oldest graves of
the earth,
Nor any thing in the myriads of spheres, nor the myriads of
myriads that inhabit them,
Nor the present, nor the least wisp that is known.

71 A native of Sumatra.

44

It is time to explain myself—let us stand up.

What is known I strip away,   1135
I launch all men and women forward with me into the
    Unknown.

The clock indicates the moment—but what does eternity
    indicate?

We have thus far exhausted trillions of winters and summers,
There are trillions ahead, and trillions ahead of them.

Births have brought us richness and variety,   1140
And other births will bring us richness and variety.

I do not call one greater and one smaller,
That which fills its period and place is equal to any.

Were mankind murderous or jealous upon you, my brother,
    my sister?
I am sorry for you, they are not murderous or jealous upon me,   1145
All has been gentle with me, I keep no account with
    lamentation,
(What have I to do with lamentation?)

I am an acme of things accomplish'd, and I an encloser of
    things to be.

My feet strike an apex of the apices of the stairs,
On every step bunches of ages, and larger bunches between
    the steps,   1150
All below duly travel'd, and still I mount and mount.

Rise after rise bow the phantoms behind me,
Afar down I see the huge first Nothing, I know I was even
    there,
I waited unseen and always, and slept through the lethargic
    mist,
And took my time, and took no hurt from the fetid carbon.   1155

Long I was hugg'd close—long and long.

Immense have been the preparations for me,
Faithful and friendly the arms that have help'd me.

Cycles ferried my cradle, rowing and rowing like cheerful
    boatmen,
For room to me stars kept aside in their own rings,   1160
They sent influences to look after what was to hold me.

Before I was born out of my mother generations guided me,
My embryo has never been torpid, nothing could overlay it.

For it the nebula cohered to an orb,
The long slow strata piled to rest it on,   1165
Vast vegetables gave it sustenance,
Monstrous sauroids[72] transported it in their mouths and
    deposited it with care.

All forces have been steadily employ'd to complete and
    delight me,
Now on this spot I stand with my robust soul.

                45
O span of youth! ever-push'd elasticity!   1170
O manhood, balanced, florid and full.

My lovers suffocate me,
Crowding my lips, thick in the pores of my skin,
Jostling me through streets and public halls, coming naked
    to me at night,
Crying by day *Ahoy!* from the rocks of the river,
    swinging and chirping over my head,   1175
Calling my name from flower-beds, vines, tangled underbrush,
Lighting on every moment of my life,
Bussing my body with soft balsamic busses,[73]
Noiselessly passing handfuls out of their hearts and giving
    them to be mine.

Old age superbly rising! O welcome, ineffable grace of dying
    days!   1180

Every condition promulges not only itself, it promulges what
    grows after and out of itself,
And the dark hush promulges as much as any.

I open my scuttle[74] at night and see the far-sprinkled systems,
And all I see multiplied as high as I can cipher edge but the
    rim of the farther systems.

Wider and wider they spread, expanding, always expanding,   1185
Outward and outward and forever outward.

---

72 "Sauria" is a division of reptiles that comprises lizards, crocodiles, and various extinct species of
   elongated-limbed reptiles. The reference here is to the belief that the last carried their unhatched
   eggs in their mouths.
73 Busses are kisses. Whitman may be deploying a variation on the semantic distinction drawn by the
   English poet Robert Herrick (1591–1674): "we buss our wantons but our wives we kiss."
74 Whitman is presumably using the term in its uncommon meaning of an opening in the roof of a
   house sealed with a lid.

My sun has his sun and round him obediently wheels,
He joins with his partners a group of superior circuit,
And greater sets follow, making specks of the greatest inside
    them.

There is no stoppage and never can be stoppage,   1190
If I, you, and the worlds, and all beneath or upon their
    surfaces, were this moment reduced back to a pallid
    float, it would not avail in the long run,
We should surely bring up again where we now stand,
And surely go as much farther, and then farther and farther.

A few quadrillions of eras, a few octillions of cubic leagues,
    do not hazard the span or make it impatient,
They are but parts, any thing is but a part.   1195

See ever so far, there is limitless space outside of that,
Count ever so much, there is limitless time around that.

My rendezvous is appointed, it is certain,
The Lord will be there and wait till I come on perfect terms,
The great Camerado, the lover true for whom I pine will be
    there.   1200

        46
I know I have the best of time and space, and was never
    measured and never will be measured.

I tramp a perpetual journey, (come listen all!)
My signs are a rain-proof coat, good shoes, and a staff cut
    from the woods,
No friend of mine takes his ease in my chair,
I have no chair, no church, no philosophy,   1205
I lead no man to a dinner-table, library, exchange,
But each man and each woman of you I lead upon a knoll,
My left hand hooking you round the waist,
My right hand pointing to landscapes of continents and the
    public road.

Not I, not any one else can travel that road for you,   1210
You must travel it for yourself.

It is not far, it is within reach,
Perhaps you have been on it since you were born and did
    not know,
Perhaps it is everywhere on water and on land.

Shoulder your duds dear son, and I will mine, and let us
    hasten forth,   1215

Wonderful cities and free nations we shall fetch as we go.

If you tire, give me both burdens, and rest the chuff of your
    hand on my hip,
And in due time you shall repay the same service to me,
For after we start we never lie by again.

This day before dawn I ascended a hill and look'd at the
    crowded heaven,   1220
And I said to my spirit *When we become the enfolders of*
    those orbs, and the pleasure and knowledge of every thing in
    them, shall we be fill'd and satisfied then?
And my spirit said *No, we but level that lift to pass and*
    continue beyond.

You are also asking me questions and I hear you,
I answer that I cannot answer, you must find out for yourself.

Sit a while dear son,   1225
Here are biscuits to eat and here is milk to drink,
But as soon as you sleep and renew yourself in sweet
    clothes, I kiss you with a good-by kiss and open the
    gate for your egress hence.

Long enough have you dream'd contemptible dreams,
Now I wash the gum from your eyes,
You must habit yourself to the dazzle of the light and of
    every moment of your life.   1230

Long have you timidly waded holding a plank by the shore,
Now I will you to be a bold swimmer,
To jump off in the midst of the sea, rise again, nod to
    me, shout, and laughingly dash with your hair.

     47
I am the teacher of athletes,
He that by me spreads a wider breast than my own proves the
    width of my own,   1235
He most honors my style who learns under it to destroy the teacher.

The boy I love, the same becomes a man not through derived
    power, but in his own right,
Wicked rather than virtuous out of conformity or fear,
Fond of his sweetheart, relishing well his steak,
Unrequited love or a slight cutting him worse than sharp
    steel cuts,   1240
First-rate to ride, to fight, to hit the bull's eye, to sail a skiff,
    to sing a song or play on the banjo,

Preferring scars and the beard and faces pitted with small-pox
    over all latherers,
And those well-tann'd to those that keep out of the sun.

I teach straying from me, yet who can stray from me?
I follow you whoever you are from the present hour,   1245
My words itch at your ears till you understand them.

I do not say these things for a dollar or to fill up the time
    while I wait for a boat,
(It is you talking just as much as myself, I act as the tongue
    of you,
Tied in your mouth, in mine it begins to be loosen'd.)

I swear I will never again mention love or death inside a
    house,   1250
And I swear I will never translate myself at all, only to him
    or her who privately stays with me in the open air.

If you would understand me go to the heights or water-shore,
The nearest gnat is an explanation, and a drop or motion of
    waves a key,
The maul, the oar, the hand-saw, second my words.

No shutter'd room or school can commune with me,   1255
But roughs and little children better than they.

The young mechanic is closest to me, he knows me well,
The woodman that takes his axe and jug with him shall take
    me with him all day,
The farm-boy ploughing in the field feels good at the sound
    of my voice,
In vessels that sail my words sail, I go with fishermen and
    seamen and love them.   1260

The soldier camp'd or upon the march is mine,
On the night ere the pending battle many seek me, and I do
    not fail them,
On that solemn night (it may be their last) those that know
    me seek me.

My face rubs to the hunter's face when he lies down alone
    in his blanket,
The driver thinking of me does not mind the jolt of his wagon,   1265
The young mother and old mother comprehend me,
The girl and the wife rest the needle a moment and forget
    where they are,
They and all would resume what I have told them.

48

I have said that the soul is not more than the body,
And I have said that the body is not more than the soul,   1270
And nothing, not God, is greater to one than one's self is,
And whoever walks a furlong without sympathy walks to his
    own funeral drest in his shroud,
And I or you pocketless of a dime may purchase the pick of
    the earth,
And to glance with an eye or show a bean in its pod
    confounds the learning of all times,
And there is no trade or employment but the young man
    following it may become a hero,   1275
And there is no object so soft but it makes a hub for the
    wheel'd universe,
And I say to any man or woman, Let your soul stand cool
    and composed before a million universes.

And I say to mankind, Be not curious about God,
For I who am curious about each am not curious about God,
(No array of terms can say how much I am at peace about
    God and about death.)   1280

I hear and behold God in every object, yet understand God
    not in the least,
Nor do I understand who there can be more wonderful than
    myself.

Why should I wish to see God better than this day?
I see something of God each hour of the twenty-four, and
    each moment then,
In the faces of men and women I see God, and in my own
    face in the glass,   1285
I find letters from God dropt in the street, and every one is
    sign'd by God's name,
And I leave them where they are, for I know that
    wheresoe'er I go,
Others will punctually come for ever and ever.

49

And as to you Death, and you bitter hug of mortality, it is
    idle to try to alarm me.

To his work without flinching the accoucheur[75] comes,   1290
I see the elder-hand pressing receiving supporting,
I recline by the sills of the exquisite flexible doors,
And mark the outlet, and mark the relief and escape.

---

75 Obstetrician, or possibly midwife.

And as to you Corpse I think you are good manure, but
   that does not offend me,
I smell the white roses sweet-scented and growing,   1295
I reach to the leafy lips, I reach to the polish'd breasts of
   melons.

And as to you Life I reckon you are the leavings of many
   deaths,
(No doubt I have died myself ten thousand times before.)

I hear you whispering there O stars of heaven,
O suns—O grass of graves—O perpetual transfers and
   promotions,   1300
If you do not say any thing how can I say any thing?

Of the turbid pool that lies in the autumn forest,
Of the moon that descends the steeps of the soughing[76]
   twilight,
Toss, sparkles of day and dusk—toss on the black stems that
   decay in the muck,
Toss to the moaning gibberish of the dry limbs.   1305

I ascend from the moon, I ascend from the night,
I perceive that the ghastly glimmer is noonday sunbeams
   reflected,
And debouch to the steady and central from the offspring
   great or small.

      50
There is that in me—I do not know what it is—but I know
   it is in me.

Wrench'd and sweaty—calm and cool then my body becomes,   1310
   I sleep—I sleep long.

I do not know it—it is without name—it is a word unsaid,
It is not in any dictionary, utterance, symbol.

Something it swings on more than the earth I swing on,
To it the creation is the friend whose embracing awakes me.   1315

Perhaps I might tell more. Outlines! I plead for my brothers
   and sisters.

Do you see O my brothers and sisters?
It is not chaos or death—it is form, union, plan—it is eternal
   life—it is Happiness.

76 That is, making a moaning sound, more normally associated with the wind.

51

The past and present wilt—I have fill'd them, emptied them,
And proceed to fill my next fold of the future.   1320

Listener up there! what have you to confide to me?
Look in my face while I snuff the sidle of evening,
(Talk honestly, no one else hears you, and I stay only a
   minute longer.)

Do I contradict myself?
Very well then I contradict myself,   1325
(I am large, I contain multitudes.)

I concentrate toward them that are nigh, I wait on the
   door-slab.

Who has done his day's work? who will soonest be through
   with his supper?
Who wishes to walk with me?

Will you speak before I am gone? will you prove already
   too late?   1330

52

The spotted hawk swoops by and accuses me, he complains
   of my gab and my loitering.

I too am not a bit tamed, I too am untranslatable,
I sound my barbaric yawp[77] over the roofs of the world.

The last scud[78] of day holds back for me,
It flings my likeness after the rest and true as any on the
   shadow'd wilds,   1335
It coaxes me to the vapor and the dusk.

I depart as air, I shake my white[79] locks at the runaway sun,
I effuse my flesh in eddies, and drift it in lacy jags.

I bequeath myself to the dirt to grow from the grass I love,
If you want me again look for me under your boot-soles.   1340

---

77 For examples of the way this phrase has fixed the attention of readers as far back as Whitman's
   time, see the reaction to it from an anonymous 1860 parodist in Contexts (p. **29**) and from
   William Dean Howells in Interpretations (p. **72**).
78 This is one of several instances in the closing sections of the poem in which Whitman uses as nouns
   words more familiarly used as verbs (see, for example, "sidle" in l. 1322). "Scud" generally refers
   to wind-driven movement, here applied to the last hours of daylight.
79 Whitman, who was 36 years old when he composed this line, was turning prematurely gray but
   hardly white.

You will hardly know who I am or what I mean,
But I shall be good health to you nevertheless,
And filter and fibre your blood.

Failing to fetch me at first keep encouraged,
Missing me one place search another,   1345
I stop somewhere waiting for you.

4

Further Reading

Further Reading

Primary Sources

Leaves of Grass is available in innumerable paperback and cloth editions. The vast majority of editions reprint the 1881 edition, but a few reprint earlier editions, especially the 1855 and the 1860. There are also expensive facsimile editions in print, typically of the 1855 edition, which is one of the finest collector's items in all of American literature. What follows is a short list of recommended texts:

Cowley, Malcolm, ed. *Leaves of Grass: The First (1855) Edition* (New York: Penguin, 1959). This inexpensive printing of the 1855 edition has proven so useful that it has remained in print nearly continuously since its publication. Though not a true facsimile, it gives a good sense of the appearance of the original edition and an accurate reprinting of its text. Cowley's introduction is informative but dated.

Kaplan, Justin, ed. *Whitman, Poetry and Prose* (New York: Library of America, 1982). The best compendium of Whitman's writings to be had in one volume, containing both the 1855 and the 1881–82 editions, as well as the subsequent verse annexes and the collected prose works (the later paperback edition includes additional material).

Loving, Jerome, ed. *Leaves of Grass* (New York: Oxford University Press, 1990). A useful, inexpensive edition of Whitman's poems presented as a facsimile of the 1881 edition.

Moon, Michael, ed. *Leaves of Grass and Other Writings* (New York: W. W. Norton and Company, 2002). This updated Norton Critical Edition, based on Harold W. Blodgett and Sculley Bradley's *Leaves of Grass: Comprehensive Reader's Edition* (New York University Press, 1965), is a useful one-volume combination of Whitman's writings and the history of Whitman criticism from his time to ours.

Murphy, Francis, ed. *Walt Whitman: The Complete Poems* (Harmondsworth, UK: Penguin, 1975). A useful, inexpensive edition of Whitman's poems.

Scholarly and Online Editions

The primary scholarly edition of *Leaves of Grass* and many of Whitman's other writings, published and unpublished, prose and verse, is New York University Press's *The Collected Writings of Walt Whitman*. It includes the following works:

The Correspondence, ed. Edwin Haviland Miller, 6 vols. (1961–77). The collected letters, professionally edited and superbly annotated. Also useful is Miller's one-volume selected edition, *Selected Letters of Walt Whitman* (University of Iowa Press, 1990). Recently discovered letters have been published in several supplements of the *Walt Whitman Quarterly Review*.

The Early Poems and the Fiction, ed. Thomas L. Brasher (1963). A collection of Whitman's remarkably conventional pre-*Leaves of Grass* poetry and his short fiction, both of which were published in the popular press and magazines.

Prose Works 1892, ed. Floyd Stovall, 2 vols. (1963–64). Contains *Specimen Days* (Whitman's loosely knit autobiography), *Democratic Vistas* (his incisive essay on postbellum American society, politics, and culture), and miscellaneous writings.

Leaves of Grass, Comprehensive Reader's Edition, ed. Harold W. Blodgett and Sculley Bradley (1965). This volume prints a modern textual edition of the work, with annotations. Its contents include the 1881 edition and various other works, including an extensive number of poems excluded from *Leaves of Grass*, annexes to post-1881 editions, and prose prefaces.

Daybooks and Notebooks, ed. William White, 3 vols. (1978). A collection of Whitman's daybooks 1876–92, miscellaneous notebooks, and unpublished writings on the subject of language.

Leaves of Grass: A Textual Variorum of the Printed Poems, ed. Sculley Bradley *et al.*, 3 vols. (1980). A variorum is especially useful with a text such as *Leaves of Grass*, which went through frequent, often major, revisions. Unfortunately, this particular one, which uses the 1881 edition as its base text, is not user-friendly and does not include periodical publication of poems or poetry manuscripts.

Notebooks and Unpublished Prose Manuscripts, ed. Edward F. Grier, 6 vols. (1984). The largest collection in print of Whitman's unpublished notebooks and manuscripts, although not exhaustive.

The Journalism, 1834–1846, ed. Herbert Bergman *et al.* (New York: Peter Lang, 1998). This is the first volume to date of Whitman's journalism published in *The Collected Writings of Walt Whitman*. It deploys a more rigorous standard of textual editing than did the miscellaneous compilations of Whitman's journalism published a generation or longer ago. Its primary advantage, however, is that it assembles all his discoverable journalism from 1834 to 1846. The second volume is to cover his period of editorship of the *Brooklyn Daily Eagle*, 1846–48.

A useful and necessary supplement to this edition is Joel Myerson's *The Walt Whitman Archive: A Facsimile of the Poet's Manuscripts*, 3 vols., 6 parts (New York: Garland, 1993), which reproduces substantial portions of the major collections of Whitman's poetry manuscripts at the Library of Congress, Duke University, University of Texas, and University of Virginia.

Also useful are two facsimile editions of major *Leaves of Grass* editions:

Golden, Arthur, ed. *Walt Whitman's Blue Book: The 1860–61* Leaves of Grass *containing his manuscript additions and revisions*, 2 vols. (New York: New York Public Library, 1968). This well-annotated facsimile edition reproduces the numerous changes that Whitman introduced into his own copy of the 1860 *Leaves of Grass* in preparing the revised text for the 1867 edition.

Pearce, Roy Harvey, ed. *Leaves of Grass* (Ithaca, New York: Cornell University Press, 1961). A facsimile edition of the 1860 edition, with a perceptive introduction. This was one of the most crucial editions in the development of Whitman's poetry, primarily because of the introduction of the "Calamus" and "Enfans d'Adam" clusters and the new poems "A Word out of the Sea" (retitled "Out of the Cradle Endlessly Rocking") and "Leaves of Grass 1" (retitled "As I Ebb'd with the Ocean of Life").

A more promising venture and one that seems likely to eclipse the *Collected Writings* edition as the most authoritative and capacious site of Whitman sources is the online Walt Whitman Archive (http://www.whitmanarchive.org/), edited by Ed Folsom and Kenneth M. Price. A monumental hypertext library of Whitmaniana, it offers or is in the process of making available the following materials:

- the texts of all editions of *Leaves of Grass* and of other Whitman writings;
- facsimiles and e-texts of poetry manuscripts;
- a hypertext biography, with links to photographs, maps, locations, and biographies of friends;
- a compendium of all contemporary reviews of Whitman's writings;
- a photo gallery containing all known photographs of Whitman;
- an updated bibliography of writings on Whitman;
- a section on Whitman's followers, including an online version of Horace Traubel's nine-volume *With Walt Whitman in Camden*.

Secondary Sources

The critical literature on Whitman, *Leaves of Grass*, and "Song of Myself" is enormous. What follows therefore is only a sampling of leading works, weighted toward scholarship of the past generation. For evaluations of the contents of these works, readers are advised to consult the *Walt Whitman Quarterly Review, American Literary Scholarship*, and *American Literature*, all of which print reviews of the latest Whitman scholarship.

Allen, Gay Wilson. *The Solitary Singer: A Critical Biography* (1955; revised ed. Chicago: University of Chicago Press, 1985). The book that established the documentary basis of modern Whitman biography and that remains the most nearly standard biography.

Allen, Gay Wilson and Ed Folsom, eds. *Walt Whitman and the World* (Iowa City: University of Iowa Press, 1995). A model of multinational analysis of Whitman, the international poet, seen through the cultural and interpretive traditions of several dozen nations.

Aspiz, Harold. *Walt Whitman and the Body Beautiful* (Urbana: University of Illinois Press, 1980). The first of the studies of Whitman as a poet of the body; articulate but lacking some of the theoretical sophistication of more recent work on the subject.

Asselineau, Roger. *The Evolution of Walt Whitman*, 2 vols. (Cambridge: Harvard University Press, 1960–62). This English version of a standard biography provides a still interesting, perceptive account of Whitman's life and poetry. It was reprinted in a one-volume edition by the University of Iowa Press in 1999.

Bauerlein, Mark. *Whitman and the American Idiom* (Baton Rouge: Louisiana State University Press, 1991). A semiotic reading of the incommensurability between physical presence and verbal representation in Whitman's early editions.

Brasher, Thomas L. *Whitman as Editor of the* Brooklyn Daily Eagle (Detroit: Wayne State University Press, 1970). A study of Whitman's most important and best documented period of journalism.

Burroughs, John. *Notes on Walt Whitman as Poet and Person* (1867; revised ed. New York: Haskell House, 1971). Noteworthy not only as first book on Whitman but also because partially ghost-written by Whitman.

Ceniza, Sherry. *Walt Whitman and 19th-Century Women Reformers* (Tuscaloosa: University of Alabama Press, 1998). An informative account of Whitman's dealings with and reception by contemporary feminists.

Dougherty, James. *Walt Whitman and the Citizen's Eye* (Baton Rouge: Louisiana State University Press, 1993). An analysis of Whitman's persona as citizen of contemporary Manhattan, with correlations drawn with leading Progressive and Modernist era painters and writers.

Eby, Edwin Harold. *A Concordance to Walt Whitman's "Leaves of Grass" and Selected Prose Writings*, 5 parts (Seattle: University of Washington Press, 1949–55). A good search tool for final editions of Whitman's writings.

Erkkila, Betsy. *Walt Whitman Among the French* (Princeton: Princeton University Press, 1980). A sophisticated study of Whitman's reception in and refraction via French culture.

Erkkila, Betsy. *Whitman the Political Poet* (New York: Oxford University Press, 1989). An excellent analysis of Whitman's politics in the light of current views.

Erkkila, Betsy and Jay Grossman, eds. *Breaking Bounds: Whitman and American Cultural Studies* (New York: Oxford University Press, 1996). An outstanding collection of sophisticated, innovative readings.

Fishkin, Shelley Fisher. *From Fact to Fiction: Journalism and Imaginative Writing in America* (Baltimore: Johns Hopkins University Press, 1985). Includes a good chapter on Whitman.

Folsom, Ed. *Walt Whitman's Native Representations* (New York: Cambridge University Press, 1994). A series of essays that relates Whitman's work to baseball, photography, dictionaries, and Native Americans.

Folsom, Ed, ed. *Walt Whitman: The Centennial Essays* (Iowa City: University of Iowa Press, 1994). A good set of essays generated by the Whitman Centennial Conference (Iowa City, 1992) on major strands of contemporary scholarship.

Giantvalley, Scott. *Walt Whitman: A Reference Guide*, 1838–1939 (Boston: G. K. Hall, 1981). An annotated secondary bibliography of criticism about Whitman.

Greenspan, Ezra. *Walt Whitman and the American Reader* (New York: Cambridge University Press, 1990). An analysis of Whitman's career as printer, journalist, and poet projected against the context of antebellum and postbellum print culture.

Greenspan, Ezra, ed. *Cambridge Companion to Whitman* (New York: Cambridge University Press, 1995). A compilation of useful essays on a variety of current critical preoccupations, supplemented by a chronology and primary and secondary bibliographies.

Hollis, C. Carroll. *Language and Style in* Leaves of Grass (Baton Rouge: Louisiana State University Press, 1983). A good literary critical reading of Whitman's art that emphasizes its roots in oratory and journalism.

Killingworth, M. Jimmie. *The Growth of* Leaves of Grass: *The Organic Tradition in Whitman Studies* (Columbia, South Carolina: Camden House, 1993). An overview of the critical tradition of Whitman historiography.
    Whitman's Poetry of the Body: Sexuality, Politics, and the Text (Chapel Hill: University of North Carolina Press, 1989). A strong reading of Whitman's body poetry.

Klammer, Martin. *Whitman, Slavery, and the Emergence of* Leaves of Grass (University Park: Pennsylvania State University Press, 1995). An informative account of the influence of slavery and race relations on *Leaves of Grass*.

Krieg, Joann P. *A Whitman Chronology* (Iowa City: University of Iowa Press, 1998). A detailed, comprehensive time line of Whitman's life.

Kummings, Donald D. *Walt Whitman, 1940–1975: A Reference Guide* (Boston: G. K. Hall, 1982). A useful annotated secondary bibliography of criticism about Whitman.

Lawrence, D. H. *Studies in Classic American Literature* (New York: Thomas Seltzer, 1923). A powerful appreciation of one remarkably original writer by another. The most interesting way to read Lawrence on Whitman is to consult the Cambridge University Press textual edition of *Studies* (2003), which prints three different versions of Lawrence's response to Whitman at three distinct times, including a previously unprinted text that responds to Whitman's homosexuality in strikingly powerful, idiosyncratic fashion.

LeMaster, J. R. and Donald D. Kummings, eds. *Walt Whitman: An Encyclopedia* (New York: Garland, 1998). A handy reference work with entries on virtually every conceivable aspect of Whitman and Whitman-related subjects.

Loving, Jerome. *Walt Whitman: The Song of Himself* (Berkeley: University of California Press, 1998). A solid, well-documented biography.

Martin, Robert K., ed. *The Continuing Presence of Walt Whitman: The Life after the Life* (Iowa City: University of Iowa Press, 1992). A good miscellaneous collection of literary critical essays.

Miller, Edwin Haviland. *Walt Whitman's "Song of Myself": A Mosaic of Interpretations* (Iowa City: University of Iowa Press, 1989). A line-by-line exegesis of the 1855 text stitched together from critics ranging from Whitman's time to our own.

Moon, Michael. *Disseminating Whitman: Revision and Corporeality in* Leaves of Grass (Cambridge: Harvard University Press, 1991). An insightful and assertive but unintegrated and not easily accessible reading of Whitman as a gay poet.

Myerson, Joel. *Walt Whitman: A Descriptive Bibliography* (Pittsburgh: University of Pittsburgh Press, 1993). A magisterial primary bibliography.

Myerson, Joel, ed. *Whitman in His Own Time: A Biographical Chronicle of His Life, Drawn from Recollections, Memoirs, and Interviews by Friends and Associates* (Detroit: Omnigraphics, 1991). A good collection of contemporary reviews and notices of Whitman by acquaintances.

Nathanson, Tenney. *Whitman's Presence: Body, Voice, and Writing in* Leaves of Grass (New York: New York University Press, 1992). An extraordinarily rich but unintegrated poststructuralist reading of the performative poetics of *Leaves of Grass*.

Perlman, Jim, Ed Folsom, and Dan Campion, eds. *Walt Whitman: The Measure of His Song* (Duluth, Minn.: Holy Cow! Press, 1998). A superb collection of excerpts from nineteenth- and twentieth-century creative writers from around the world "talking back" to Whitman.

Pollak, Vivian R. *The Erotic Whitman* (Berkeley: University of California Press, 2000). An interesting biographical-critical study of gender, sexuality, and "textual sex" in Whitman's writing.

Price, Kenneth M. *Whitman and Tradition: The Poet in His Century* (New Haven: Yale University Press, 1990). A sophisticated influence study of Whitman and his age, informed by critical taste both in Whitman's era and in our own.

Price, Kenneth M., ed. *Walt Whitman: The Contemporary Reviews* (New York: Cambridge University Press, 1996). The best collection in print of nineteenth-century reviews of Whitman's writings.

Reynolds, David S. *Walt Whitman: A Cultural Biography* (New York: Knopf, 1995). A massively documented study of Whitman and *Leaves of Grass* understood contextually against the popular and sophisticated culture of the time.

Rubin, Joseph Jay. *The Historic Whitman* (University Park: Pennsylvania State University Press, 1973). Still a useful biography of Whitman's pre-*Leaves of Grass* years.

Thomas, M. Wynn. *The Lunar Light of Whitman's Poetry* (Cambridge: Harvard University Press, 1987). A New Historicist reading of Whitman as artisan-poet increasingly out of sorts in an age of industrial capitalism.

Zweig, Paul. *Walt Whitman: The Making of the Poet* (New York: Basic Books, 1984). An absorbing literary biography of Whitman as author of *Leaves of Grass* up to the end of the Civil War, much better as a critical reading than as a work of scholarship.

Index